DISOBEDIENT WOMEN

Anastasia Valecce

DISOBEDIENT WOMEN

Decolonial Movements of Afro-Queer Puerto Rican Artists

University of Florida Press / Gainesville

This book will be made open access within three years of publication thanks to Path to Open, a program developed in partnership between JSTOR, the American Council of Learned Societies (ACLS), University of Michigan Press, and The University of North Carolina Press to bring about equitable access and impact for the entire scholarly community, including authors, researchers, libraries, and university presses around the world. Learn more at https://about.jstor.org/path-to-open/.

Cover: Art by Rosenda Álvarez Faro. Cover design by Mindy Basinger Hill.

Published in the United States of America

31 30 29 28 27 26 6 5 4 3 2 1

DOI: https://doi.org/10.5744/9781683406631

Library of Congress Cataloging-in-Publication Data

Names: Valecce, Anastasia, 1980– author
Title: Disobedient women : decolonial movements of Afro-Queer Puerto Rican artists / Anastasia Valecce.
Description: Gainesville : University of Florida Press, 2026. | Includes bibliographical references and index.
Identifiers: LCCN 2026018880 (print) | LCCN 2026018881 (ebook) | ISBN 9781683406631 hardback | ISBN 9781683406303 paperback | ISBN 9781683406051 ebook | ISBN 9781683407393 pdf
Subjects: LCSH: Sexual minority activists—Puerto Rico | LGBT activism—Puerto Rico | Art movements—Puerto Rico | Art movements—Caribbean Area | BISAC: ART / Caribbean & Latin American | HISTORY / Caribbean & West Indies / General
Classification: LCC HQ73.3.P84 V35 2026 (print) | LCC HQ73.3.P84 (ebook)
LC record available at https://lccn.loc.gov/2026018880
LC ebook record available at https://lccn.loc.gov/2026018881

UF PRESS

University of Florida Press
PO Box 140239
Gainesville, FL 32614
floridapress.org

GPSR EU Authorized Representative: Mare Nostrum Group B.V, Doelen 72, 4831 GR Breda, The Netherlands, gpsr@mare-nostrum.co.uk

For my children, Noah and Iris—

May the dreams we dare to live in the present
become the ground of your tomorrows.
May they nourish both your boldest desires
and your quietest hopes,
so that you may shape this world anew
by living—
unapologetically,
disobediently—
the life I gave you,
the life you gave me,
and the life that calls you.

CONTENTS

FIGURES

ACKNOWLEDGMENTS

No book comes to life in solitude. This one is no exception. It is the result of collective energy—of love, care, and creative complicity.

To Noah and Iris, my two luminous companions: you remade me from the inside out. I began this book before you were imagined, and I sent its final version to press when you were almost four and two and a half. You were with me for months in Puerto Rico—tiny, resilient, joyful presences reminding me what endurance and tenderness look like. You are my greatest teachers, especially as I wrote on motherhood, femininity, and becoming.

To Wilay, my other pillar and coconspirator in love and life: our way of walking together defies the patriarchal script. May it offer our children a vision of gender-equal love rooted in care, creativity, laughter, and mutual growth.

I extend my deepest gratitude to the artists whose brilliance and generosity sustain these pages—Gisela Rosario Ramos/Macha Colón, Awilda Rodríguez Lora, Helen Ceballos, and Awilda Sterling-Duprey. Your work, your words, and your trust made this project possible. Over time, what began as research became kinship.

I would also like to thank Spelman College and the Department of World Languages and Cultures for granting me a sabbatical in Fall 2024 that allowed me to complete the manuscript; the UNCF/Mellon Residency Program for supporting my research in Puerto Rico and making possible the podcast, the artists' roundtable, and my participation in *La Cumbre Afro* at the University of Puerto Rico–Río Piedras. Thank you to The Gordon Zeto Center, UNCF/Mellon, and Spelman for additional grants and faith in my work. And thanks to Stephanye Hunter and the University of Florida Press for championing this project with care and conviction.

There are presences less visible yet vital—friends who functioned as family in Puerto Rico: Velissa, Luis Daniel, Rebeca, Gerardo, Mildred, Lío—thank you for meals, laughter, childcare, wine, furniture, and love. To the friends always present across distance and time, and to those in Atlanta—Juan Carlos and Cynthia, Rafa and Mariana, Fernanda, Mariangela, Rosita—your warmth held me together. Thanks to Atlanta Bread in Smyrna, where I wrote entire chapters from opening to closing; Basil Couvaras and his team, thank you for your hospitality and care. And to Shawn and Russell, whom my children call grandpas, for your steadfast love, generosity, and grace.

To the colleagues and interlocutors who shaped this work—Kadiri Vaquer Fernández, Juan Carlos Rodríguez, María Mercedes Carrión, Jossianna Arroyo, Yolanda Martínez-San Miguel, Mabel Cuesta, Ramón Rivera-Servera, Rosita Scerbo, Larry La Fountain-Stokes, Consuelo Martínez Reyes, Jessica Pabón-Colón, nibia pastrana santiago, Nelson Maldonado-Torres, Charlie Geyer, Mayra Santos-Febres, Aurora Lauzardo, and Zaira Rivera Casellas—thank you for the conversations, your readings, your provocations, and your generosity. Gratitude as well to the Performance Studies Group sponsored by The Resources and Research Center (TRRC) and the Office of the Provost at Spelman College—Aku Kadogo, Kathleen Shaag, Cicely Kelley, and Phyllis Kimberleigh Jordan—for conversations that bridged scholarship and embodiment. Finally, eternal gratitude goes to Julio González-Ruiz (1971–2021) and José Quiroga (1959–2024), whose intellect, generosity, and friendship continue to reverberate in this book.

If this project is about disobedient women and collective becoming, its making was no different. Writing it was a communal act of care—an anticapitalist practice grounded in love, not productivity. For all those whose names may not appear but whose presence shaped me: thank you. Finally, to my family of origin—my father Vito, my siblings Luisa and Alessandro, my nieces and nephews (my other children) Sofía, Alberto, Arianna, and Mattia—and in memory of my mother, Anna: *Mamma,* everything I am, was first possible through you. *Grazie.*

INTRODUCTION

Undisciplined Measures

Between Movement, Femininities, and Queerness

> ¡Soy pata, soy puta, pero nunca corrupta!
> [I am queer, I am a whore, but I will never be corrupted!]
> DJ Perra Mística

A girl dances provocatively wearing a pink wig, a beret—a symbol of combat and militancy—and a Puerto Rican flag bikini within a crowd that is dancing, singing, and celebrating. DJs work at their stations to sustain the reggaetón music while a scantily dressed crowd of people dance and twerk to the urban rhythms, until one of the DJs, known as Perra Mística,[1] takes the microphone and shouts to the multitude the epigraph that opens this introduction: "¡Soy pata, soy puta, pero nunca corrupta!" [I am queer, I am a whore, but I will never be corrupted!][2] After this declaration, people cheer and continue dancing while Perra Mística twerks with a bare-chested hooded woman, and people dance and vogue—among them the artist and founder of LaBoriVogue artivist lab, Edrimael Delgado Reyes.[3] This was the night of July 24, 2019, and the crowd had gathered in front of the cathedral in San Juan, Puerto Rico, for a historic *perreo combativo* [combative twerking] to protest and demand—and that night, to obtain, under the slogan "Ricky renuncia" [Ricky resign]—the resignation of then-Governor Ricardo Rosselló.

That night, Perra Mística's declaration not only claimed queerness and sexuality as unapologetic forms of self-definition but also turned politics itself into a site of moral confrontation. If, as the quote suggests, corruption—not queerness—is the true moral transgression, Perra Mística's statement reordered long-standing hierarchies that have historically framed queerness, pleasure, and female sexuality as moral flaws. By contrast, here corruption is identified as the ethical failure, while queer embodiment and sexual disobedience become assertions of integrity, coherence, and justice.

The protests had begun on July 14 and took many creative forms—from protesting while salsa dancing, doing yoga, or kayaking, to the more traditional *cacerolazos* [pot banging]—that centered largely around La Fortaleza, the governor's residence. Though often portrayed as spontaneous by the media, the mobilization was organized in part by groups such as the Grupo de Trabajo de Género and Colectivo Queer. It was fueled by civic outrage over nearly nine hundred pages of leaked Telegram messages between Rosselló and close allies, published by the Centro de Periodismo Investigativo. The chats revealed grotesque misogyny, homophobia, transphobia, fatphobia, and even jokes about the thousands who died in the aftermath of Hurricane María—deaths that exposed governmental negligence and corruption.[4]

What began as widespread indignation soon took the shape of embodied resistance, as the most visible participants in the protests were LGBTQ+ collectives—especially women, trans women, and femme individuals.[5] Femininity itself, expressed through dance and public performance, became a politicized tool of protest grounded in the profound misogyny that shaped those moments. On the steps of the cathedral, bodies moved in direct refusal of a government that openly upheld patriarchal, misogynistic, heteronormative, and colonial values. As Zorimar Rivera Montes (2024) observes, the control of bodies—particularly female and feminized bodies—has been central to Puerto Rico's colonial history. The 2019 uprising revealed how those most targeted by that history—Black people, queer people, all women—did not just claim public space, but moved through it freely, asserting new visions for the island's future as "improper" colonial subjects (Rivera Montes 2024, 124).

The perreo combativo, however, generated backlash. Several conservative, sexist, and classist reactions to the protest—particularly the moral panic provoked by nonnormative bodies dancing and exposing themselves in public space—stemmed not only from the location but from the visibility of women and nonbinary bodies reclaiming pleasure while protesting. The protest, organized by a queer youth collective, constituted a legitimate political performance that challenged heteropatriarchal, religious, and colonial structures. However, the indignation centered on three main elements: *where* the perreo occurred (a public, religiously sacred space), *who* performed the perreo (intersectional queer people), and *how* the performances functioned through the excess of feminine energy and the visibility of the expression of sexual desire.

Nevertheless, the Catholic Church not only failed to release any statement condemning the leaked chats but, as Edrimael Delgado Reyes observes, it has historically played an ongoing role in repressing sexual and gender freedoms, demonstrating that queer, feminist resistance is crucial—not peripheral—to Puerto Rico's broader political struggle.[6] Ultimately, the radical joy and embodied disobedience of that night—through dancing, twerking, and public misbehavior—made visible a form of protest rooted in movement, femininity, and queerness. It was an undisciplined act of decolonial resistance, reclaiming space and imagining liberation on queer and feminist terms.

Framing the Argument: From Crisis to Creation

The events of the 2019 perreo combativo and its aftermath address the main concerns of this book. I examine performative undisciplined measures—radical acts of movement, femininity, and queerness—as powerful forms of decolonial resistance that confront and dismantle epistemic violence (Grosfoguel 2003). This form of epistemic violence privileges the white, Christian, able-bodied, cisgender, heterosexual male—typically from the United States or the Global North and socially and economically validated by neoliberal standards—as the universal subject and legitimate producer of knowledge. I analyze how the undisciplined measures in the artistic works discussed in this book propose new practices of worldmaking in the Puerto Rican archipelago. Centering the work of four Afro-queer women multidisciplinary artists, this study examines how their performances, visual practices, and lived experiences challenge patriarchal, heteronormative, and colonial structures through a decolonial feminist lens that has the aim of dismantling patriarchal structures within and through revolutionary movements (Fauzia and Amenta 2024, 22). Through case studies of Gisela Rosario Ramos/Macha Colón, Awilda Rodríguez Lora, Helen Ceballos, and Awilda Sterling-Duprey, the book illuminates how embodied disobedience, radical joy, and the reclamation of marginalized identities function as tools for collective survival and the imagining of alternative futures amid ongoing crises, historical trauma, and systemic neglect. Ultimately, it argues that art is not merely a form of commentary, but a necessary mode of political action—one that enables new ways of being, relating, and remembering within and beyond colonial constraint.

The Afro-queer Puerto Rican women artists examined—Rosario Ramos/ Macha Colón, Rodríguez Lora, Ceballos, and Sterling-Duprey—mobilize their bodies and movements, both literal and metaphorical, as tools of decolonial resistance, collective memory, and identity affirmation, across diverse disciplines, methodologies, generations, and economic contexts. Through interdisciplinary and undisciplined artistic practices, their performances engage dance, visual culture, and corporeality to reclaim agency and visibility in a society shaped by colonialism, heteropatriarchy, racism, and neoliberal violence. In doing so, they participate in "the cultural and material dimensions of feminist and queer politics" through which "a livable future for the marginalized and everyone else" becomes imaginable (Rivera Velázquez and Decena 2024, 11). Therefore, these artistic movements function not only as aesthetic expressions but also as acts of artivism, challenging social norms and reconfiguring space, gender, and the political imagination.

These artistic interventions are urgent responses to a sociohistorical context marked by feminicide, transphobic violence, colonial neglect, and the systematic erasure of marginalized bodies from public life. Feminist and queer approaches, as Rivera Velázquez and Decena argue, "spotlight the connectedness of our practice of joy, resistance, and survival in the face of racist, patriarchal, capitalist, misogynist, homophobic and transphobic Caribbean politics" (2024, 7). By centering queer, Black, and feminine experiences, the artists in this study challenge dominant narratives and offer decolonial tools for survival, proposing radical alternatives for community, belonging, and justice in Puerto Rico.

The 2019 protests serve as a catalytic moment for these concerns. When demonstrators took over the plaza and cathedral in San Juan with a perreo combativo, they activated a political grammar rooted in the body. Movement—particularly queer, femme, and unruly movement—became a weapon against the entangled structures of religious, patriarchal, homophobic, and class-based oppression. This embodied rebellion centered the visibility of queer women and femme subjects whose performances of nonnormative femininity contested what is permissible, legible, or respectable in public space. As Arnaldo Cruz-Malavé observes, perreo combativo transforms reggaetón's hypersexualized dance into a queer and decolonial mode of protest. Its radical potential lies in its power to "expose and unmake" the normative frameworks of Puerto Rican identity shaped by colonial and patriarchal ideologies (2023). Through aesthetics of disobedience, protesters used pleasure and irreverence as collective acts of refusal and reimagination (2023). The artists examined in this book extend this same ethos into their creative practices.

As Adriana Garriga-López argues, these creators do not simply work across disciplines; they embody *in-disciplinariedad,* or undiscipline, defying aesthetic and social norms alike (Homar and pastrana santiago 2022, 76). Their art enacts a refusal of containment by using the body to open critical conversations about queerness, femininity, and sexuality—conversations often silenced in Puerto Rican public discourse. Like the protesters of 2019, these artists blur the line between public and private, occupying urban, domestic, institutional, and digital spaces in ways that unsettle normative spatial logics. Their work envisions the "queer home" not as a fixed site but as a mobile and porous structure of support, resistance, and possibility. Their movements are *wild* in the Halberstam and Nyong'o sense: untamed, disobedient, and generative (2018).[7] These performances do not merely symbolize resistance—they enact it through corporeal presence, unruly gestures, and a defiant aesthetic of disorder.

The perreo combativo of July 24, 2019, thus serves as both a historical turning point and a symbolic foundation for this book's analysis. The collective refusal performed that night—through twerking, voguing, chanting, and occupying a sacred space—resonates with the dissident aesthetics and feminist politics expressed in the works of Rosario Ramos/Macha Colón, Rodríguez Lora, Ceballos, and Sterling-Duprey.[8] Each artist reclaims movement as an instrument of decolonial resistance, queers both urban and intimate spaces, and foregrounds the racialized and sexualized body as a site of vulnerability and power. Their interventions reject the colonial disciplining of femininity and the invisibilization of Black and queer lives by generating alternative epistemologies rooted in performance, desire, and radical joy.

In dialogue with the perreo combativo, these artists mobilize *indisciplinariedad* as a political and aesthetic strategy that resists containment. They perform this resistance through their bodies, their art, and their everyday lives. In doing so, they create a living archive of Afro-queer feminist resistance in Puerto Rico—one that unsettles colonial temporality and affirms the body as both archive and agent of transformation. As I will expand in the chapters, Rosario Ramos/Macha Colón's strategies of radical joy, Rodríguez Lora's performance of Wonder Woman in a Puerto Rican flag bikini (recalling the outfit worn during the protest that opened this introduction), Ceballos's uses of her female body and nudity, and Sterling-Duprey's connection to music, space, and movement—all echo the political imagination that took place so forcefully with the perreo combativo. They remind us that art is not peripheral to politics but rather one of its most potent and necessary forms: a source of historical memory, present agency, and future possibility.

Chronologies of Colonial Control: An Afro-Queer Feminist Framework for Puerto Rico

The historical relationship between Puerto Rico and the United States, established in 1898 following the Spanish-American War and the US invasion, unfolds within what Jossianna Arroyo calls a "neoliberal temporality." As articulated in Arroyo's book *Caribe 2.0*, this temporality suspends Puerto Rico in a colonial present where subjugation endures, and political resolution is perpetually deferred. This manipulation of time sustains Puerto Rico's status as an unincorporated territory (a commonwealth since 1952) while obscuring the ongoing nature of American imperialism. In response, the Afro-queer Puerto Rican women artists featured in this study enact what may be called *dissenting politics*—artistic practices that resist colonial chronologies by rejecting assimilation and the binary logics of US hegemony. Their work aligns with María Lugones's theorization of the "coloniality of gender," which reveals how colonial power structures impose gender as a mechanism for organizing labor, property, cosmologies, and knowledge systems (Lugones 2010, 748). Black queer femmes in Puerto Rico experience this coloniality through their exclusion from normative womanhood—what Hortense Spillers describes as the "ungendering" produced by the colonial "theft of the body" (Spillers 1987, 67). This exclusion manifests through the racialized and heteronormative hierarchies that privilege whitened, cisgender, and middle-class ideals of femininity, while rendering Black and queer embodiments as excessive, improper, or invisible. For example, Puerto Rican media and beauty industries have historically celebrated mestiza femininity as a national ideal, marginalizing Afro–Puerto Rican and queer women's bodies as deviations from the norm. The artists examined here—such as Awilda Rodríguez Lora and Gisela Rosario Ramos/Macha Colón—disrupt those exclusions by centering the abject, performative, and desiring Black femme body as a site of resistance and knowledge production. These artistic interventions are thus ontological acts that defy colonial and gendered logics, envisioning alternative ways of being beyond neoliberal subjectivity and imperial categorization.

Drawing from performance studies, visual culture analysis, and decolonial feminist theory, this book explores how Afro-queer Puerto Rican artists mobilize the body as a site of political resistance and futurity. A salient example of historical gendered violence in Puerto Rico is the reproductive experimentation conducted on Puerto Rican women during the 1960s, when the birth control pill was tested without informed consent and with serious life-threatening effects for many Puerto Rican women and babies. As Laura Briggs compellingly argues in *Reproducing Empire* (2002), the US colonial administration has long instrumentalized Puerto Rican women's reproductive capacities for biopolitical experimentation and population control. From sterilization campaigns to contraceptive trials, Briggs demonstrates how reproductive politics have been central to US imperial strategies in the Caribbean, positioning Puerto Rican women's bodies as both objects and instruments of governance. Eileen Suárez Findlay, in *Imposing Decency* (2000), similarly documents how moral and legal discourses targeted the sexuality of working-class and Afro-Caribbean women to construct a racially stratified colonial order. As Rivera Montes underscores, these logics of "decency" continue under neoliberal colonial rule, reinforcing a feminized obedience that maintains the coloniality of power (2024, 106). Collectively, these studies illuminate how respectability politics and sexual regulation have served as tools of social control and mechanisms for defining Puerto Rican national identity in opposition to a racialized and gendered "other." The artists examined here critically engage with this archive, not only resisting its legacies but also reimagining queer and feminine futures through Afro-Caribbean visual and performative practices.

Amid this entangled history of reproductive control, fiscal violence, and structural abandonment, artists and activists have developed practices that do not simply respond to crisis but reimagine the very terms of political engagement and survival. I argue that the Afro-queer Puerto Rican women artists studied here enact radical forms of decolonial resistance by challenging the gendered, racialized, and temporal logics of US imperialism through visual and performative practices.

This book particularly focuses on a series of contemporary events that underscore the ongoing effects of Puerto Rico's colonial status. The implementation of the Puerto Rico Oversight, Management, and Economic Stability Act (PROMESA) in 2016 and the establishment of the Fiscal Control Board (La Junta) mark a significant moment of neoliberal governance wherein fiscal austerity was imposed without democratic accountability. Hurricanes Irma and María in 2017 further exacerbated the island's vulnerabilities, disproportionately affecting marginalized communities, particularly women. As Rima Brusi, Yarimar Bonilla, and Isar Godreau (2018), Yarimar Bonilla and Marisol LeBrón (2019), and Godreau and Bonilla (2021) argue, these crises exposed the intersection of disaster capitalism, colonial neglect, and gendered inequalities. The imposition of austerity measures directly impacted public services, including education and healthcare, and catalyzed mass protests throughout

2016 and 2017. These mobilizations laid the groundwork for the 2019 protests that led to Governor Ricardo Rosselló's resignation. These protests—marked by the leadership of queer women and nonbinary artists—signaled a new era of grassroots political resistance.

Subsequent events further intensified the island's crisis: the earthquakes in early 2020, the COVID-19 pandemic (2020–23), persistent blackouts under LUMA Energy, and widespread gentrification. These conditions have exacerbated precarity, particularly among women and working-class communities, revealing the entanglements of gender, colonialism, and systemic violence. Scholars such as Rivera Montes (2024), Contreras Capó (2021), and Rocío Zambrana (2021) argue that debt functions as a contemporary mechanism of colonial domination, disproportionately affecting women and LGBTQ+ communities.

The events of August 31, 2016, when President Barack Obama appointed the seven members of La Junta under PROMESA, marked a pivotal moment in this trajectory. With sweeping authority to revise budgets and prohibit public strikes, the board exacerbated the liquidity crisis, leading to devastating cuts, particularly in education. The University of Puerto Rico (UPR) became a focal point of resistance, with students and faculty organizing strikes and protests against La Junta and its measures. In September 2017, Hurricane María devastated the island's already fragile infrastructure. The Puerto Rico Electric Power Authority (PREPA), weakened by budget cuts and workforce reductions, was ill-equipped to respond. The hurricane destroyed the power grid, leaving all 3.4 million residents without electricity. Governor Rosselló initially downplayed the death toll, aligning with President Donald Trump, who delayed his visit, misrepresented the devastation, and prioritized fiscal concerns over human lives. While official reports cited sixteen deaths, independent studies later estimated nearly 5,000 fatalities due to delayed aid and inadequate infrastructure. San Juan Mayor Carmen Yulín Cruz estimated that some areas would remain without power for four to six months, with all the extenuating consequences that it brought. On September 24, Puerto Rico's Governor Rosselló estimated that the damage from Hurricane María in Puerto Rico was probably over $8 billion. Approximately 80 percent of the territory's agriculture was lost due to the hurricane, with agricultural losses estimated at $780 million.[9] The reality is that even nowadays the archipelago is far from recovery. Many homes are still destroyed after Hurricane María, as FEMA [Federal Emergency Management Agency] aid was inadequate; the electric grid remains outdated; and schools, hospitals, and roads are in disrepair.

This mismanagement fueled public outrage. But it was the 2019 leak of misogynistic, homophobic, and violent private chats between Rosselló and his inner circle that catalyzed widespread protests. Hundreds of thousands took to the streets, chanting "Ricky renuncia" [Ricky resign], "y llévate la Junta" [and take the "Junta" with you]. The protests were characterized by three key features: they were led predominantly by queer, trans, and nonbinary individuals; they foregrounded the role of women and femmes in political resistance; and—as analyzed in the opening of this book—they used perreo and reggaetón as tools of subversion and communal empowerment. On July 24, 2019, the massive perreo combativo [combative twerkathon] on the steps of San Juan's cathedral symbolically challenged both colonial and patriarchal authority. Rosselló resigned that night. Activists declared "el perreo ganó" [twerking won], circulating slogans like "sin perreo no hay revolución" [there is no revolution without perreo]. While some criticized these embodied protests as vulgar, such responses only revealed entrenched anxieties about gender, sexuality, and public space.

From 2019 to 2023, Puerto Rico endured further crises: deadly earthquakes, rising femicides and violence against trans women of color, the disappearance of numerous young women, and ongoing infrastructural collapse.[10] The health care system, education, and housing sectors continue to suffer under the weight of colonial neglect and neoliberal governance. The intersections of Puerto Rican nonsovereignty and coloniality reveal how economic and sociopolitical events are structurally tied to the archipelago's colonial condition. Debt and austerity function as instruments of control, targeting the most vulnerable. As Aurora Santiago-Ortiz asserts in "Testimonio as Stitch Work," Hurricane María "removed the colonial veil," exposing both local dysfunction and federal abandonment (2021, 122). Rivera Montes (2024) critiques the rhetoric of "resilience" as a neoliberal tool that privatizes responsibility for structural failure, while Zambrana links debt to racialized and gendered disposability. The artists studied in this book take up these critiques not only to resist but to imagine otherwise, advancing Afro-queer feminist practices as tools for rethinking embodiment, sovereignty, and community.

The historical and political conditions outlined here directly inform the artworks analyzed in this book. My focus from 2013 to 2023 marks a prolonged and compounding era of crisis in Puerto Rican society, one that continues to produce far-reaching consequences across the archipelago. In fact, although this book engages with key historical events from 2016 onward to understand Puerto Rico's sociopolitical context, I have chosen to frame its scope within the decade spanning 2013 to 2023. The decision to begin in 2013 reflects a political inflection point: it was a moment marked by renewed waves of protest and resistance across the archipelago. That year, Puerto Rico experienced a series of significant mobilizations, particularly around issues of public education, austerity, and labor rights. Students, faculty, and staff throughout the University of Puerto Rico protested tuition increases, budget cuts, and the looming threat of privatization—continuing a legacy of resistance rooted in the 2010–11 student strikes. On March 15, 2013, teachers demonstrated in front of the governor's mansion in opposition to proposed cuts to retirement benefits. Days later, police officers staged a similar protest over their own pension concerns. On December 19, members of the Puerto Rico Teachers' Federation occupied the Senate floor in an attempt to block Governor Alejandro García Padilla's pension reform legislation. Despite their efforts, the bill was signed into law on December 24. These mobilizations occurred amid a worsening economic crisis and growing discontent with austerity and colonial governance. Simultaneously, feminist and queer activism gained visibility, with organizations such as La Sombrilla Cuir and the Coalición Amplia de Búsqueda de Equidad (CABE) becoming increasingly vocal in their demands for gender and sexual justice. I understand the protests of 2013 as a pivotal threshold—both political and affective—that helped lay the groundwork for future mass mobilizations, including the anti-PROMESA demonstrations of 2016 and the "Ricky Renuncia" uprising of 2019, culminating in the energies that carry us into the present.

Within this context, I pay particular attention to how sexuality and gender nonconformity function as sites through which colonial subjects are both represented and reimagined. These narratives not only confront entrenched colonial power structures but also articulate alternative visions of identity, embodiment, and resistance. While the featured artists began their practices before 2013, the decade between 2013 and 2023 represents a turning point in Puerto Rican cultural and political life. This period's converging crises provide both the context and urgency for the emergence of queer Black women and femmes as protagonists of the contemporary art scene. These artists engage in layered forms of movement—political, physical, metaphorical, and digital—that resist immobilization and erasure. Their irreverent gestures, visual interventions, and corporeal performances insist on presence, refusing marginalization through embodied disobedience.

In light of these overlapping histories of colonial violence, economic extraction, reproductive control, and gendered exclusion, the artistic practices explored in this book emerge as radical acts of resignification. These works do not merely respond to crisis; they reframe the very terms under which colonial subjects become legible. By centering the unruly, desiring, and resistant Black femme body, these artists disrupt the temporality of neoliberal crisis and the expectations of colonial respectability. As such, their practices rearticulate embodiment as a site of political imagination and refusal. I argue that these aesthetic and corporeal acts constitute insurgent theorizing—rooted in the material realities of racialized and gendered oppression, yet oriented toward speculative, liberatory futures. Within this matrix of crisis and creativity, dispossession and defiance, Afro-queer feminist aesthetics articulate new modes of belonging and political possibility in contemporary Puerto Rico.

Theoretical Lineages and Decolonial Cartographies

The theoretical conversations that animate this book emerge from an interdisciplinary constellation of thinkers whose work traverses, rather than inhabits, fixed disciplinary boundaries. These thinkers engage in dialogues that refuse containment, generating frameworks that are at once decolonial, queer, performative, and feminist. For the sake of tracing a genealogy—while acknowledging its porousness—I draw from decolonial thought (Mignolo, Quijano, Maldonado-Torres, among others), queer theory (Halberstam, Muñoz, Butler, Decena, Saketopoulou, and Pellegrini, among others), and performance theory (Dolan, Franko, Rivera-Servera, Santana, and Taylor, among others), all refracted through an intersectional feminist lens (Briggs, Lugones, Sharpe, and Suárez Findlay, among others). These lineages do not delineate separate territories but rather chart an entangled cartography in which ideas migrate, overlap, and reconfigure one another—mirroring the decolonial, embodied, and relational methodologies that guide this study.

Decolonial thought, particularly the work of Walter Mignolo, Aníbal Quijano, and Nelson Maldonado-Torres, provides crucial conceptual tools for unpacking terms such as coloniality, neocolonialism, and decoloniality. These thinkers help illuminate how race, gender, geography, and epistemology are structured under global capitalism and imperialism. Applying their insights to Puerto Rico reveals how coloniality continues to inform its social, cultural, and artistic life. Rocío Zambrana's analysis of debt as a contemporary mechanism of colonial control (2021), along with Ramón Grosfoguel's critique of Eurocentric epistemologies (2003), deepens this understanding by linking economic precarity to enduring systems of racial and gendered dispossession. This is how, for example, Grosfoguel's analysis of Puerto Rico as a "modern colony" clarifies the critique embedded in Helen Ceballos's portrayals of undocumented

Afro-Caribbean subjectivities in her performances. These frameworks make legible how performance in Puerto Rico operates as a form of intervention within these structures of power.

Equally vital is the scholarship of Zorimar Rivera Montes, Celiany Rivera Velázquez, Laura Briggs, and Eileen Suárez Findlay, whose work highlights the entwinement of gender, capitalism, and colonialism. Their insights were pivotal in interpreting the artistic labor featured here as a gendered, embodied critique of colonial capitalist logics. Foundational texts by Jossianna Arroyo, Lawrence La Fountain-Stokes—whose interviews and lectures on Awilda Rodríguez Lora have been invaluable, Arnaldo Cruz-Malavé, Yolanda Martínez-San Miguel, Marisel Moreno, Rubén Ríos-Ávila, Sandra Ruiz, and Aurora Santiago-Ortiz further provided the sociopolitical and queer theoretical groundwork for reading the body as a site of resistance. These thinkers enabled me to theorize the bodily vocabularies of these artists not simply as aesthetic practices, but as decolonial gestures that expose and reframe the social constructions of womanhood, Blackness, and femininity under colonial capitalism.

Queer and affect theory, particularly the work of José Esteban Muñoz, Jack Halberstam, Tavia Nyong'o, and Sara Ahmed, has also been essential. Muñoz's vision of utopia as a queer horizon (2009) informs how this book interprets artistic practices as imaginaries of alternative futures. Halberstam's contributions (2005, 2011, 2020) have helped theorize queer embodiment as mobile, performative resistance that traverses and reconfigures space. The volume *Wildness* (Halberstam and Nyong'o 2018) opened interpretive pathways for reading the affective and temporal disruptions in the work of Gisela Rosario Ramos and Rodríguez Lora. Ahmed (2006) conceives queerness as a spatial and affective orientation, a concept embodied in Rosario Ramos's persona, Macha Colón,[11] where queerness emerges not just as identity but as disorientation, redirection, and affective refusal.

These theoretical insights grounded my interpretations of bodily experiences mediated through cultural and political contexts, particularly in relation to gender, race, and sexuality. They guided my readings of Macha Colón's sonic and visual performances, Awilda Rodríguez Lora's *La Mujer Maravilla* and *Sustento* as feminist and queer interruptions to hegemonic representations of womanhood, and Helen Ceballos's work on migratory and queer diasporas. They also inform the analysis of racial and gender disobedience in Awilda Sterling-Duprey's practice, where abstraction and gesture become vehicles for memory, resistance, and visibility.

Nadia Ellis's dialogue with Muñoz's theory of queer utopia and her engagement with diaspora, care, and aesthetics deepened my own interpretive lens—especially in reading how these artists navigate belonging and futurity amid displacement. Alongside Jill Dolan's theory of utopia in performance and Grosfoguel's framing of utopia as a critical decolonial gesture further allowed me to locate embodied artistic practices as hopeful worldmaking. Ellis's writing allowed me to critically connect queer futurity with the embodied experience of displacement and desire. Ana-Maurine Lara's critical work on race, gender, and sexuality—especially her analyses of LGBTQ+ protest and ritual in the Dominican Republic—offered a comparative Caribbean framework through which to theorize urban space, embodiment, and decolonial resistance. Her insights resonate with the performative strategies of Rodríguez Lora and Ceballos, whose works likewise engage spiritual, corporeal, and social registers of disobedience.

This project also engages broader conversations in Caribbean cultural studies. Rosamond King, Angelique Nixon, Carolyn Cooper, Édouard Glissant, Nadia Ellis, Ana-Maurine Lara, and Pat Saunders are key interlocutors. King's work on Caribbean sexualities and violence offers context for understanding gendered visual representation and repression, particularly in Rodríguez Lora's practice. Nixon's analysis of diaspora and tourism highlights the racialized spectacle that artists like Ceballos confront. Cooper's studies of dancehall and the "vulgar" body offer valuable comparisons to the performances of Sterling-Duprey and Rosario Ramos, particularly in their sonic, affective, and embodied disruptions.

These conversations destabilize reductive notions of Puerto Rico as peripheral, instead locating the island within an archipelagic Caribbean framework. Drawing from Édouard Glissant's conception of the Caribbean as a geography of relation, opacity, and movement (1990), this book reads the Puerto Rican archipelago not only as a site of colonization but also as a space of theoretical and artistic generation. Shared colonial histories and cultural subalternity across the region have engendered aesthetic responses that contest imposed hierarchies of race, gender, and sexuality. In this light, queer performance and visual art emerge as powerful epistemologies of resistance, pleasure, and futurity.

Caribbean-centered queer theory—particularly the work of Cruz-Malavé, José Quiroga, La Fountain-Stokes, and Decena—has shaped my understanding of queer diasporic embodiment and aesthetics. Decena's most recent work (2023) provides tools for interpreting ritual, syncretism, and spiritual practices in the performances of Ceballos and Sterling-Duprey, including their queer engagements with Santería, Yoruba cosmologies, and Marian iconography.

These theoretical frameworks represent only a part of the intellectual scaffolding that undergirds this project. Nevertheless, there is a conspicuous lack of academic production on the artists included here. This study responds to that absence by carefully selecting and then centering the queer Afro–Puerto Rican women artists included in this study—across four generations and intersectionally different among one another—within the recent artistic and sociopolitical landscape of the Puerto Rican archipelago. Their work is analyzed in relation to the social, economic, and cultural shifts that transformed Puerto Rico between 2013 and 2023—a decade marked by austerity, crisis, and resistance. These artists offer not only critique but also affective, embodied strategies of survival and transformation. Their practices envision alternative configurations of gender, race, queerness, embodiment, and beauty, articulating worldmaking strategies rooted in resistance, memory, and joy.

Their works demand a rethinking of what it means to embody femininity, Blackness, queerness, and resistance within a colonial and patriarchal context. Rather than simply reflecting political realities, these artists intervene in them. Their work reclaims public and intimate spaces, resignifies femininity and Blackness, and queers aesthetic discourses. My aim, then, is not to "apply" theory to their art, but to read these performances as theory—as situated, embodied, and affectively charged acts of knowledge-making. Scholars such as Lawrence La Fountain-Stokes, Susan Homar, nibia pastrana santiago, Zorimar Rivera Montes, and Celiany Rivera Velázquez have recently made important contributions—particularly between 2021 and 2024—to the study of artists like Awilda Rodríguez Lora, Awilda Sterling-Duprey, and Gisela Rosario Ramos. However, critical scholarship on Helen Ceballos remains scarce, and a more sustained body of work on all the artists featured in this book is still notably limited. My own 2018 publication on Rosario Ramos's *El hijo de Ruby* stands among the few existing texts. This scholarly gap reflects broader patterns of erasure within Latinx and Caribbean studies, where Black, queer, and feminist artistic labor often remains understudied.

This book seeks to break that silence by foregrounding performances that defy normativity and produce new grammars of disobedience, visibility, and embodied knowledge. These artists resignify womanhood, reclaim public and intimate spaces, and reorient aesthetic discourse toward embodied justice. Their work invites us to think of art not as passive representation but as active transformation—a medium through which life, agency, and desire are reimagined and made possible.

This is not an exhaustive study, and these are not the only artists engaging in such practices, nor does this book claim to be the first or only intervention of its kind.[12] Rather, it is a situated intervention that foregrounds the contributions of four queer Afro–Puerto Rican intergenerational women artists to contemporary conversations on decoloniality, embodiment, and futurity. By situating their bodies, gestures, and voices within the political present of a colonized island, this book argues that their performances are not simply responses to oppression—they are aesthetic and political acts of worldmaking. Through their radical reimaginings of femininity, resistance, and joy, these artists transform Puerto Rico into a generative site for imagining queer, feminist, and decolonial futures. This book, then, is more than an academic exercise. It is an invitation—to scholars, students, artists, and readers—to think, feel, and disobey in concert with those who dare to undiscipline and queer the world to make space for freedom, for pleasure, and for joy. It asks us to imagine freedom not as an abstraction, but as a viable decolonial queer female/femme future of existence, and as an embodied, collective, and joyful practice.

Establishing a Shared Vocabulary: Artivism, Queerness, Decolonial Futures, Movement, and Femininities

To frame the chapters that follow, this introduction establishes a shared vocabulary by clarifying several key concepts—*artivism, queer/Afro-queer, coloniality/temporality/futurity, movement,* and *femme/feminine/women.* These terms ground the theoretical and political lens through which Afro-queer Puerto Rican women artists are analyzed. Far from being static labels, they intertwine and denote positionalities, epistemologies, and interpretive methods that center the body, performance, and movement as central tools of resistance and social transformation.

The artists examined in this book are best understood as *artivists,* following Eva Aladro-Vico's (2018) definition of artivism as the use of art to foster social change and transformation. Artivism diverges from conventional aesthetic traditions through its political commitments and entanglement with the material realities of marginalized lives. Its forms are hybrid and unclassifiable, resisting aesthetic and ideological containment. The artists use disobedient gestures to intervene in public and institutional spaces, to generate decolonial imaginaries, and to envision alternative futures. Their work critiques political inaction and highlights the precarities faced by queer communities, women, and other structurally excluded populations.

Emerging from this artivist framework is a theorization of *queer* that moves beyond identity politics and into the realm of epistemology and resistance. This book proposes the construction of an Afro-queer canon rooted in embodied artistic and political praxis. Drawing on Halberstam's understanding of queer as a mode of refusal and a way of knowing (2011), I approach queerness here as an antinormative force that disrupts legibility, coherence, and disciplinary regimes. The queer visual, sonic, and performative practices analyzed throughout this book act as collective disobedience against aesthetic discipline, colonial frameworks, and capitalist logics of productivity. These works do not seek to include or exclude anyone from metaphorical or discursive closets. Rather, echoing Celiany Rivera Velázquez and Carlos Ulises Decena (2024), queerness operates as a shifting and destabilizing force—a geopolitical dislocation and transposition, an "umbrella" that resists taxonomic violence. Queer thus becomes a method for sensing, feeling, and thinking otherwise: a messy, joyful, incoherent, and radically relational mode of becoming.

The artists featured here channel this queer potential through a specifically Afro-queer, Puerto Rican, and femme lens, revealing how visuality itself can be a form of resistance. Their work reimagines visuality itself as a form of endurance, unsettling historical attempts to control Black femme bodies. Their work values joy, community, memory, and beauty, embracing what Halberstam (2011) describes as the disruptive power of the nonproductive and the deviant. Their voices, gestures, and images transform space and suggest radically different futures.

Foregrounding the autonomy of Black and queer subjects, the performances studied here render bodily presence as protest. Their gestures offer visibility, but also survival strategies, alternative forms of pleasure, and resistance to the forces of erasure that mark Puerto Rican colonial life and opposition to colonial and capitalist obliterations. The art analyzed here does not merely represent Afro-queer realities; it performs interventions in cultural and political discourse. These "irreverent," "rebellious," and "wild" bodies challenge heteronormative and colonial constraints and move through space in ways that are difficult to fix, contain, or neutralize. Through their undisciplined gestures, these artists question fixed ideas of femininity, refusing the temporal and social expectations imposed by patriarchal, heteronormative logics (Halberstam 2005). Their bodies are not passive representations but active tools for redefinition—porous, dynamic, in constant transformation and movement, and therefore more difficult to contain and control. Their undisciplined gestures refuse the timelines, behaviors, and appearances demanded by cisheteropatriarchal systems. In so doing, their bodies are transformed into active agents of critique—porous, fluid, and irreducibly dynamic.

Themes such as motherhood, community, oral memory, and unofficial histories emerge as critical motifs, articulating an anticapitalistic, decolonial aesthetic in which difference becomes a generative resource. These works do not simply depict Afro-queer realities; they enact them. They present new modalities of survival and belonging, using embodied joy and aesthetic rebellion to imagine decolonial futures. These movements are not just cultural expressions; they are political gestures. They speak directly to the condition of the Puerto Rican archipelago as a colonized territory, revealing how art can function as a decolonial strategy with tangible effects on society, culture, and politics.

The works examined in this study, thus, do not merely reflect on *coloniality* but enact resistance to it. Drawing on Muñoz's (2009) distinction between possibility and potentiality, I argue that these performances open up a queer potentiality grounded in the capacity to imagine futures not yet realized but sensed. Their movements articulate an aesthetic and political refusal to accept the limits imposed by capitalist temporality and colonial spatiality. In these gestures, art becomes a tool for dreaming otherwise. It sheds light on a political present defined by exploitation and abandonment and gestures toward the possibility of radically different futures.

In line with Jill Dolan's (2005) notion of utopia in performance, this volume proposes that imagining queer futures becomes a critical method for rethinking Puerto Rico's colonial status within a "modern/colonial world-system" (Mignolo 2000). If, as Grosfoguel argues, Puerto Rico functions within a "modern/colonial/capitalist world-system" and Puerto Rico is a "modern colony" (2003), then the subaltern perspectives of these women artists illuminate forms of global coloniality that persist long after formal colonization. This includes the global coloniality that endures systems of power, domination, and exploitation that originated with European colonialism but that continue to shape global socioeconomic and cultural relations (Quijano 2000). The artworks studied here expose a common story of a political colonial tradition that always aimed to control the bodies in the Puerto Rican archipelago.

These works speak from the racialized, feminized, and geographic margins to expose the colonial histories of bodily control. By reclaiming the language of movement—physical, metaphorical, aesthetic—they simultaneously make visible the effects of imperial domination and propose collective strategies for survival. The euphemism of Estado Libre Asociado [Commonwealth] is thus contested; instead, these performances envision alternative cultural and political possibilities for the archipelago. Their moving bodies act as tools of critique of coloniality, gender, and race through lived, embodied experiences of those whose lives are shaped by those very forces.

As Grosfoguel (2003) reminds us, capitalism is inseparable from systems of racial and gendered domination. The performances in this study render these structures visible through embodied aesthetic resistance. They do not seek assimilation but instead craft new imaginaries rooted in Afro-queer, femme, and feminist survivance. These works are acts of memory and rupture, privileging the geopolitical body as a site of knowledge production. The women artists featured here resist neoliberal forms of Caribbean exploitation and articulate their critique from within the periphery of the modern/colonial/capitalist world-system. Their moving bodies represent a critique of their reality from the geopolitical experience and memory of coloniality (Mignolo 2000). The convergences of performance, queer identity, and movement address the need to create new heterarchical thinking (Kontopoulos 1993) and spaces for life in the shadow of colonialism's persistence, to better understand social structures in their complexity, and the ways they are entangled with heterogeneous hierarchies and capitalism as a historical system.[13] The works of these women artists are interconnected by these convergences.

This book offers new frameworks for understanding identity and the body as sites of decolonial intervention against heteronormative, patriarchal, and oppressive systems of value. By theorizing women's bodies, femininity, and femme as flexible, inclusive categories, it resists narrow definitions rooted in cis heteronormativity. I use the term *woman* expansively, recognizing femininity and femme identity as expressive modes available to anyone who claims them, regardless of gender identity, biological features, or sexual orientation. While the artists featured in this book identify as queer cisgender women and/or advocate for queer life through their artistic practices, their work fosters broader forms of solidarity. Their performances imagine a world in which all women—cis, trans, femme, straight, Black, disabled, older, of varying class backgrounds, or otherwise marginalized—are seen, heard, and valued. And this inclusivity is only possible through a queer lens.

Feminine bodies—cis, trans, Black, queer, heterosexual, of a specific social class, young, or old—are often deemed vulgar or unruly when they defy norms. They are marked as excessive when they resist expectations of modesty, docility, and propriety. This book centers these four Afro-queer Puerto Rican multidisciplinary artist *mujeres desobedientes*, whose visual and performative languages—across video, filmmaking, music, visual art, dance, and performance—embody undisciplined femininities. Through physical, digital, political, domestic, and metaphorical movements, these artists defy, deconstruct, and reimagine dominant understandings of beauty, femininity, and respectability. Their practices engage with and contest the sociopolitical structures that attempt to control Black, queer, and feminine bodies in Puerto Rico. In doing so, they provoke what Jill Dolan calls a "utopian performative" (2005), offering audiences moments of collective recognition and imagined potential.

The visibility and impact of these artists are intimately tied to their movements—understood in expansive terms as performative, physical, political, digital, and affective gestures across public, communal, and domestic spheres. These movements are often labeled as irreverent, rebellious, or improper because they transgress the gendered and racialized boundaries imposed by heteronormative colonial logics. For queer, Black, female, and femme bodies—as well as for other marginalized Puerto Rican subjects—movement is both a physical necessity and a radical aesthetic strategy, as explored in Dávila and Ramirez's anthology *Nuyorican and Diasporican Visual Art* (2025). Within Puerto Rico's colonial context, it carries a double meaning: displacement and creative resistance. Marisel Moreno's *Crossing Waters* (2022) extends this analysis by describing the Caribbean Sea as a militarized and racialized border that simultaneously connects and divides, disrupting romanticized myths of paradise and exposing the realities of climate change, poverty, anti-Blackness, sexism, homophobia, hunger, and war that drive migration. Moreno introduces the concept of "liquid borders" (2022, 3), which she further develops into "the process of bordering" (4), as ways of understanding mobility, dislocation, and constraint. I read these liquid, metaphorical, and material processes within the Puerto Rican performance and visual art context. Movement in these artistic works functions not merely as geographic transition but as an embodied politics, with queer and Black artists deploying movement to articulate alternative futures that resist both assimilation and erasure. This is what Moreno terms "uneven mobilities" (4), which I link to both disobedience and the aesthetic of disorder that defines the work of the artists in this study.

These artists visually and performatively challenge normative timelines and resist "straight time" (Halberstam 2005). In contrast, their expressions of femininity resist socially sanctioned roles and expectations, rendering their movements legible as undisciplined. By focusing on their artistic gestures and movements, I propose that they carve out movable spaces—fluid, queer, and hybrid—where femininity and queerness coexist and merge. Yet their work shifts the emphasis from occupying space to moving through spaces—claiming a presence that is neither static nor easily contained. Instead, their movements make space porous, dynamic, and resistant to capture. Their performances form a powerful critique of coloniality and offer speculative blueprints for different futures.

In this way, this book contributes to a growing body of scholarship that links Afro-Caribbean performance to decolonial theory, queer studies, and feminist thought. In doing so, this study imbues the intersectional female body (at the intersection of race, age, class, gender, and sexual identity) with values that capitalism and colonialism—in this case in the context of the Puerto Rican archipelago—have stripped from it. Through their undisciplined movements, the women artists studied here provoke, resist, and reimagine. Their performances are not only cultural expressions but acts of geopolitical critique and social transformation. Through the practices of these *mujeres desobedientes,* we are invited to imagine new modes of visibility, collectivity, and becoming.

Similarly, other aspects emerging from the Afro-queer female body are addressed in the works analyzed in this study: motherhood, community, support systems, belonging. These elements are framed within an anticapitalistic perspective, in which difference functions as a resource rather than a source of alienation. Central to this framework is the recuperation of collective oral memory and unofficial histories, which serves as a vital decolonial strategy. These artists, therefore, offer more than an Afro-queer feminist body of work; they articulate tools of decolonial survival that illuminate Puerto Rico's condition as a US-occupied territory. These artistic movements thus propose decolonial acts with an impact on arts, society, culture, and politics.

The term *Afro–Puerto Rican* is used here in alignment with how the artists self-identify, whether as Afro–Puerto Rican or Afro-Dominican Puerto Rican, as in the case of Helen Ceballos. These identities are not reducible to phenotype but are anchored in shared cultural, historical, and ancestral experiences. In their work, Blackness operates not merely as a marker of identity but as a conduit for complex negotiations with memory, neighborhood, geography, and social belonging. This is why artists such as Gisela Rosario Ramos/Macha Colón, Awilda Rodríguez Lora, and Awilda Sterling-Duprey were included in the exhibition *Puerto Rico Negrx,* which opened at the Museo de Arte Contemporáneo de Puerto Rico (MAC) [Museum of Contemporary Art of Puerto Rico], on October 20, 2023 and ran until September 1, 2024, curated by Marina Reyes Franco and guest curator María Elena Ortiz of the Modern Art Museum of Fort Worth.[14]

Puerto Rico Negrx has been the first institutional exhibition in Puerto Rico to foster an intergenerational dialogue and provide historical context for the work of self-identified Black Puerto Rican and diasporic artists, presenting works from the 1990s to the present. The curators drew inspiration from Edwin Velázquez's pivotal 1996 exhibition *Paréntesis: Ocho artistas negros contemporáneos,* which challenged dominant narratives that either folklorized or erased Blackness altogether. *Puerto Rico Negrx* not only updated these conversations for the present moment but expanded them to include diverse gender identities and sexualities. Featuring over thirty artists and collectives—including Daniel Lind Ramos, Juan Sánchez, Glendalys Medina, and Las Nietas de Nonó, among others—the exhibition employed a broad range of media such as painting, sculpture, installation, performance, video, and archival materials. It explored critical themes like identity, spirituality, displacement, food sovereignty, migration, post-plantation legacies, reggaetón, and Afro-Caribbean resistance.

What stands out about *Puerto Rico Negrx,* beyond the artistic quality of the works presented, is the exhibition's capacity to expand and complicate our understanding of race and Blackness within the Spanish Caribbean.[15] This is especially significant when considering Blackness outside the context of the United States, and particularly within the colonial framework of Puerto Rico. These same considerations guided the selection of artists featured in this book. The artists' expressions of *Negritud* challenge the pervasive whitening tendencies and the linguistic strategies used in Spanish to evade the term "negro/negra/negrx," and instead foreground the possibilities for inter-Caribbean and transgeographic solidarities beyond the US imaginary.

The analysis of these artists' movements theorizes the utopian potential, queer futurities, and political aesthetics inherent in queer Afro–Puerto Rican interdisciplinary performance, with particular emphasis on their spatial and temporal interventions in the public sphere. These artistic expressions resist not only sexism and homophobia, but also ageism, fatphobia, and transphobia. Femininity, here, is understood as a floating signifier—one that can be claimed by women who are frequently denied it, including older, fat, and trans individuals. Through their work, these Afro-queer women artists articulate new modes of cultural disobedience that interrogate coloniality and offer alternative ways of existing in a society marked by systemic violence and erasure.

Their art resists a cultural logic that contributes to the institutional invisibility of women—particularly queer Black women—as well as to the normalization of sexual violence and feminicide, which occurs at an alarming rate.[16] For this reason, it is crucial to clarify at the outset how I use terms such as queer, Afro-queer, feminine/femme/ women, coloniality, and temporality/futurity/movement—not as fixed categories, but as fluid, intersectional, and politically charged frameworks that shape both the interpretive approach and the decolonial commitments of this book.

In sum, the convergence of artivism, queerness, Afro-Caribbean identity, and embodied movement in the work of these women artivists reveals the transformative power of aesthetics as a political and decolonial practice. Their performances do not merely represent oppression; they enact resistance. Through movement, voice, and presence, these artists carve out material and imagined spaces for freedom, care, and collective becoming. By foregrounding the entangled histories of coloniality and embodiment, this book offers a decolonial feminist methodology rooted in the lived experiences and radical aesthetics of Afro-queer Puerto Rican women and femmes. Through their bodies in motion, these artists offer both a critical reading of the present and a visionary gesture toward not-yet-imagined futures.

Disobedience as Method: Embodied Research, Feminist Kinship, and Decolonial Approaches

This book emerges from over a decade of fieldwork, critical research, and embodied witnessing in Puerto Rico, beginning in 2008 and intensifying from 2013 to the present. During this time, I closely followed the evolving trajectories of the artists featured in these pages, immersing myself in the island's political and cultural landscape while deepening my engagement with performance studies, decolonial theory, and queer feminist thought. Rather than treating these artists' works as static objects of analysis, I theorized alongside their practices, approaching performance as a living, generative, and ever-evolving site of inquiry. I witnessed how their embodied vocabularies, aesthetic interventions, and community-based actions transformed the sociocultural fabric of the Puerto Rican archipelago. From this sustained encounter emerged this study: a cartographic and theoretical project that maps how queer Afro-Caribbean women in Puerto Rico deploy performance as a mode of worldmaking—refusing normative representations of womanhood while forging decolonial ways of existing, relating, and resisting.

The genesis of this book is rooted in a personal act of disobedience: my decision in 2013 to leave a marriage that demanded I relinquish my intellectual pursuits in favor of a domestic life that I did not desire in that moment. Choosing instead to spend that Christmas in Puerto Rico, away from the expectations of my Southern Italian hometown, marked a turning point. It was there that my queer, undisciplined movements—personal and intellectual—began to take shape more consciously. It was also then that I started encountering the disobedient women who would shape this book.

In Puerto Rico, my academic interest in visual art and performance converged with these personal ruptures. Since 2013, I have returned to Puerto Rico almost every year, nurturing enduring ties with the artists whose works—unbeknownst to me then—would later form the core of this study. I attended their performances, listened to their stories, and followed how their aesthetic and political practices interrogated the entanglements of femininity, coloniality, social norms, and the political history of the island. As a scholar of Latin American and Caribbean studies, I became particularly attuned to how these dynamics manifested in Puerto Rico—a Caribbean territory bound by US colonialism.

The intellectual inquiry began with a set of fundamental questions: How and why did performances by queer Afro–Puerto Rican women compel me to think about coloniality? In what ways did the colonial condition of Puerto Rico shape their responses, and how did their artistic interventions differ from other geopolitical contexts? I was struck by the provocative presence and cultural power of femme and feminine bodies in these works. What made their presence resonate so forcefully? What aesthetic and embodied tools were they deploying? And how did their performances confront, reflect, or transform Puerto Rico's colonial and patriarchal legacies? And more in general, how do "undisciplined femininities" contribute to resistance and redefinition of cultural and sociopolitical rules?

This book responds to these questions through a methodology that is both intellectual and profoundly personal. Over the years, I cultivated meaningful relationships with the artists featured in these pages—relationships marked by dialogue, mutual care, and shared moments. I approached the artists not simply as subjects of study, but as collaborators. My scholarship thus unfolded not in isolation but through conversation—intellectual, artistic, and affective—across time, being more relational than extractivist.

For example, I first met Gisela Rosario Ramos/Macha Colón at a *bombazo* in Río Piedras, where we spoke about her documentary *El hijo de Ruby,* which later became the subject of a published article and the foundation of chapter 1 in this book. I encountered Awilda Rodríguez Lora outside the Conservatorio de Música in San Juan. Our conversation about her performance project *La Mujer Maravilla* led me to discover her recorded works, which immediately resonated with unspoken yet familiar narratives. Over time, we shared meals, ideas, and community at her home, La Rosario, and through virtual gatherings during the COVID-19 pandemic.

I met Helen Ceballos after seeing her perform at a university conference in Mayagüez. Her embrace and enthusiasm made me feel as though we had known each other for years. We continued to connect at exhibitions, gatherings, and meals—spaces where her generosity and artistic urgency became unmistakable. I first encountered Awilda Sterling-Duprey after already knowing her work and having decided she belonged in this project. Our first in-person meeting—over dinner and margaritas at *Panucho* in Santurce—confirmed the sense of kinship I had long felt through her art. During an extended stay in Puerto Rico from December 2023 to April 2024, we spent more time together, deepening our conversations and expanding my understanding of her philosophy of art and life.

The formation of this book is also intimately tied to my experiences of motherhood. Between 2021 and 2023, I became a mother, twice, with a previous pregnancy loss in 2019. My extended stay in Puerto Rico from December 2023 to April 2024, with a toddler and a breastfed newborn, became a physically and emotionally demanding exercise in navigating colonial infrastructure while balancing childcare, fieldwork, and writing. Daily acts such as grocery shopping, driving, or sleeping were imbued with the burdens of colonial precarity. Yet motherhood also expanded my interpretive lens. I began to understand works such as *La Mujer Maravilla* by Rodríguez Lora or *Cuerpos fronterizos* by Ceballos through the lived experience of maternal embodiment. Macha Colón's *jayaera* became a source of resilience; Rodríguez Lora's notion of *sustento* took on new meanings; and the communal networks that surrounded me echoed the very strategies these artists deploy in their performances. Even silence—especially in Sterling-Duprey's *en-cierro* and . . . *blindfolded*—emerged as a critical form of survival and resistance charged with new value.

Throughout this journey, I maintained ongoing dialogues with each artist. We met individually and collectively. A recorded podcast with all of them on March 7, 2024, at the recording studio of the Taller Comunidad La Goyco in

San Juan became a foundational thread of this book. I shared drafts of each chapter with the artists, generating vibrant exchanges that also shaped my readings and revealed the book as a collaborative act of thinking and making. Their feedback informed the book's theoretical framework and sharpened its critical perspective.

Writing this book while navigating postpartum embodiment and solo parenting in a colonial context became its own kind of performance. As Awilda Rodríguez Lora put it during our recorded group conversation at La Goyco on March 7, 2024: "Le metiste *la cuerpa*" [You put your body into it—with the queer variation of the word "body," "cuerpo" as "cuerpa"]. The intellectual labor of this project is inseparable from the disobedience that first brought me to Puerto Rico—and resonates with the aesthetic-political disobedience at the heart of the artists' work. Whether through the rupture of divorce or the transformation of motherhood, I found myself returning to the same animating question: what does it mean to live—and live fully—on one's own terms?

As *la performera* 2.5 reminds us, *sustento* is not only nourishment but action, verb, and community—embracing the future while holding the past with love (chapter 2). Remembering how I met these women is not merely anecdotal; it is a methodology. It marks the affective, embodied, and intellectual grounds from which this book was born. And it affirms a common denominator across these chapters: disobedience.

The selection of the artists featured in this book is the result of a long and evolving journey through Puerto Rico's vibrant and complex artistic landscape. Rather than presenting an exhaustive list of all deserving contemporary creators in the archipelago, this study highlights four artists whose work remains academically understudied yet deeply significant within the intersection of art, activism, and decolonial thought. These include established multidisciplinary artists such as Gisela Rosario Ramos/Macha Colón and Awilda Sterling-Duprey, alongside a younger generation with robust bodies of work—namely Awilda Rodríguez Lora and Helen Ceballos.

The selection was guided by three criteria: (1) the extent to which each artist's practice engages with movement—physical, political, conceptual—as a site of inquiry into gender, race, sexuality, and coloniality; (2) the depth and consistency of their creative output; and (3) the ways in which their work enriches intergenerational understandings of contemporary Puerto Rican cultural production. The chapters follow a circular structure: beginning with Rosario Ramos/Macha Colón (b. 1967) and ending with Sterling-Duprey (b. 1947), while centering Rodríguez Lora (b. 1977) and Ceballos (b. 1986) in the middle chapters. This structure reflects the artists' intergenerational relationships, including mentorships and collaborations that shape their practices.[17]

These artists are best understood as *artivists*—where art and activism are inseparable from the colonial realities of Puerto Rico. Their works respond critically to the island's ongoing crises, particularly those intensified since 2016, while drawing from long-standing histories of resistance. Most of the pieces discussed here were created between 2013 and 2023, though earlier works are referenced to trace aesthetic evolutions and thematic continuity. Together, they offer a powerful, intersectional, and multigenerational perspective on queer Afro-Caribbean visual and performance cultures. Their work not only represents but enacts disobedience—against colonialism, patriarchy, heteronormativity, and racialized gender norms. Their performances are central to this book's conceptual and critical framework.

This book was born from embodied proximity: from returning, listening, and staying with the discomforts, joys, contradictions, and urgencies of Puerto Rico's artistic and political life. As mentioned, my methodology is rooted in queer feminist, decolonial, and performance-based epistemologies. It is grounded not only in theory but in intimacy, collaboration, and care. Rather than observing from a distance, I moved alongside the artists—research as kinship, as co-presence, as an ethics of mutual exchange. It is grounded in the ethics of reciprocal exchange and the affective labor of building trust—over meals, in living rooms, at performances, on WhatsApp, during pandemics, while breastfeeding, and across oceans. This approach rejects extractive models of knowledge production in favor of a situated, embodied, and community-engaged practice of critical witnessing.

The project thus emerges as both a scholarly intervention and a collective gesture. It is a cartography of resistance, tracing how queer Afro-Caribbean women in Puerto Rico craft new ways of being through performance. It is also a deeply personal chronicle of how disobedience—in life, in research, in art—becomes a method. These pages are the result of years of dialogue, movement, and shared refusals. They are also a testament to the transformative potential of feminist kinship and creative survival within and beyond colonial terrain. Ultimately, this book asks, How can we learn from those who refuse, who insist on living otherwise? The answers lie not only in the performances themselves, but in the lives and communities that make them possible. This work is an archive of these artists' productions, but it also affirms disobedience not merely as a subject matter, but as a praxis.

And this, too, is a scholarly method.

Embodied Narratives: Mapping the Chapters

As previously mentioned, the choice of these specific artists and the order in which I study them is deliberate. I focus on four artists who primarily live and work in Puerto Rico, selecting two well-established figures—Gisela Rosario Ramos/Macha Colón and Awilda Sterling-Duprey—and two younger artists—Awilda Rodríguez Lora and Helen Ceballos. The book opens and closes with the more established artists, who have both influenced and collaborated with the younger ones. This circular structure reflects a generative intergenerational dialogue, highlighting the continuities and transformations within queer feminist artistic practices in Puerto Rico.

The performances analyzed in this book are grounded in movement—through bodies, urban and political spaces, and networks of care and resistance. Their force lies in how they question the ways women are spoken about and treated, how femininity is constructed, and the potential and limits that performative movements have for political transformation. The book is composed of an introduction, four central chapters, and a conclusion.

Chapter 1, "Filming, Performing, and Singing Disobedient Femininities: Gisela Rosario Ramos and Macha Colón," examines the multimedia work of Rosario Ramos/Macha Colón. I analyze her directorial projects—*El hijo de Ruby* (2014) and *Perfume de gardenias* (2021)—as well as her alter ego Macha Colón's performative persona and musical productions, focusing especially on "Jayá" and *Tanquecito de amor* (2011). The chapter explores how Rosario Ramos's art reimagines femininity, sexuality, and embodiment through irreverent movement, humor, and visual poetics.

Chapter 2, "Wonder Woman Dances Every Day: The Radical Movements of Awilda Rodríguez Lora," focuses on Rodríguez Lora's ongoing performance project *La Mujer Maravilla* (2013–), as well as *La Rosario* (2014–), *Bailar todos los días* (2015–), and *Sustento* (2019–). Rodríguez Lora's performances enact a queer feminist politics of sustenance, care, and community through movement, sound, and presence, challenging dominant representations of race, gender, and coloniality.

Chapter 3, "Entre Islas: Shifted Geographies, Displaced Borders, and the Queer Caribbean Movements of Helen Ceballos," traces a cartography of the transdisciplinary work of Ceballos, a Dominican-born, Puerto Rico–based performer and cultural organizer. Drawing from her experiences as an undocumented migrant and queer Afro-Caribbean woman, her work interrogates the borders of identity, nation, and belonging. The study goes from *Sitiada* (2010) to the most recent works, such as *Cerezas por papeles* (2021), *Cuerpos fronterizos* (2021), *Fue esa la vía* (2021), and *Rito de paso/comen de mí* (2022–23), among others. The chapter also considers her work as a *gestora cultural* showing how Ceballos's practice combines performance, writing, photography, curatorial work, and cultural managing to create a poetics of embodied displacement and Caribbean resistance.

Chapter 4, "Artistic Articulations: The Visual Movements of Awilda Sterling-Duprey," analyzes key performances such as *Reggaetón lento* (2010), *Maelo en el cuerpo* (2015), *Transparente desnudez* (2015), and *Soy la reencarnación de un alma esclavizada* (2021), as well as the most recent projects *Lacks Criticality* (2018–23), and . . . *blindfolded* (2019–23), among others. Sterling-Duprey's practice merges visual arts, Yoruba spirituality, and improvisational movement to explore Blackness, womanhood, and colonial memory. Her abstract aesthetic gestures construct a decolonial language that reclaims visibility and affirms Black female embodiment.

The conclusion, titled "Estoy Jayá," revisits the central arguments of the book and considers the broader cultural and political implications of the artists' work. While acknowledging the limitations of a single-volume study, it gestures toward a wider landscape of queer Afro-Caribbean artists who are shaping the island's vibrant queer Afro-Caribbean art scene. The book closes as an open invitation to continue thinking about gender, performance, and liberation through disobedient, embodied, and collective forms of art making.

Movements of Disobedience: A Conclusion

In this book, I bridge movement and queer space theory to propose an Afro-queer framework that centers performance—understood through movement and visual aesthetics—as a critical lens for examining the sociopolitical weight carried by Afro-queer women's bodies. These movements are shaped by the intersecting forms of precarity, including race, class, gender, ethnicity, age, sexuality, and disability. The artists studied here embody, in different ways, these layered vulnerabilities as they queer the urban, domestic, and public spaces they inhabit, reclaiming mobility as a form of resistance.

The project underscores how deeply the artists' personal expression of their internal worlds can resonate outward and influence an entire culture of multiple movements. Thus, it unfolds along two intertwined axes. First, it highlights how queer Afro–Puerto Rican women artists reclaim both physical and metaphorical space as part of a broader cultural, political, and social movement toward

Puerto Rico's decolonization. Second, it examines how their work generates aesthetics and narratives that defy heteronormative logic, echoing Halberstam's call for a "queer adjustment" to the ways we conceptualize time and space (2005, 6). Yet these artists do more than demand space—they traverse, disrupt, and transform it. Through embodied gestures and performative acts, they challenge dominant structures that seek to marginalize them, asserting new ways of being, seeing, and imagining femininity, identity, and belonging within Puerto Rican society.

The book thus centers the performances of women too often rendered invisible or expendable by a sexist, racist, and heteronormative society—including within LGBTQ+ spaces. These artists disobey, misbehave, and defy the boundaries of what is socially permissible for women. Their artistic "misbehaviors" enact a queer wildness—borrowing the term from Halberstam and Tavia Nyong'o—that reclaims public space through bodily presence, movement, and dissent. Whether through Gisela Rosario Ramos/Macha Colón's plural, playful reimaginings of femininity; Awilda Rodríguez Lora's radical self-love and embodiment of Black and Brown queer womanhood; Helen Ceballos's explorations of displacement, migration, and diasporic queerness; or Awilda Sterling-Duprey's choreographic interrogations of Blackness and femininity—each artist deploys movement as a decolonial strategy. Dancing, performing, and moving becomes a political force. Their bodies become sites of resistance, redefinition, and renewal. Their movements are not merely physical—they are political. These artists claim space not merely to exist, but to imagine and enact alternative futures. In doing so, these Afro-queer women artists transform marginalization into a generative force. Their work maps a Puerto Rican present haunted by colonial neglect and envisions a common future shaped through the embodied, unruly movements of *disobedient women.*

ONE

Filming, Performing, and Singing Disobedient Femininities

Gisela Rosario Ramos and Macha Colón

> Déjate de cosas
> Tú sabes la que hay
> Agárrame las tetas
> y bésame que ya . . .
> [Quit messing around
> You know what's up
> Grab my tits
> and kiss me already . . .]
>
> Macha Colón
>
> "Tú sabes la que hay"
>
> Song from the album *Tanquecito de amor*

> I am an undisciplined artist [. . .]
> I want to move people.
>
> Gisela Rosario Ramos/Macha Colón / From the podcast recorded with the author on March 7, 2024

Onstage, a fat woman wearing bold, colorful clothing and artfully applied glittery makeup—Macha Colón—unapologetically loud and luminous—sings with full-bodied bravado, voice raspy and commanding: "¡Agárrame las tetas!" Just then, a tray of *carne frita* [fried pork] is passed to her from the audience, like an offering. Without missing a beat, she reaches out, grabs a piece, and bites into it mid-verse. The grease glistens on her fingers as she chews and sings, her pleasure both sonic and gustatory. Her body, her hunger, her voice—everything insists on presence, on being seen and being felt. The air is thick with laughter, tension, recognition, music, sweat, and singing. From the audience, a sixty-year-old woman who moments earlier passed the *carne frita* to the singer—Awilda Sterling-Duprey—cuts through the moment with her own raw declaration: "Gisela, ¡Agárrame las tetas!" It's not an interruption but a joining-in, a fierce echo. Her voice rises in support, but also as a reclamation, a demand for embodiment, for visibility, for touch and tenderness on her own terms, following the vibe and guidance of the song. The stage and the audience collapse into each other for a brief, radiant second. The line between performance and life blurs—here are women, aging, fat, Afro-queer, unruly, desiring—refusing shame, refusing being silenced.[1]

The first disobedient woman featured in this book is the queer Puerto Rican interdisciplinary artist Gisela Rosario Ramos (she/her, b. 1967), known artistically as Macha Colón.[2] Throughout her career, Rosario Ramos has declared her disobedience across various platforms—including a podcast recorded on March 7, 2024, in which she joined all the artists featured in this book and me. The epigraph that opens this chapter comes from that conversation, where she links her identity as an "undisciplined artist" to her artistic imperative to "move people." Movement, both literal and metaphorical, is central to her work. It defines the way she produces her art and how she seeks to connect with her audience. Her visual, musical, and performative expressions articulate the power of irreverent motion—motions that traverse the public sphere and challenge the boundaries of what is considered acceptable or beautiful.

Through practices of radical joy and embodied disobedience, Rosario Ramos proposes alternative tools for queer survival.[3] Her work occupies and mobilizes both physical and digital spaces to affirm a femininity that celebrates its own existence—one that resists and redefines imposed standards. Rosario Ramos dismantles binary understandings of gender and patriarchal norms, reshaping conventional ideals of beauty, love, and community. She reimagines Puerto Rican queer femininity as joyful, resistant, and gloriously nonconforming. Her body of work offers a new geography of womanhood—one that resists neat categorization and insists on the legitimacy of bodies often deemed incomplete, imperfect, or wrong by dominant society.[4]

This chapter centers on the representations of femininity that Rosario Ramos constructs through her diverse artistic practices: her filmmaking, music, performance, and the overall aesthetic of Macha Colón. Specifically, I examine two major aspects of her creative output: her work as a film director and her persona as a performer and singer. As a filmmaker, Rosario Ramos has directed works in various genres, including the short documentary *El hijo de Ruby* [Ruby's son] (2014) and her first fiction feature film *Perfume de gardenias* (2021).[5] As Macha Colón, I will focus on the visual and sonic components of her performances, paying particular attention to her aesthetics and to two songs, "Jayá" and "Tanquecito de amor," from her 2016 album *Tanquecito de amor* [Little Tank of Love], originally recorded in 2011.[6]

Her artistic works are the result of her intellectual growth since her college years. Rosario Ramos studied Black and Puerto Rican studies and film and media studies at Hunter College in New York City, where she also worked as a documentary editor. Upon returning to Puerto Rico in 2002, she became involved in television production, served as artistic and programming director at Casa de Cultura Ruth Hernández, organized cultural events, continued to edit, and developed her music and film career. In her biography for the National Association of Latino Arts and Cultures (NALAC), she writes: "Mi trabajo nace de mi cuerpo. Cuando crecí, me inspiraron figuras como Madonna, pero pronto me di cuenta de que nunca iba a ser como ella, no por falta de talento, sino porque no era rubia ni delgada." [My work comes from my body. When I was growing up, I was inspired by figures like Madonna, but I quickly realized that I would never be like her—not because I lacked talent, but because I wasn't blonde or skinny.][7] Through this reflection, Rosario Ramos makes clear that her art arises from a politics of embodiment that challenges dominant ideals of whiteness, thinness, and femininity.

Rosario Ramos is an artivist whose work aims to dismantle systems of fatphobia, racism, sexism, homophobia, and patriarchy.[8] This chapter will explore how her aesthetic and artistic practices confront and expand the meanings of femininity beyond the confines of heteronormative and patriarchal frameworks. Through her films, songs, music videos, and performances, Rosario Ramos offers powerful new ways—in a decolonial, anticapitalistic, and anti-heteronormative way—to express and celebrate sexuality, gender identity, gender fluidity, femininity, and beauty.

Disobedient Femininities on Screen: *El hijo de Ruby*

In the final scene of *El hijo de Ruby* (2014), a short documentary directed by Gisela Rosario Ramos, a young man opens and twirls a wide, flowing white skirt in time with the rhythm of a *bomba* drum.[9] The viewer immediately recognizes the dancer as the same person from earlier scenes—Lionel "Lío"

Villahermosa—but now adorned in a garment traditionally worn by women in Puerto Rican *bomba* dance. His movements not only define the rhythm but also articulate a transformation: from previous performances in masculine attire to a final act that embraces femininity through embodied expression. With this striking visual gesture, Rosario Ramos challenges binary and patriarchal representations of gender and queerness. Through Lío's performance, she offers an alternative cinematic narrative of queer masculinity and femininity—one that is fluid, embodied, and defiant of normative expectations. The skirt becomes more than a costume; it is a symbolic tool that allows for a reimagining of who can be feminine and how femininity can be expressed and celebrated on screen.[10]

El hijo de Ruby centers on the story of Lionel "Lío" Villahermosa, a contemporary Puerto Rican artist, as he reconstructs his family history—particularly his relationship with his father, Ruby, a talented bomba dancer who struggled with drug addiction and was largely absent from Lío's life. The film's title, *El hijo de Ruby* [Ruby's Son], emphasizes this connection: Lío's identity is framed through his father, not only biologically but also artistically and emotionally. The documentary unfolds through four distinct bomba performances, each corresponding to a different rhythm and emotional state, mapping Lío's journey of self-discovery and familial memory.[11] These dance sequences act as narrative anchors that trace Lío's process of healing, reconnection, and self-affirmation as Lionel Villahermosa, but also as *el hijo de Ruby.*

The final dance, performed in a traditional skirt, adds a powerful layer of meaning. It is a moment of transformation that not only honors his father's legacy but also asserts Lío's own identity through a queered embodiment of Puerto Rican cultural tradition. By integrating gender nonconforming performance into a folkloric practice often associated with heteronormative frameworks, *El hijo de Ruby* reclaims bomba as a site of resistance, healing, and self-expression. Rosario Ramos thus offers a deeply moving and politically resonant portrait of queer identity rooted in cultural memory and performance.

Nothing in *El hijo de Ruby* explicitly anticipates or reveals Lío Villahermosa's gender identity or sexual orientation. Although the documentary offers intimate glimpses into Lío's childhood, family life, and emotional struggles, his identity remains unmarked until the final scene. There, without warning or explanation, Lío appears wearing a traditional bomba skirt, ready to dance. The moment is not presented as a revelation, confession, or spectacle—it simply unfolds as the film's natural epilogue, a quiet culmination of memory, healing, and artistic expression.

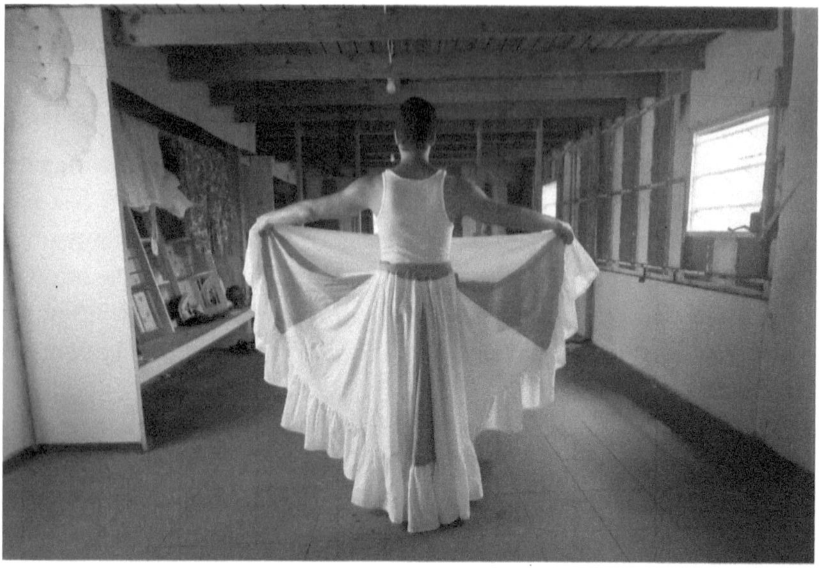

FIGURE 1.1. From a scene of *El hijo de Ruby*. Photo credit: Ángel G. Flores Rodríguez. Courtesy of Ángel G. Flores Rodríguez.

This understated choice by director Gisela Rosario Ramos is deliberate. Divided into four bomba dance sequences, each marked by distinct rhythms, colors, settings, and camera movement, the film is not centered on sexuality. Rather, it crafts a layered narrative through dance, aesthetics, and embodiment. Rosario Ramos resists framing this as a "gay film," opting instead for a portrayal where queerness emerges not through exposition but through presence. Lío is not portrayed within the limits of familiar stereotypes—he is neither the flamboyant gay man, which would put him "a polite distance from the viewer" (Venkatesh 2016, 5)—nor the token queer figure. He is a complex individual whose story speaks to vulnerability, resilience, and creative survival. He is a masculine-presenting man who, in the final dance, confidently expresses a feminine aspect of himself—without labels, justification, or apology. His choice to wear a skirt while dancing bomba does not signal imitation but authenticity. He is not playing a woman; he is a man dancing bomba in a skirt, fully inhabiting his identity through the freedom of movement.

The improvisational nature of bomba further reinforces this message. Each swirl of the skirt marks a different emotional resonance, a shifting spatial presence that gestures toward the fluidity and multiplicity of identity. Rosario Ramos crafts a space where Lío's femininity is not a departure from his masculinity but a reclamation of wholeness. The absence of narrative explanation liberates the queer subject from the burden of visibility-as-difference and opens up a space where queerness is simply lived.

This subtle but powerful shift challenges dominant cinematic conventions. As Vinodh Venkatesh argues in his analysis of "new maricón cinema," contemporary Latin American queer film is moving away from explanatory storytelling and toward sensory, affective engagement. Rather than foregrounding identity, these films invite viewers to feel their way into queerness, dissolving ethical distance and promoting empathetic connection.

In *El hijo de Ruby,* this shift is especially resonant. Viewers are drawn into Lío's journey and may feel an unexpected intimacy with him. The final scene surprises not because it "reveals" anything new, but because it breaks with the expectation that queerness must be disclosed or justified. Rosario Ramos reframes the narrative terrain to suggest that queer existence needs no preamble—it can simply be. From the beginning, the film anchors Lío's story in loss: the murder of his father Ruby, a man he barely knew, whom he first saw as a homeless figure on the street. Yet Ruby also left behind a legacy: he was a celebrated bomba dancer. Through this cultural inheritance, Lío rebuilds a fragmented history and, in doing so, claims his identity as *el hijo de Ruby.* But it is only in the final dance—in a skirt—that Lío fully realizes his personal and artistic lineage. It is in queering bomba that he reconnects with his father, and with himself.

Rosario Ramos, thus, uses the structure and aesthetics of the documentary to challenge patriarchal spaces and heteronormative logic. Drawing on José Esteban Muñoz's concept of *disidentification,* Lío resists assimilation and rejection alike. Instead, he finds a third path: he navigates a society that marginalizes difference by inhabiting it visibly, joyfully, and on his own terms, or—as Power-Sotomayor (2020) puts it—he is "listening to [his] flesh," creating a choreosonic landscape that allows him to claim not space itself, but a relation to space and place, to exist and to be. The film does not present queerness as identity politics but as an embodied performance of freedom, resistance, and survival.

In doing so, *El hijo de Ruby* offers what Ramón Rivera-Servera calls "new landscapes of inequality"—spaces where queer subjects find ways to exist, to move, and to be seen. Rosario Ramos gives Lío room to be complex and unfinished, rooted in both personal and cultural memory, yet open to transformation. Her documentary reclaims bomba as a medium not only for healing but for imagining new forms of being in the world—forms that embrace contradiction, fluidity, and radical presence.

In *El hijo de Ruby*, Gisela Rosario Ramos proposes a radical rethinking of how femininity and queerness are embodied and perceived on screen. Rather than foregrounding identity through overt exposition, the film invites the viewer to encounter queerness as an affective, aesthetic, and political force. The final dance sequence—where Lío Villahermosa performs bomba in a skirt—resists the spectacle of coming out or revelation. Instead, it gestures toward what Jacques Rancière calls the "emancipated spectator": one who actively interprets what they see, questioning assumptions and reconfiguring meaning beyond the "obviousness of the visible in order to sketch a new topography of the possible" and get to what he defines as a "transformed sensation" (2011, 49, 56). This viewer is not a passive recipient, but a participant in creating new "topographies of the possible." This transformation in spectatorship aligns with José Esteban Muñoz's notion of queerness as a horizon of possibility—a way of sensing that something is missing in the world as it is.

The invisibility of Lío's sexual orientation throughout most of the film, and the understated but powerful final dance, become acts of resistance against rigid binaries and social norms. Lío's last dance escapes the rigidity of the present.[12] The final performance, set indoors, evokes intimacy and collectivity. As Muñoz suggests, dancing makes us "less like ourselves and more like each other," dissolving individual boundaries and forging shared futures (2009, 66). Lío's skirt movements do not merely signal a personal expression—they transform the space, reformulating how we understand identity within bomba's cultural framework. These movements, then, propose possible alternatives that highlight how close we are despite differences, and that can bring us together instead of separating us. The "us" in the film is the audience that is transported to that space whenever the film is watched. Thus, the audience represents the Muñotian potential future that allows us to imagine a possible future or, said in another way, that "allow[s] us to experience or feel the world as it should be" (Rivera-Servera 2012, 35). By queering bomba, Lío expands its expressive possibilities. This performance both softens gender binaries and offers a vision of a liberatory art form deeply rooted in Afro-Caribbean oral and musical traditions. As Juan Cartagena argues, bomba connects youth to ancestral knowledge through rebellion (2004), and Lío's fluid embodiment serves as both remembrance and defiance to remember his own oral history without ignoring the complexity and multilayered reality that race, gender, and queerness constitute within the bomba context, claiming space, thus, for queer existence without apology.[13]

However, this reimagining of the tradition sparked controversy. When Lío first danced bomba in a skirt in 2012, initial responses were tempered by respect for his father, a revered bomba figure. But as Lío continued performing, criticism—especially from men in the bomba community—intensified. Supporters like singer Ángela Flecha also became targets of misogynistic backlash. The gendered nature of this response reveals how deeply bomba remains entangled with patriarchal structures. While Lío was granted a limited space for transgression because of his lineage, Flecha's vocal support was met with overt hostility—illustrating how expressions of femininity, whether embodied by cis women or queer men, are still punished within traditional frameworks. Even if the act of writing a hateful comment on Facebook does not necessarily correspond to a real intention of hurting someone, "language is an expression of agency" (Rodríguez 2003, 69). The question is how we can educate the community and stop a global culture that constantly belittles, humiliates, and despises women. These events indeed reflect broader social dynamics: femininity remains porous and vulnerable to attack, whether expressed by women or queer individuals. Hatred directed at the female body—cis or trans—extends to anyone perceived as occupying femininity in ways that challenge normative expectations.

This animosity, often masked as tradition or humor, reinforces systems of control and exclusion. As Juana María Rodríguez reminds us, identity is not fixed but "situated in motion"—it is spatial, embodied, and often contested (2003). Queer bodies moving through public spaces generate "spaces of dissension," moments that expose social tensions and unsettle dominant narratives. *El hijo de Ruby* becomes one such space, offering a visual and emotional terrain where Lío can exist fully—without needing to justify his masculinity, femininity, or queerness.

Still, visibility can be fraught. Allyship, when not accompanied by a commitment to dismantling binary thinking, may replicate the very systems it seeks to oppose. The 2012 bomba song "El Gay" from the album *Tiempo al tiempo*, released by Los Rebuleadores de San Juan, exemplifies this tension. Though possibly intended as inclusive, the song reinforces stereotypes and underscores the need for nuanced, liberatory representations like Rosario Ramos's film.

The song "El Gay" by Los Rebuleadores de San Juan opens with a repeated chorus that narrates the story of a man judged for wearing a skirt while dancing bomba in a *batey*, the traditional community space for this Afro–Puerto Rican genre. While the lyrics appear to defend Lío Villahermosa's right to express himself freely, they also reflect a problematic reinforcement of stereotypes. For instance, the song stresses that "the problem is not that he is gay, but that he dances *bomba* backward"—a phrasing that subtly upholds heterosexual norms and portrays queerness as a deviation. Similarly, phrases like "pluma pluma pluma gay" evoke clichéd representations of gay identity through the image of flamboyance, undermining the song's supposed support with homophobic undertones. Los Rebuleadores de San Juan is a respected bomba group, and their attention to Lío's case signals his significance within the tradition. Yet, the figure of Jerry Ferrao—lead singer and a known provocateur—complicates this support. Ferrao may have used the song more to provoke debate than to offer genuine solidarity.[14] Regardless of intent, *El Gay* situates Lío's identity solely within the frame of his sexual orientation, erasing the broader richness of his artistry and individuality.

Lío responded by dancing publicly to *El Gay* in 2012, dressed in a skirt, re-appropriating both the song and the space he occupied.[15] In bomba, the dancer communicates with the lead drum to set the rhythm, a dialogue traditionally charged with sensual tension. Lío's performance queers this relationship, embodying femininity from a masculine-presenting body and transforming the exchange into one of joyful, queer desire. His public assertion of identity—through movement, costume, and presence—disrupted the normative codes of bomba and incited strong responses from both critics and supporters.[16]

This embodied defiance is visually and politically crystallized in Gisela Rosario Ramos's 2014 short documentary *El hijo de Ruby*. The film not only documents Lío's journey but also interrogates the language used to defend or condemn queer existence. It challenges those who, even when supportive, reproduce binary, patriarchal logics. Through careful aesthetic choices, the documentary queers the visual and sonic space of bomba, allowing Lío to occupy it on his own terms.[17] His skirted dance in the final scene functions as both artistic and political gesture—demanding visibility and redefining what is considered "irreverent" behavior in the public sphere.

El hijo de Ruby thus becomes a space of resistance, proposing alternative grammars for understanding queerness and femininity—especially in contexts where such expressions are marginalized or punished. *El hijo de Ruby* stages a powerful intervention in Puerto Rican cultural discourse. It challenges how we see, how we move, and how we imagine futures where queerness is not just tolerated but celebrated. This documentary is a political act of resistance that moves toward liberation by questioning the "virility of the nation" (Ríos Ávila 2009),[18] and does so by opening new possibilities for the multifaceted understandings of femininity beyond the exclusive relegation of it to the female body.

Through dance, memory, and presence, the film sketches a world where identities are fluid, traditions can transform, and liberation emerges in motion.

Rosario Ramos's work contests the idea that femininity belongs only to female bodies and instead celebrates it as a powerful mode of disobedience, agency, and redefinition. This ongoing project of cultural transformation continues in her later work, most notably her 2021 fiction film *Perfume de gardenias,* which expands her vision of liberated, irreverent femininities.

Disobedient Femininities on Screen: *Perfume de gardenias*

Gisela Rosario Ramos approaches femininity from a queer perspective, allowing it to be embodied by all kinds of bodies, regardless of gender. In her work, femininity and queerness are deeply intertwined. In *El hijo de Ruby,* this intersection is explored through a masculine body expressing femininity, while in *Perfume de gardenias* (2021), Rosario Ramos examines femininity, womanhood, and queerness through the often-overlooked lenses of age and death. Even here, however, she does so by highlighting how her characters move through space in pursuit of radical joy.

Perfume de gardenias is a Caribbean story about death, created by a mostly female production team and featuring the work of artists from various disciplines, including those responsible for the elaborate artistic funeral installations shown in the film. A coproduction with Colombia, the film is an interdisciplinary and multimedia project—reflecting the broader artistic vision of its creator. Notably, Rosario Ramos uses both her legal name and her artistic persona, Macha Colón, in the credits: Macha is credited as the film's director, while Gisela appears under her technical roles, such as producer and editor. This dual identity signals not only the film's artistic foundation but also Rosario Ramos's decision to embrace and integrate both sides of her creative self. By allowing Macha to step beyond the realm of concerts and performances, Rosario Ramos asserts her artistic maturity and rejects the dichotomy that once separated the "serious" Gisela from the "extravagant" Macha. Through *Perfume de gardenias,* audiences encounter a more liberated and empowered version of both personas. This evolution enabled Rosario Ramos to explore themes rarely addressed in Puerto Rican, Latin American, or global cinema: aging, queerness in later life, lesbianism, illness, and death. The film centers on a group of elderly women as a tribute to the matriarchal structure that defines many Puerto Rican families.

The story follows Isabel, a woman in her eighties who has spent years caring for her ill, ex-military husband. After his death, she organizes a uniquely creative funeral that attracts the attention of her community. This prompts Toña, a neighbor, to recruit her into a collective of women who design and assist in local funerals. With each ceremony, Isabel's artistry grows, as she incorporates personal elements that honor each deceased individual. However, tensions arise, leading to a split within the group and temporarily halting Isabel's work. She then begins to care for Julia, a terminally ill lesbian neighbor marginalized by the community. Julia makes a final request, which Isabel initially refuses—until she reflects on the natural cycles of death and renewal. In the end, Isabel returns to her artistic calling, while Toña adopts a more conventional role elsewhere.

In this study, I focus on the aspects of *Perfume de gardenias* that resonate most strongly with Rosario Ramos's broader body of work: diverse representations of the female body, varied expressions of femininity, and nuanced portrayals of queerness. I examine how these themes are conveyed through the film's use of visual imagery, music, religious symbolism, tradition, language, and bodily movement.

THE FEMALE BODY AND AGEISM

In *Perfume de gardenias,* Gisela Rosario Ramos—through her artistic persona Macha Colón—both embodies and dismantles traditional, social, and religious representations of the female body. From the film's conception, she breaks with conventional norms by casting elderly women in the leading roles, notably giving veteran actress Luz María Rondón her first lead performance at the age of eighty-eight. Rather than selecting a well-known or institutionally recognized figure, Rosario Ramos's decision highlights her consistent artistic ethos: to center marginalized voices and challenge societal expectations about age, visibility, and creative potential.

This philosophy is echoed in the closing credits song *Tanta vanidad* [So Much Vanity], performed by Macha Colón, where the lyrics reflect the irrelevance of socially imposed timelines and affirm the pursuit of personal joy. Rosario Ramos's work repeatedly affirms that value and fulfillment are not confined to youth, fame, or traditional success. Her choices signal to the audience that *Perfume de gardenias,* while ostensibly a fictional story about older women in a working-class Puerto Rican neighborhood, is in fact a layered reflection on gender, aging, and social marginalization.

Throughout the film, Rosario Ramos juxtaposes traditional gender roles with subtle subversions. For example, in the opening scene, Isabel is portrayed performing domestic tasks—feeding her unconscious husband, cooking, cleaning, embroidering a religious message, and finally relaxing in a rocking chair while watching the news and embroidering a "Dios me ama" [God loves me] message on a piece of fabric (1:18–3:32)—all of which reflect patriarchal norms. However, these seemingly mundane moments are infused with political and emotional subtext. As Isabel hangs laundry, a neighbor asks if she felt the recent earthquakes, to which Isabel responds with fear—suggesting not just concern for natural disasters but also the broader instability and neglect experienced by Puerto Ricans in the wake of political crises.

Simultaneously, while she is still embroidering the religious message "Dios me ama," Isabel watches a televised protest demanding justice for Keishla Rodríguez Ortiz, a young pregnant woman murdered by her lover, former Puerto Rican boxer Félix Verdejo, in May 2021. The protesters call for gender justice and a curriculum inclusive of gender perspectives. This moment connects private domestic life with broader feminist struggles, suggesting that even within traditional roles, women like Isabel are aware of, and affected by, structural violence. Isabel, even while embroidering the religious phrase "God loves me," does not live in a blind dogma of faith; instead, she understands contemporary political and social events. These subtle overlaps between private life and public crisis critique the often-invisible burdens assumed by women—from household labor to the ever-present threat of gender-based violence.[19]

These narrative techniques recur throughout the film, often embedded in passing dialogue, background music, or visual metaphors. This layering mimics the real-life challenge of disrupting patriarchal systems, where resistance often occurs in the margins or beneath the surface. One example is the funeral of Isabel's husband. As a former military man, his death might traditionally demand solemnity and public mourning. Instead, Isabel channels her grief into floral artistry, accompanied by a religious hymn about trust in God and the passage of pain. Her joyful creativity disrupts expectations of how an older widow should behave, carving out space for emotional expression beyond sadness. This moment becomes emblematic of the film's larger message: that joy, particularly for older women, is radical and often socially misread. A brief shot of a wall filled with family photographs further reinforces the notion that women's bodies are closely monitored from youth, framed by societal expectations of behavior, appearance, and emotion.

Ultimately, *Perfume de gardenias* is a poetic and politically charged exploration of how female bodies—especially those of older women—navigate and resist the limits imposed by religion, patriarchy, and tradition. Rosario Ramos constructs a cinematic space where alternative narratives can flourish, highlighting the power of ordinary gestures and quiet resistance in reimagining womanhood, aging, and creative agency.

MOTHER AND DAUGHTER

Several scenes in *Perfume de gardenias* (10:10–11:45, 26:26–27:43, 32:51–34:08, 41:03–42:35, and 44:40–45:55), as mentioned, subtly insert subversive subtexts to challenge conventional narratives about female roles, and as explored in this section, particularly through the dynamic between Isabel and her daughter Melanie. Though never explicitly stated, Melanie appears to live abroad—likely in the United States—as suggested by her English expressions and her status as a visitor. Their relationship is marked by tension, impatience, and mutual criticism. For instance, Melanie often treats Isabel as outdated or incapable, especially with technology or domestic routines. For example, she scolds her for using chlorine in the laundry or questions her understanding of digital devices. Yet Isabel, seemingly sweet on the surface, also embodies a passive-aggressive, hypercritical stance toward her daughter. She frequently undermines Melanie with backhanded comments, such as questioning why she no longer uses a camera or implying she doesn't visit enough when she compliments her mother's cooking.

This cycle of veiled criticism and defensiveness reflects deeper generational and gender-based tensions. Isabel often mocks or dismisses Melanie's ideas, sometimes calling her "crazy," while Melanie, in turn, trivializes these interactions, treating her mother as someone too old to engage meaningfully. These microaggressions surface even in ostensibly warm moments, like during a shared meal or casual conversation. In another scene, Isabel critiques Melanie's appearance in front of others, to which Melanie responds with weary resignation—underscoring how normalized this dynamic is for her. Even when Melanie tries to show affection or interest, Isabel responds critically, only later backtracking with comments that appear conciliatory but still carry undertones of judgment.

Whoever is a daughter and has or had a mother can recognize and identify with the tension between the love and the conflict that often define the mother/daughter relationship. In all these scenes, we see Isabel being a real mother with real flaws, and we see her daughter Melanie expressing her lack of patience with her mother. However, despite the persistent tension, the film also provides glimpses of tenderness. In one moving scene (52:00–53:06), Melanie asks Isabel if she misses her late husband and breaks into tears. The silence and mutual gaze that follow communicate a profound, wordless understanding. Another emotional moment occurs as Melanie prepares to leave and wistfully notes that her mother never made her *sorullos,* a nostalgic reference that highlights how food, memory, and maternal love intertwine.

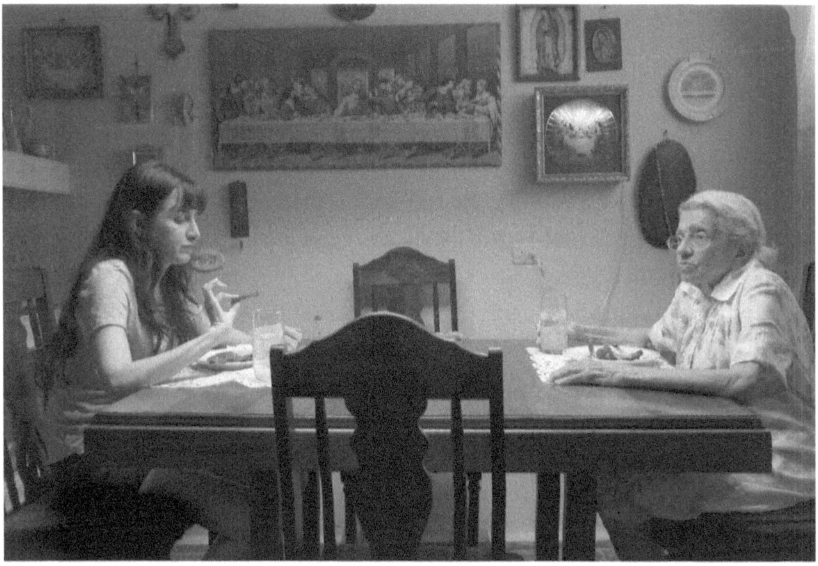

FIGURE 1.2. Picture of a moment between Isabel and her daughter Melanie while eating dinner. From a scene in *Perfume de gardenias*. Photo credit: David Correa. Courtesy of 3 Gardenias Inc.

By portraying the mother-daughter relationship in all its contradiction—love, irritation, mutual care, and disappointment—Rosario Ramos refuses to romanticize motherhood. Instead, she offers a more complex and honest depiction. Isabel is not the idealized, self-sacrificing mother often expected in popular narratives. She is flawed, sharp-tongued, and at times emotionally manipulative. Similarly, Melanie is not the dutiful daughter society envisions—she is independent, unmarried, and childless, unafraid to express her frustrations.

This realism serves a larger political function: by depicting female characters outside idealized norms, Ramos opens space for a broader range of expressions of womanhood. The mother and daughter are allowed to be human—imperfect, emotional, and complex. In doing so, the film liberates the female body from restrictive social roles and creates room for alternative, more truthful representations of women's lives.

FEMALE MASCULINITY

Femininity in *Perfume de gardenias* is portrayed as multifaceted and diverse, offering alternative modes of existence that challenge normative gender roles. One of the most striking examples is Julia, Isabel's neighbor, whose embodiment of what Jack Halberstam terms "female masculinity" resists conventional expectations of both femininity and queerness. Halberstam argues that such representations in film are crucial because they expose and subvert dominant gender ideologies, particularly within patriarchal and even lesbian contexts, where masculinity often remains a contested terrain. Julia, a butch lesbian, exemplifies a form of femininity that integrates masculine traits not as mimicry of male power, but as a form of resistance to gender conformity and misogyny.

In a community where most women are portrayed as caretakers—devoted to their homes, ailing husbands, and neighbors—Julia stands out. She assumes tasks traditionally coded as masculine: mowing the lawn, cleaning the front yard, taking out the trash. She even offers to help Isabel with household maintenance, prompting Isabel's rejection based on the idea that such responsibilities belong to men. Despite her son's disinterest in caregiving, Isabel clings to the belief that a male figure should assume those roles, preferring the idea of masculine help—even when unavailable—over accepting assistance from a woman who unsettles her heteronormative worldview.

Julia's difference makes Isabel uneasy, not only because of her masculine-coded actions but also because her sexuality defies the heteronormative feminine ideal. When Julia approaches Isabel to offer help with the outside of the house, she also mentions that Isabel should be careful with their neighbor Toña and her entourage. That suggestion provokes tension between the two women, culminating in a powerful exchange where Isabel accuses Julia of impropriety for hosting young women at her house, masking judgment under the guise of moral superiority. Julia responds defiantly: "¡Pero no le tengo miedo al placer! ¡Coño!" [At least I'm not afraid of pleasure! Goddammit!] (27:45–29:04). In this moment, Julia not only calls out the hypocrisy of religious and moralistic policing but also reclaims pleasure as a right for nonnormative femininities. Her outburst becomes a small but potent act of rebellion against the heteropatriarchal order that seeks to regulate women's desires and bodies.

Isabel's discomfort with Julia reveals an internalized misogyny—an inability to recognize femininity beyond heterosexual and submissive frameworks. Rosario Ramos, through these nuanced character interactions, invites viewers to rethink rigid definitions of gender. By presenting a fluid spectrum of femininities—some aligned with traditional caregiving roles, others defined by resistance and queerness—*Perfume de gardenias* opens a space to imagine more inclusive, tolerant ways of living and relating.

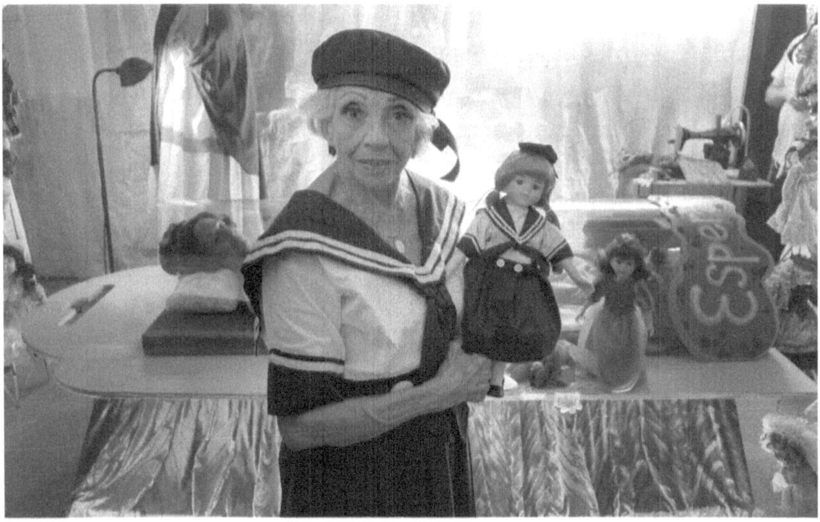

FIGURE 1.3. Picture of the character of Isabel dressed up as a doll for a doll-themed funeral. From a scene in *Perfume de gardenias*. Photo credit: David Correa. Courtesy of 3 Gardenias Inc.

AGED AND TRANS FEMININITIES

In *Perfume de gardenias*, femininity is not confined to the cisgender female body. Rather, it is presented as a complex, evolving space through which Rosario Ramos invites viewers to reflect on, critique, and reimagine societal norms around what is considered feminine. A particularly telling scene unfolds when Isabel agrees to wear a doll-like outfit originally intended for a trans woman who refuses to wear it, deeming it ridiculous. Isabel, made up with false lashes and styled hair, is then complimented by her friend Juana: "¡Qué bella! ¡Casi pareces una jovencita!" [How lovely! You almost look like a young girl!] Her shy yet pleased expression is juxtaposed with a close-up of another woman from the circle, Tata, who appears stern and later walks away from the funeral in disapproval (49:31–49:44 and 52:08–52:29).

This contrast reveals deeper tensions around age, femininity, and social expectations. While Tata typically supports Isabel's creative funeral arrangements, she disapproves when Isabel herself becomes a decorative element—when she reclaims a more youthful, joyful version of herself. This disapproval reflects broader societal discomfort with older women expressing playfulness or sensuality, particularly in the context of widowhood. The final shot of Isabel's serious, distant gaze suggests an internalized guilt, highlighting how women are often pressured to suppress joy and self-expression if it does not align with ageist, patriarchal expectations.

The scene also explores the intersections of ageism and transphobia. The trans woman's refusal to wear the dress (48:12–49:29) and her demand for fair compensation become a moment of agency and resistance. When Toña tries to convince her with a patronizing tone, the trans woman firmly asserts herself: "Mira, bebx, yo lo que quiero es que se me pague el cash de antemano, porque yo no voy a hacer de ridícula para que se me den $20 nada más, ¿entiendes?" [Look bebx, all I want is the cash. Up front. I am not going to play the fool for a measly 20 bucks. Got it?] Toña responds with a slur—"¿Quién trajo a la inepta esta sin futuro?" [Who brought this no-future stupid girl?]—but the trans woman dismisses the insult with humor and leaves the situation without compromising her dignity.

This moment is crucial for its portrayal of queer, feminine agency. The character not only rejects caricature and exploitation but also reclaims space on her own terms. By using inclusive language ("bebx") and asserting her value as a laboring subject, she challenges both the binary logic of gender and the patriarchal control over feminine expression. Through these layered portrayals, Rosario Ramos critiques the societal policing of femininity across lines of age, gender identity, and sexuality. The film champions the right to joy, autonomy, and self-representation for all women—cis, trans, older, and queer—offering a powerful reflection on how femininity can be reimagined beyond rigid, exclusionary norms.

A QUEER SONG FOR A QUEER FILM

The doll-dress scene in *Perfume de gardenias* seamlessly transitions into a new sequence underscored by the song "El arca de Mima" (49:30), composed and performed by Puerto Rican queer artist Mima specifically for the film. This atmospheric electro-folk piece, introduced through a metaphorical list of tropical fruits, serves as a meditation on the sociopolitical conditions of the Puerto Rican archipelago, particularly its colonial history and the cyclical nature of economic and cultural exploitation. Although the song's rhythm may feel light and lyrical, its core is a mournful reflection on the depletion of both natural resources and cultural memory.

Mima's song functions as a *queer lament*, not only in its thematic resistance to heteronormative, capitalist frameworks, but also in the broader sense of queerness defined by Jack Halberstam—as a way "to live life otherwise," beyond conventional norms of gender, sexuality, and time (2011, 2). Through poetic and dreamlike lyricism, Mima critiques colonial legacies, capitalism, and ecological loss, while also envisioning alternate futures.

The song opens with a poignant observation about the disappearance of fresh fruit, a metaphor for the archipelago's eroded self-sufficiency and the loss of connection to the land:

Es rara la fruta fresca
que aquí se da a conocer
hay mucha que da placer
y poca que ya aparezca.
[It is rare, fresh fruit
that becomes known here
there are many that give pleasure
and few that still appear.]

In a later stanza, Mima describes the fruit's future as "perverse," its seed "too much for a verse and too little for history." This line encapsulates the paradox of Puerto Ricans' colonial condition: an archipelago small in size but dense with an often-erased or overlooked history. The metaphor of seedless fruit emerges as a powerful image of capitalist modernization—convenient, marketable, but ultimately sterile. Seeds, as emblems of regeneration and futurity, are rendered absent, symbolizing a future denied to the Puerto Rican archipelago. Thus, the singer proposes her song as utopia for whoever "que se jaye" [feels good inside out].[20]

As the song progresses, Mima files a poetic *querella*—a formal complaint—about the disappearance of native fruit, echoing the disappearance of collective memory and self-determination. The narrative turns personal as the singer confesses that singing this story suffocates her—it is, after all, "the end of her kind." Yet she ends on a note of hope: "Algún día crecerá otra cosa" [Someday something else will grow]. This is not resignation, but a gesture toward possibility, toward imagining a postcolonial, queer future.

The inclusion of "El arca de Mima" in the film is far from incidental. Rosario Ramos, herself a cultural producer deeply attuned to the role of music in political storytelling, places the song at a pivotal moment in the narrative. Its themes—grief, land, memory, and resistance—resonate with the emotional and symbolic trajectory of Isabel, the film's protagonist. Just as Mima mourns the fruit and what it represents, Isabel mourns her husband while beginning to reimagine her life and femininity beyond widowhood. But throughout the film, Isabel tends her garden—a space of beauty, creation, and reflection—as an unconventional way of mourning. Moreover, these scenes are visually distinct: bathed in warm light and soft focus, they evoke a dreamlike atmosphere that complements the ethereal tones of Mima's song. The garden becomes a metaphor for potential and regeneration, aligning with the song's insistence that something else will grow, despite—or because of—what has been lost.

The song and film both operate as critiques of colonialism, patriarchy, and heteronormativity, but they also function as proposals for new ways of living. Isabel challenges societal expectations placed on older women and widows. Her creative work and play with femininity—in particular, the doll-dress scene—marks a moment of personal liberation, as she reclaims joy, beauty, and self-expression on her own terms. Similarly, Mima's song queers traditional musical structures and content, offering a sonic landscape that disrupts normative narratives and proposes alternative rhythms of existence.

Ultimately, grief—personal, political, ecological—is at the heart of both *Perfume de gardenias* and "El arca de Mima." Yet within that grief lies the possibility for transformation. As Elizabeth Freeman theorizes in *Time Binds,* revisiting the past and engaging with nonlinear temporalities allows for a redefinition of the present—a queering of time itself. In this sense, both Mima and Isabel engage in performances of loss that are also performances of hope, community, and queer existence.

As Joshua Chambers-Letson reminds us, performance holds the power "to sustain some fragment of lost life in the presence of a collective present . . . and to draw people together" (2018, xvii). In *Perfume de gardenias,* Isabel's journey and Mima's song come together to create a collective narrative of resistance and reimagination. The choice to include "El arca de Mima" at the film's midpoint underscores femininity as a structuring force—one that sustains both the story's emotional arc and its political vision.

In closing, movement—both literal and metaphorical—validates the protagonists' agency. Mima metaphorically travels the island through her lyrics, mourning and remembering; Isabel begins to move through her community with renewed purpose, asserting her autonomy despite resistance from her family and neighbors. Both narratives culminate in the understanding that "for something new to grow, something else must die"—be it outdated norms, systems of domination, or internalized limitations. Together, they call for the cultivation of new forms of life, creativity, and queer futurity.

Rosario Ramos, through a tool that she knows very well, such as music, creates a metanarrative and, from the platform of the song, summarizes, reflects on, and anticipates the evolution of the protagonist and of her story. This communication between the audiovisual happens, as mentioned, during the highest point in which Isabel's explores her femininity. Femininity, though, becomes a pillar of the film, a backbone that sustains, from the middle of the plot, what happened prior and what will happen next. Shortly after this moment, Isabel's relationship with Julia will evolve, intertwining femininity and queerness.

FEMININITY, QUEERNESS, AND POLITICAL GRIEF IN *PERFUME DE GARDENIAS*

Perfume de gardenias is rich with references to queerness, woven throughout both its narrative and visual textures. These allusions appear in subtle gestures and explicit moments, signaling a broader critique of heteronormative norms and making space for alternative forms of kinship, intimacy, and resistance. One such moment occurs when Isabel visits her neighbor Tata. During this visit, Tata's son, portrayed with both macho posturing and flamboyant mannerisms, engages in exaggerated, performative banter that hints at queerness (29:55–31:05). This suggestion is reinforced by what he's watching on television: a music video of the song "Todo en su sitio" [Everything in place] by queer artists Eduardo Alegría and Macha Colón, whose work critiques normative gender and sexual identities.[21] As for Mima's song, this song functions as a metanarrative that reveals the paradox of an apparent heterosexual order. Tata's mockery of her son and her labeling him as a "sinvergüenza" [a shameless good-for-nothing] and a "borrachón" [drunk] not only plays on stereotypes of masculinity but subtly opens space for queerness within the domestic sphere. This scene also parallels another moment in the film that reveals the contradictions of normative appearances—Tata insists that her health is fine while a surreal tower of prescription bottles fills the frame—a visual indictment of a healthcare system where the commodification of human life has become normalized.

Other nuanced references surface in Isabel's funeral arrangements, like the shoe-shaped coffin for a deceased shoemaker. The camera lingers on a sign that reads "ZA-PATERIA," which, when split visually as in the film, hints at "patería"—a colloquial term for queerness in Spanish. Moreover, Rosario Ramos intentionally populates the film with queer and trans performers and artists such as Lío Villahermosa, Helen Ceballos, Pó Rodil, Awilda Rodríguez Lora, Eduardo Alegría, Mima, Carla Cavina, Pati Cruz, and others, making the very fabric of the film a reflection of contemporary Puerto Rican queer life. These choices render queerness not just thematic, but also materially present, grounded in lived cultural and artistic practices.

The theme of queerness crescendos in the film's final act, through Isabel's evolving relationship with her lesbian neighbor, Julia. Unlike Julia, who is visibly ill but absent from Toña's list of dying neighbors, Isabel begins to see her not as an outsider but as someone deserving care and companionship. This gesture challenges the moral and social order enforced by Toña, whose obsession with control and "assisting" deaths veers into authoritarian territory. Toña's maniacal obsession with order and control makes visible the difficulty of queerness existence. While Toña sees her mission as divinely sanctioned, it reflects what Martin F. Manalansan calls the "regimens of control" that attempt to regulate messy, queer lives (2018, 494, 496). Julia, on the other hand, embodies a queer disruption of these norms—her illness, her humor, her resistance to religious convention, and ultimately, her choice in how she wants to die—all challenge dominant frameworks of morality, femininity, and death.

A pivotal moment comes when Isabel chooses to stay and care for Julia rather than leave town with her son. This decision comes after a break in the relationship with Toña caused by the unexpected way that Toña handled the death of one of their neighbors. The relationship between Isabel and Julia deepens, built on conversations about love, marriage, and death. Julia critiques the institution of marriage with sharp wit and irony, pointing out the limitations placed on queer lives. Her refusal to conform, even in death, inspires Isabel to rethink her own sense of duty, faith, and agency. When Julia dies, her farewell is not one of despair but a beautifully orchestrated moment of queer care, joy, and autonomy. Isabel, once resistant to deviation from religious and social norms, becomes a facilitator of this radically different goodbye—one that does not deny faith, but redefines its place in a more inclusive and liberatory framework.

During one of their interactions, they connect through poetry in apparently opposite ways, and the moment reveals they have more in common than they think. Isabel mentions that she likes the sixteenth-century author Santa Teresa de Jesús, and Julia responds with verses by a Puerto Rican poet from the twentieth century, Julia de Burgos. Despite the differences between the two chosen authors, they were both reformers, activists, and feminists of their time. Similarly, Isabel and Julia, despite their different ways of living life, are both advocating for a way of living that deconstructs the imposed social heteronormative parameters—Isabel by allowing herself to enjoy life despite being a widow, and Julia by living her sexuality freely and by deciding when she wants to die.

In the final scenes, Isabel removes a certificate honoring her late husband and replaces it with her own handcrafted artwork—a carved gardenia framed with embroidered details and signed with her name. This symbolic act marks a reclamation of space, identity, and authorship. Isabel's journey—facilitated by her connection with Julia—becomes a metaphor for queer survival and reinvention. The substitution of the art piece on the wall of her home makes Isabel reclaim her space, reaffirms her passions and talents, and breaks with the past to begin a new future. All this is possible only through the death of her husband first, then through the death of the neighbors she decorated their funerals for, and lastly through Julia's different way of living and dying. Actually, it is precisely through Julia's queer way of living that Isabel finds a way to live following her free will. Julia's queer death addresses "the relationships among body, power, and subjection" translated into the survival script of Isabel (Arroyo 2023, 109).

The film's final funeral, for Julia, becomes an overt political statement. Rosario Ramos incorporates a poster reading "Por los 4,645. Para que descansen en paz y justicia" [For the 4,645. May they rest in peace and justice], referencing the estimated deaths following Hurricane María and the inadequate governmental response. The altar includes red shoes and a rainbow flag—symbols of feminist and queer mourning—and the guests receive miniature Puerto Rican flags in both color and black and white.[22] These details extend the film's personal grief into a broader collective mourning, implicating the colonial and neoliberal structures that continue to shape life and death in the Puerto Rican archipelago. Rosario Ramos creates multiple spaces in *Perfume de gardenias* to keep talking about a natural disaster that in the geography had even heavier consequences due to the political incompetence and disinterest. The fact that these references are subtle, contained in a secondary dialogue, or placed on a poster at the margin of a frame metaphorically speaks about the political effort to erase a collective memory of a trauma that directly speaks about a constant inefficiency and neglect.

In post-Hurricane María Puerto Rico, mourning and grief have taken on layered meanings, shaped not only by the massive loss of life and destruction but also by the political and economic realities of neoliberalism. Drawing from Christina Sharpe's concept of "the hold," which explores how Black life is continually shaped by the afterlives of slavery, we can see how Puerto Rican grief exists in a space of both suspension and dispossession. Mourning in this context is not just about individual loss but about the loss of a future, of security, and of autonomy. The neoliberal restructuring of the Puerto Rican territory—through austerity measures, mass privatization, and displacement—has created what Sharpe calls a "wake," a continuous state of crisis and survival where grief is never allowed to settle. Instead, it is interrupted, co-opted, or even commodified by the very forces that produced it.

However, at the same time, grief has become a space of resistance, the ritual, the ceremony, the way we celebrate lost lives and remember (Arroyo 2023, 114). Mourning in Puerto Rico has been made public, collective, and political. The protests that emerged post-María, particularly in 2019 with the ousting of Governor Ricardo Rosselló, reveal how grief can be mobilized into action. The refusal to let deaths be ignored—whether from the hurricane or from neoliberal neglect—speaks to a kind of insurgent memory, one that fights against erasure and demands accountability. Thus, in post-María Puerto Rico, grief exists in the hold—suspended between trauma and resilience, between imposed disaster and collective defiance. It is both an imposed condition and a tool for imagining futures beyond neoliberalism's grasp (Sharpe 2016).[23]

The final scene of the film brings together the central symbols of grief and mourning in the Puerto Rican context. Grief and mourning—protagonists in *Perfume de gardenias*—converge during Julia's funeral, which also becomes a symbolic funeral for the nation. This moment reflects what Yarimar Bonilla calls "sites of melancholia that necessitate, in the collective survival script, responsive social action" (Arroyo 2023, 114). Agency against neoliberal economies and the state does not preclude precarious existence (Arroyo 2023, 115). However, Rosario Ramos proposes a celebration of the funeral of suffering itself, in order to open new, possible ways of living.

Julia dies of cancer, a metaphor for the political, economic, and sexist "cancer" that affects everyday life in Puerto Rico. Yet, Ramos suggests a shift in how mourning is practiced. Like Isabel and Julia, she proposes a queer mode of breaking with social expectations—or what Christina Sharpe describes as "wake work," in which mourning becomes a collective experience. With this film, Ramos invites us to understand that for something new to be born, something must die—within a space of decay that, through interactive processes and community, can transform death into something spectacular, ritualized, and visible, much like the problems that afflict the Puerto Rican archipelago (Arroyo 2023, 119).

In *Perfume de gardenias,* the characters engage in this transformation by organizing artistic funeral-parties, which—as Joshua Chambers-Letson puts it—create "a condition for a practice of being with, in which the misfit's loneliness becomes the condition for a relation of being together in difference" (2018, xiv). Similarly, Isabel defies the loneliness that society expects from an older widow and instead builds a community that is queer precisely because it is "together in difference."

Julia's funeral ends with a chorus chanting, "¡Qué perra, qué perra, qué perra mi amiga!" [What a fierce bitch, bitch, bitch, my friend!], signaling how wake work (Sharpe 2016) is tied to celebration, companionship, community, and gathering (Arroyo 2023). This is followed by a song performed by Macha Colón that emphasizes the importance of being true to oneself—because in the end, we are all going to die. While we may not be able to choose how or when we die, we can choose what to leave behind through our actions.

Toña reappears during the end credits in a small mountain neighborhood. She cannot maintain control unless others grant her that space. Once again, Ramos highlights the necessity of collective unity in order to live freely—and finds in queerness a way to imagine new forms of existence. The funerals in *Perfume de gardenias* serve as an homage to a timeless, suspended present that becomes the articulation of a new political signification (Arroyo 2023, 132).

In the closing song, Rosario Ramos affirms the importance of feeling good about oneself and invites the viewer to love one another as the only viable path to societal transformation. The film concludes with Mima's "El arca de Mima"—a song previously heard during one of Isabel's decorated funerals and analyzed earlier in this chapter—reiterating the necessity of letting go in order to create new possibilities. Public mourning here becomes a form of resistance, an insurgent memory that defies erasure and demands justice. The film resists the neat resolution of closure, instead offering a more honest, messy, and politicized vision of what it means to remember—and to live—otherwise.

QUEER REIMAGINATIONS

Rosario Ramos understands femininity from a queer standpoint and, in *Perfume de gardenias,* allows femininity to become "disobedient" by inhabiting any type of body. She explores femininity, womanhood, and queerness from the unusual and powerful perspective of ageism and death. In this film, Ramos represents the female body from multiple angles: through the lens of aging, the complexities of mother-daughter relationships, and the social expectations placed on women—how they should mourn, how and when they should mother, and what it means to embody femininity. The film brings to the screen a diversity of representations of the female body, varied expressions of femininity, and multiple ways in which queerness can be visually and narratively articulated. These elements are intricately connected in *Perfume de gardenias* and are beautifully rendered through the use of visual symbolism, music, religion, tradition, and spoken and bodily language.

The representation of the female body, the visual vocabulary of femininity, and Ramos's exploration of queerness on screen serve as a means to revisit, reimagine, and interrogate tradition, language, religious faith, and the broader social order. The film thus becomes a space in which to imagine an end to Puerto Rican grief. *Perfume de gardenias* is, ultimately, a film that dreams of a better queer future—one capable of breaking away from patriarchal structures and, as Mima's song suggests, of letting go in order to allow something new to grow. This "something else" holds the potential to imagine alternative futures for Puerto Rico and for the queer community.

While *El hijo de Ruby* (2014) marked an initial attempt to represent queerness on screen and to imagine a possible future for queer individuals in a predominantly sexist and homophobic society, *Perfume de gardenias* (2021) offers a more expansive, layered, and critical approach. It deconstructs and challenges a society deeply entrenched in homophobia, misogyny, transphobia, ageism, and sexism. Moreover, *Perfume de gardenias* brings to the screen both Gisela Rosario Ramos and Macha Colón—whose music and performance art predate these films, but who find a shared and meaningful space in this 2021 production. Together, they articulate a politics of queer presence and aesthetic resistance both on screen and onstage that—as explained in the following sections—affirms the power of collective creativity in imagining new ways of being.

Music, Performance, and Video Aesthetic: Becoming Macha Colón

Macha Colón emerged as Gisela Rosario Ramos's alter ego several decades ago. When Rosario Ramos was nineteen, she moved to New York, where she lived for two decades. It was during this formative period that Macha Colón was first conceptualized and shortly thereafter brought to life. In a September 2019 interview with Cuban journalist Yoani Sánchez,[24] Rosario Ramos explained the distinction between her two personas: Macha as the funny and irreverent performer, and Gisela as the more serious, behind-the-scenes filmmaker. Over time, however, and with each performance, video, concert, and film project, Rosario Ramos increasingly came to understand that she wanted Gisela and Macha to become one—collaborating, fusing identities, and working together in harmony.

Sánchez titled the interview *Macha Colón: Sin pelos en la lengua* [Macha Colón: Without mincing words], a phrase that captures the defining feature of Rosario Ramos's artistic and political expression: outspokenness. In the interview, Macha Colón discusses her lifelong resistance to the social and political constraints that attempted to force her to conform within a racist, homophobic, and fatphobic world. Embracing her natural hair became a declaration of her identity as an Afro–Puerto Rican woman—an assertion that also underpins the social and political dimensions of her audiovisual work. Noting the general absence of social critique in Puerto Rican film production, Rosario Ramos recognized the need to explicitly define her work as queer. This label not only reflects the core of her creative energy but also serves as a gesture of representation: creating space for a queer artistic community in Puerto Rico, where no one would feel compelled to hide or feel ashamed of their identity.

In this section, I analyze Gisela Rosario Ramos's work as Macha Colón, focusing specifically on her music, performances, and video clip productions. Much like the fusion of Gisela and Macha, her interdisciplinary artistic output resists strict categorization. Instead, it forms a unified body of work with a singular goal: to dismantle binaries, challenge sexism and patriarchy, and carve out a joyful, livable space for the queer community.

To that end, I study the impact of Macha Colón's work as a singer, performer, and video artist by analyzing the soundscapes she creates. Through her music and audiovisual productions, she constructs a political space using her Afro–Puerto Rican-fat-queer body as a performative and radical statement. I examine how she moves within public, artistic, and visual spaces, achieving her artistic and political purpose through her physical presence—whether in public performances, onstage during concerts, or in the visual choreography of her video clips. In all these spaces, Macha Colón subverts normative aesthetics and challenges conventional notions of femininity. Through her irreverent and joyful bodily movements, she claims a mobile, uncontrollable space that defies confinement—opening it up for herself and for those who move with her.

Thus, her work—as a filmmaker, as explored in the previous section, and as a singer, performer, and video maker—offers a unique and disruptive perspective on womanhood, gender identity, beauty, love, and femininity. It challenges normative frameworks through disobedient behaviors and irreverent gestures. Rosario Ramos's work in these various forms demonstrates how Macha Colón occupies and transforms public space. Through her "undisciplined" femininity and exuberant movement, she redefines the parameters of womanhood and reimagines how the feminine body can exist, resist, and move in the world.

THE SONGS

I begin this section by analyzing the songs "Jayá" and "Tanquecito de amor" from the album *Tanquecito de amor* [Little Tank of Love], recorded in 2011 and released on March 8, 2016.[25] The aim of this analysis is to highlight the representations of femininity, self-love, and sexual desire, as well as the critique of normative social standards that Gisela Rosario Ramos has advanced throughout her musical production—understood here as an interplay of lyrics, performative aesthetics, and sonic choices.

Through these songs, Rosario Ramos crafts a sense of community that dismantles stereotypes and traverses marginalized neighborhoods. This sense of community emerges through the lyrics, the persona of Macha Colón, the music videos, and the sounds and melodies themselves. These elements are not easily separable; rather, they often overlap in both her creative process and in this analysis.

As discussed earlier in this chapter, Macha Colón frequently points to the centrality of her plus-size body in her work. She notes how, as a plus-size person, both fashion and popular cultural icons often felt out of reach. The visual, performative, and artistic dimensions analyzed here seek to challenge normative standards of whiteness, body shape, and femininity, proposing alternative ways of embodying feminine icons—particularly through strategies often dismissed or marked as undesirable. Macha achieves this not only through the visual imagery in her videos, album covers, and performances, or through the lyrical content of her songs, but also through her sonic experimentation. Her music plays with rupture—breaking with sonic norms to open up other possibilities of listening and perception. In doing so, she questions conventional notions of authority in the music industry and agency in the creative process. Her aesthetic choices evoke what Przybylski (2023, 19) conceptualizes as "sonic sovereignty," wherein experimental sounds "break with linear time" and offer new avenues for storytelling. In these sonic landscapes, untold, erased, and rejected narratives are reclaimed—what Przybylski calls "the sound of decolonization" (22). Specifically, Macha Colón's music confronts binary understandings of femininity rooted in heteronormative and patriarchal ideologies, while simultaneously challenging fatphobia, racism, sexism, homophobia, and patriarchal control. Her soundscapes—interwoven with lyrics and visual aesthetics—thus propose new modes of expressing sexuality, gender identity, gender fluidity, femininity, and beauty.

The album *Tanquecito de amor* (2016) consists of eight songs: "Maldita sea" [Damn her], "Divino amor" [Divine love], "Jayá," "Si Superman se deprime" [If Superman gets depressed], "Hiroyuki," "Tusa" [Worthless person], "Tú sabes la que hay" [You know what's up], and "Tanquecito de amor" [Little tank of love]. Song lengths range from 2:02 ("Tusa") to 13:20, with the final track ("Tanquecito de amor") consisting of a 4-minute song followed by a 9-minute hidden track.

These psychedelic punk-rock compositions can be grouped into two main thematic categories: those that explore love, sex, and sexual desire; and those that emphasize self-love, self-care, and community. For instance, songs like "Maldita sea," "Divino amor," "Hiroyuki," and "Tú sabes la que hay" fall into the former, advocating for sexual freedom and open expressions of desire. In contrast, "Jayá," "Si Superman se deprime," and "Tanquecito de amor" foreground themes of self-care, mental health, and collective well-being. This section focuses on "Jayá," the album's most popular track, and "Tanquecito de amor," which gives the album its title. Both songs embody Macha Colón's artistic ethos: radical joy, self-love, and nonconforming beauty.

"Jayá" became a major hit in Puerto Rico, popularizing a term that had previously circulated only within rural mountain communities. In the interview with Cuban journalist Yoani Sánchez, Rosario Ramos explains that the term *jayá* originally referred to someone who was well dressed or attractive. In her reinterpretation, however, Macha Colón expands the meaning: *jayá* comes to signify a deeper state of well-being, one that begins with embracing one's body—including clothing choices regardless of size—and culminates in a sense of harmony with the universe.

In doing so, Macha intentionally disregards formal grammar and dominant linguistic norms, resignifying a term historically seen as substandard. The term *jayá* is rescued "in relation to locations and traditions once considered 'vulgar'" (P. Saunders 2022, 9). In this way, Rosario Ramos foregrounds "cultural traditions that began as modes of resistance to colonial and postcolonial oppression or as the release valve needed for poor people to express themselves, their joys, and their sufferings" instead of becoming "cultural commodities and experiences for locals (particularly those from the middle classes) and tourists alike" (P. Saunders 2022, 9). Rather than becoming a sanitized commodity for middle-class consumers or tourists, "Jayá" becomes a hymn to radical joy and resistance for the marginalized.

The song offers this shared mantra of radical joy, bringing together queer communities in celebration, particularly during events such as the tenth anniversary of "Jayá" in 2022. The *jayaera* is both a state and a performative act that, through social media and collective celebration, enables this song (and as I will explore later, its video) to generate a new language of queer self-love and care.

"Tanquecito de amor" is also a declaration of self-love. The artist describes herself as a "little tank of love," reclaiming a term often used pejoratively to describe larger bodies. Macha Colón reconfigures this image into one of strength, resilience, and affection. The song celebrates love in all its forms, including the radical act of showing affection publicly: "voy por la calle, caminando, lentamente, de la mano, de mi amor" [I walk down the street, slowly, hand in hand, with my love] (1:25–1:37). In doing so, the song champions the right to love and be loved openly, beyond societal constraints.

The track also includes a hidden narrative that begins at the 4:25 mark and lasts until 13:20. In this extended spoken segment, Macha recounts a surreal dream featuring salsa legend Ismael "Maelo" Rivera (d. 1987). In the dream, Rivera appears first as a snake-messenger and then as a spiritual figure reminding Macha to care for her friends. She later recalls feeling uplifted when her friend, queer Puerto Rican singer Mima, brought her to a *barrio* where people were "cantando, bailando, riendo, gozando" [singing, dancing, laughing, enjoying]. This act of community care restores her sense of self.

In the narrative's climax Macha asks Mima how she came to be feeling better, and Mima explains: "en el barrio nos sentimos libres, porque en el barrio podemos bailar, nadie te pregunta cómo y quién somos . . . no importa que te gusten ellos y ellas, porque en el barrio se ve todo igual" [in the neighborhood we feel free; we can dance, and no one asks who we are . . . it doesn't matter if you like women or men, because in the neighborhood, everyone is the same] (8:28–10:11). Rosario Ramos then closes the piece by dedicating it to "los barrios que están desapareciendo en Puerto Rico" [the neighborhoods that are disappearing in Puerto Rico]. The track becomes a sonic manifesto of community, unity, and resistance to gentrification. It calls for territorial defense, framing the *barrio* as synonymous with community. Drawing on the works of Fernando Picó, Pedro Lebrón Ortiz, and Ángel "Chuco" Quintero, this analysis understands the *barrio* as a site of historical marronage and contemporary countermarronage, where self-sufficiency, mutual aid, and Afro-Caribbean spiritual practices challenge the encroachment of neoliberal development and tourism.[26]

This theoretical framework directly informs my analysis of Macha Colón's "Tanquecito de amor," a song that centers neighborhood, territory, and community as fundamental sites of resistance and as rightful spaces of existence. Through this track, Macha Colón evokes spaces that are constantly under threat—whether through displacement, gentrification, or institutional policies that seek to absorb them into state-sanctioned, regulated frameworks. Her music underscores the urgency of defending these communities, whose ongoing resistance—expressed through land occupation, mutual aid networks, and the reaffirmation of Afro-Caribbean cultural and spiritual practices—extends the long legacy of marronage. It is within this genealogy of resistance that the work of Gisela Rosario Ramos gains relevance.

"Tanquecito de amor" becomes not only a love letter to the island, its people, its music, and its traditions, but also a vessel for self-care, self-love, and love directed specifically toward the queer community. In the song's final track, Rosario Ramos guides the listener through the often-forgotten or marginalized barrios of Puerto Rico, such as La Perla and Santurce, highlighting these spaces as sites where community can be found—communities that are nonjudgmental, that allow individuals to be and to love freely, and that are grounded in a present shaped by joy, care, and queer kinship. As Jack Halberstam (2005) argues, the present is the temporality in which queerness resists the linear demands of heteronormative adulthood. In Macha's track, healing occurs in the present—through dance, music, and community. This irreverent, Halberstamian present opens the possibility for the utopian future José Esteban Muñoz (2009) envisions: a future that emerges through the incompleteness of the queer now. In this light, *Tanquecito de amor*, both the album and its final track, offers a framework for imagining political and cultural transformation rooted in queer artistic practices on the island.

THE VISUAL AESTHETICS OF MACHA COLÓN

In her work, Macha Colón mobilizes her Afro–Puerto Rican female body in what Nora Chipaumire described in a 2014 TEDx Talk as a "collision course with power, with masculinity, with whiteness [. . .] often refuting its presence. So, [the body] is a gloriously terrible fact, a weapon, a laboratory, an experiment, a theory, a cultural and global imperative, and always potentially disruptive."[27] To create with the body is to explore, uncover, comprehend, and critique. As Chipaumire suggests, making art with the body is also experiencing with the body—it is theoretical, practical, experimental, critical, and, crucially, dangerous (5:25–5:38). Although Chipaumire speaks of the Black African female body in a different geographical context, Macha Colón's Afro–Puerto Rican body carries a similar disruptive potential. Her aesthetic power derives not only from nonconformity, but from the fact that her body is never static. Whether onstage, in a music video, or moving through urban space, hers is a dynamic body in motion—a body that carries a specific aesthetic, that demands to be seen—a body that cannot be ignored.

In performance, Macha wears garments altered to fit her body—clothes originally designed only in smaller sizes. These outfits often feature deep necklines, sheer fabrics, and overt nods to the commodification of female nudity, engaging critically and ironically with the fashion industry's standards. Her presence onstage constitutes a living critique of an industry that erases fat bodies while simultaneously eroticizing and profiting from slender ones. Slimness in fashion is marketed as the prerequisite for female desirability—an ideal that reinforces the notion that women should occupy less space and exist primarily for the heterosexual male gaze.

By contrast, Macha Colón's large, queer, female body in motion offers a counternarrative that is as disruptive as it is necessary. As Ellen Messer-Davidow observes, to act "otherwise" than in accordance with the status quo is, inherently, provocative (Gardiner 1995, 4, 23–25). Macha has spoken of the many negative reactions she has received throughout her career—especially from men—who reject the presence of an Afro-fat body onstage.[28] Her provocative body possesses agency and aims to be legible on its own terms. This agency, as understood by Gardiner, is rooted in an individual's capacity for self-determination realized through decision and action (1995, 25). But as Patrocinio P. Schweickart argues, personal discontent and the desire for change only become political when they resonate with others and are reciprocated. Transformation, particularly in the face of patriarchy and sexism, requires both individual and collective agency: "my personal agency, and the collective agency of a political movement" (Gardiner 1995, 229).

Indeed, Macha Colón's performances consistently foster and include the Puerto Rican queer community. In doing so, her political body transcends its physical form and becomes a visual message for the community—a call to action born from a place of dissident femininity. This is how Rosario Ramos takes up Judith Butler's challenge of asking, "Which bodies come to matter?" (1993, x). Through the deconstruction of femininity and normative ideas of how women should look and behave, Macha Colón expands the meaning and function of her body into a collective that imagines a political future and provokes cultural transformation. Her inclusive aesthetic asserts the presence and persistence of queer life within the same patriarchal space that seeks to erase it.

In this section, I examine Macha Colón's aesthetics as they manifest in her artistic work, with particular attention to how her visual language deploys the body as a performative platform designed to provoke and challenge the foundations of heteronormative society. I focus specifically on her appearance in Sánchez's interview, the album cover for *Tanquecito de amor,* and the video for what is perhaps her most well-known song, "Jayá."[29]

When Yoani Sánchez interviews Gisela Rosario Ramos in the short documentary *Macha Colón: Sin pelos en la lengua,* the first image of the artist shows her applying makeup. In a following scene, large circles of purple, green, blue, and gold frame her eyes, blending into fuchsia tones on her cheeks; metallic gold lipstick and a touch of blue glitter above her eyebrows complete a striking and extravagant look. Rosario Ramos begins her interview by speaking about her Afro hair and her mother's obsession (mirroring that of an entire country) with straightening it—an act she interprets as a denial of African heritage. Interspersed with the interview are scenes of her preparing her appearance. She applies false lashes and dons a voluminous, colorful outfit as she speaks about her drive to create work that addresses gender, queerness, and race. Her looks directly inform her artistic statements: her hairstyle, clothing, and accessories carry the same messages that she visually articulates as an artist—on screen, in photographs, and in video.

The visuals accompanying her albums and performances, in fact, underscore her irreverent aesthetic. For instance, the cover of *Tanquecito de amor* (2016) features an out-of-focus photograph of what appears to be Macha, her hair mid-motion as she shakes her head.

The blur conveys energy and movement—perhaps a prelude to the rhythmic intensity of the music. The album and group names are emblazoned in vibrant colors, accompanied by three fuchsia, tear-shaped diamonds, which might recall the sweat and disorder from dancing at these songs and at her concerts. Against a black background, the figure's blue-toned image stands out, signaling a departure from the representational imagery of previous visuals toward abstraction. This abstraction opens space for varied interpretations and relational possibilities, effectively conveying the vibrant, chaotic incompleteness that characterizes queer existence.

On the other hand, in the video clip for "Jayá," Macha becomes a queer reverend, ultimately presiding over a series of queer weddings. Here, Macha is not just a performer—she becomes a goddess, a life coach, a spiritual leader for the queer community. Through this transformation, she demonstrates that other forms of femininity are not only possible but already real and necessary. Her poses and performances project a "queer futurity" (Muñoz 2009) that is anchored in the present, pushing back against normative constraints through radical joy—or, as Macha herself puts it, through jayaera. In the "Jayá" video,

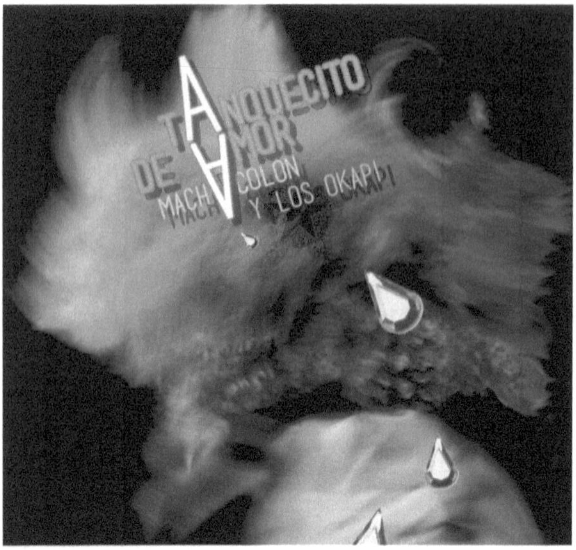

FIGURE 1.4. Cover for the album *Tanquecito de amor*. Design: Gisela Rosario Ramos/ Macha Colón. Photo credit: María González. Courtesy of the artist.

Macha Colón constructs a visual and performative language that, through a dance across several public spaces in San Juan, builds a queer community and questions gender and femininity from a decolonial perspective. Her work traverses film, song lyrics, photography, and video with a consistent goal: to resist the austerity and colonial pressures imposed on Puerto Rico by capitalism and patriarchy. This resistance is expressed through joy and pleasure while imagining a livable queer future. As Rocío Zambrana argues:

> Debt functions as a form of coloniality [. . .]. In contemporary Puerto Rico [. . .] debt actualizes, updates, reinstalls the colonial condition. [. . .] [I]t actualizes, adapts, reinscribes race/gender/class posited by the history of colonial violence that produced the modern capitalist world. [. . .] "Interruption," on the other hand, seeks to name attempts to turn coloniality inoperative [. . .] requiring unbinding the world posited by capital/coloniality. As Frantz Fanon argues, "Decolonization, which sets out to change the order of the world, is clearly an agenda for total disorder." (2021, 10–12)

Zambrana, like Muñoz, Halberstam, and Nyong'o, values interruption and disorder as tools for rearticulating the social order. Yet she warns that subversion alone can reinforce existing hierarchies. Decolonization, she reminds us, requires *disorder*—a dislocation of entrenched power. Practices like "land rescue, defiant refusal, queer laziness" are strategies to disarticulate and rearticulate the world anew (Zambrana 2021, 14).

Macha Colón's joyful queer aesthetic is one such strategy. She sings the value of being *jayá* while dancing in the ruins of a colonized space with glitter on her skin and revolution in her and her community's hips. Her decision to reclaim and reinvest the slang word *jayá* with political and affective meaning empowers a term historically relegated to sublanguage. This reappropriation functions as a metaphor for the so-called impropriety of the queer community. As Halberstam reminds us in *The Queer Art of Failure*, it is through "imperfection" that new modes of connection and survival emerge.

In the "Jayá" video, Macha is presented as a queer reverend at just 44 seconds into the 6:45 runtime. She begins to sing and dance in the streets, gradually gathering more participants into her choreography. By the 2:48 mark, a growing crowd joins her in Río Piedras, the university neighborhood historically targeted by government austerity. Her decision to bring jayaera to this space reclaims it as a site of resistance. Thus, through dance, joy, and by being in order with the universe they are able to create a disruption into the capitalist and colonial way of living.

From the Río Piedras neighborhood, she moves to a new scene where she and her band welcome couples to be married. The marriages she officiates include not only same-sex and queer couples, but playful and fantastical pairings—like a girl with her dog, a woman with her mask, and another with her mirror. The video ends with a big party of all these couples dancing on the final notes of the song while Macha wishes "como siempre mucha felicidad para todos, mucha paz, pero sobre todo, [. . .] mucho pero mucho amor" [as always much happiness, a lot of peace, but especially [. . .] lots and lots of love] (5:33–5:55), recalling the motto of famous Puerto Rican astrologer and queer icon Walter Mercado. This joyful queering of matrimony breaks with normative tradition and affirms alternative life paths outside of heteronormative adulthood (Halberstam 2005). It is a celebration of queer existence in the present, and a vision for a future rooted in love, joy, and resistance.

Macha's work becomes a living archive, a way of storing and transmitting knowledge that disrupts binary conceptions of masculinity and femininity. As Diana Taylor theorizes, the body becomes a "repertoire" of embodied practice (Taylor 2003), and as Esiaba Irobi writes, it is "a site of multiple discourses [. . .] grooved into it" (Irobi 2006, 3). This knowledge is not only intellectual—it must be experienced through embodied performance. Through her queer femininity, Macha discovers new strategies for being. A difficult task, if—as Calvin L. Warren argues—Black people "incarnate nothing in a metaphysical world" and their nothingness is both fascinating and terrifying (2018, 21). While Warren centers Blackness specifically, his insight resonates with the queer community, who similarly face erasure and ontological exclusion, prompting theorists like Muñoz and Halberstam to locate queer being in futurity and failure.

Zimbabwean performer Nora Chipaumire warns us that making art with the body is dangerous. Macha Colón's work is indeed dangerous—to a world that fears what it cannot contain. And tragically, many queer Puerto Ricans continue to pay the price of visibility in a society where their bodies are seen as threats. As Larry La Fountain-Stokes writes in *Queer Ricans,* many lesbians have fled the island seeking safety and freedom elsewhere (2009, 64). But Macha Colón, like the artists I explore in the following chapters, is an Afro-queer woman who creates a space where migration is not the only alternative from the island and for the community. She proposes practices of radical joy as a tool of queer survival while staying in Puerto Rico.

She does so, for example, by creating events and spaces for jayaera. For example, in December 2022, to celebrate the tenth anniversary of the release of the song "Jayá," she hosted *el templo de la jayaera,* inviting the community to gather and rejoice.[30] Through her irreverent movements and performances, she proposes new rituals, alternative femininities, and a stage for queer Afro–Puerto Rican fat bodies. Her performative, aesthetic, and visual movements function as an interruption to colonial capitalism and heteronormativity. Then, as a "disobedient, irreverent" woman, she lays the groundwork for a collective queer memory—one rooted in radical joy and aimed at future generations.[31]

The Future Is Jayaera

We have seen—throughout these sections, how Macha Colón's visual and performative aesthetics dismantle the normative logics that have long governed gender, race, beauty, ageism, and sexuality in Puerto Rico. Through her deliberate embrace of extravagance, irreverence, and joy, she offers not only critique but also possibility—a visual language of resistance grounded in the Afro-Caribbean, queer, fat, and femme body. Her work reveals how the pursuit of pleasure, laughter, and collective celebration can become a powerful mode of political action and resistance, unsettling the austerity of colonial and patriarchal regimes.

What emerges from Macha's *jayaera* is not simply a refusal to conform but a blueprint for living otherwise. Her stage—when she performs or when she directs—becomes a temple; her body, an archive; her performance, a call to arms. In reappropriating the term *jayá,* she summarizes her artistic philosophy and transforms what was once marginal and maligned into a force of empowerment. And in doing so, she reminds us that alternative futures are not only imaginable—they are already underway, unfolding in the bodies and movements of those who dare to dance at the edge of respectability.

To center Macha Colón in this analysis is to assert the urgency of attending to voices and visions often dismissed by dominant narratives. Her work as filmmaker, singer, and performer defines and values disobedient femininities, and challenges us to expand the contours of what counts as resistance, what qualifies as knowledge, and who is permitted to take up space. In the context of an island marked by coloniality, debt, and displacement, jayaera and disobedience emerge as a vital strategy of survival and joy—a refusal to be erased, and a celebration of all that persists in spite of erasure. Macha's aesthetic project is not simply about being seen. It is about reshaping the very terms of visibility, about demanding a future where queer, Afro-Caribbean, fat, and femme bodies are not just tolerated but revered. In her world, to be *jayá* is a vision, a ritual, a manifesto. The future, she insists, is already here. And it is loud, glittered, and unapologetically *jayao.*

TWO

Wonder Woman Dances Every Day

The Radical Movements of Awilda Rodríguez Lora

> I am not exotic,
> I am exhausted.
> Yto Barrada

> [M]ovement is the cornerstone of my work.
> I feel that movement generates movement [. . .]
> it is about moving things, and things are moving within us even in stillness.
> This generates life, circulation, air, intestines, digestion . . .
> all of these are natural parts of us, part of our humanity,
> always observing movement as a generator of transformation.
> Awilda Rodríguez Lora / From the podcast recorded with the author on March 7, 2024

"I am not exotic, I am exhausted," reads the print on a black shirt worn by Awilda Rodríguez Lora during one of her performances. This stark statement encapsulates how Rodríguez Lora transforms her body, nudity, attire, and movement into radical tools of resistance. Ramsey Burt, in his essay "Genealogy and Dance History," asks, "How could radical, experimental performance practices transform these [performing] bodies into sites of resistance?" (2004, 29). Rodríguez Lora (she/her, b. 1977), the second disobedient woman featured in this book, responds with her body and practice. She uses her movement to enact experiences of connection, reflection, and community as political gestures of both resistance and existence.

Her performances challenge normative understandings of the queer, Black, female body, using it as a site of intervention and a catalyst for rethinking femininity—across cis, trans, nonbinary, and queer identities. Her work disobeys the social norms and aesthetic codes that regulate womanhood and the female body. If, as Burt notes, "bodies are produced through the intersection of codes of the social and the aesthetic" (2004, 34), Rodríguez Lora confronts this production through what can be called epistemological disobedience—a refusal rooted in her own experiences of exoticization as a Caribbean dancer trained for television.

Born in Mexico to Puerto Rican parents and raised on the island, Rodríguez Lora studied and worked in the US, the Caribbean, and Latin America. Now based in San Juan, she creates performances that question gender norms, sexuality, sexual violence, and care. Through sound and movement—live and on video—she intervenes in colonial legacies, patriarchal expectations, and intersecting oppressions of race, class, gender, and sexuality.[1] Her rejection of the way her Afro-Caribbean body was consumed in media led her to embrace disobedience as an artistic and political method. Her work aligns with what Patricia Saunders calls "a wide range of possibilities for exploring and reinterpreting the power of consumption . . . to frame what citizenship and belonging mean for Black Caribbean subjects" (P. Saunders 2022, 22). In doing so, Rodríguez Lora embodies what Zakiyyah Iman Jackson describes as an "ontological absence"—a paradoxical visibility that marks Black queer bodies as disruptive, as tropes of disorder (2018, 619). Through her choreographed disobedience, Rodríguez Lora intervenes in dominant visual economies that render Black queer feminine bodies both hypervisible and erased. In *Wildness*, Halberstam and Nyong'o propose wildness as a mode of queer being that resists institutional definitions of gender and sexuality. It is ungovernable, chaotic, and transformative. Rodríguez Lora's body—Brown, queer, often half-dressed—represents this wildness. Her presence enacts disorder and embodies sexual difference in visual, tangible ways.

Rodríguez Lora—also known artistically as *la performera*—uses movement, video, and sound to explore, what she defines, the "economy of the body." Her work stages bodies that are culturally unwanted and politically erased, reclaiming their right to be seen, felt, and heard. She creates what Burt calls "potential for agency within discourses of theater dance" (2004, 34). Building on Julia Kristeva's concept of abjection[2]—the violent rejection of otherness that stabilizes the subject—Rodríguez Lora's performances cross and dismantle normative boundaries. Halberstam and Nyong'o observe that when not erased, the Black feminine sublime often reappears as abject or mythical (2018, 622). Rodríguez Lora occupies this abject space, reclaiming it through vulnerability and public nudity, destabilizing the commodification of queer feminine bodies in art and life. Judith Butler, in *Bodies That Matter*, links abjection to gender, showing how queer expressions are excluded to maintain heteronormative binaries. Rodríguez Lora interrogates these exclusions through her performances, connecting them to the colonial violence endured by Puerto Rico and the queer women who inhabit it. Her work speaks from the margins and against the hypersexualization and silencing of feminine bodies of color.

In this way, Rodríguez Lora's work offers a critique of contemporary Puerto Rican society and proposes a vision of queer life in the colony. Arnaldo Cruz-Malavé calls this "el cuerpo coral de la comunidad" [the choral body of community] (2023, 329), a collective space that both devours and silences the abject. Cruz-Malavé asks if the abject can find a space outside the binary logic of sacrifice. Rodríguez Lora with her work answers: if the subaltern cannot speak—as Gayatri Spivak argues in her 1988 essay—she can still create a space through her body. Her performances disrupt colonial logic and reclaim space through movement.

La performera emerged in 2008 during a residency in Chicago. Rodríguez Lora sought to separate her identity as a Caribbean dancer from her evolving identity as a performance artist. As Halberstam and Nyong'o argue, "going wild" involves both liberation and vulnerability (2018, 600). She turned the exoticism imposed on her into a wild aesthetic that reclaims agency and intimacy. Reflecting on this transformation, Jodi Byrd—via Halberstam and Nyong'o—warns that the "wild" can be quickly co-opted into the status quo unless it actively resists (2018, 612). Between 1996 and 1999, Rodríguez Lora performed on television, later rejecting the industry's narrow beauty standards. With *la performera,* she crafted a new relationship to her body—one that embraced wildness and fragility, building community through exposure. Thus, Rodríguez Lora's body becomes what Julietta Singh defines as an "errand," both a message and its embodied delivery (Halberstam and Nyong'o 2018). Her performances carry an anticolonial "errand," reclaiming embodiment, queerness, and resistance as public interventions. As Halberstam and Nyong'o frame it, this "wild erranding" gestures toward "an ungovernable future-present" (2018, 569), where performance reimagines both physical and emotional landscapes.

This chapter examines Rodríguez Lora as both a multimedia artist and cultural entrepreneur. Through queer, dance, performance, and decolonial theories, I explore how her work breaks the norms that regulate public, domestic, and urban spaces. Her pieces offer visions of a queer future, addressing sexual violence, gender stereotypes, and the systemic marginalization of feminine people. As Patricia Saunders argues, public performance carries profound semiotic weight in Black diasporic communities, especially when enacted by women. Rodríguez Lora's body becomes a tool of intervention, transmitting a message of resistance and possibility from the perspective of a Caribbean, queer cis woman of color.

Like the other women in this study, Rodríguez Lora is a multidisciplinary artist: performer, choreographer, filmmaker, educator, and cultural organizer. Her work, though composed of distinct pieces, forms a conceptual continuum shaped by two key themes: motherhood and community. As she explained in the podcast conversation with the other artists and myself on May 7, 2024: "No quisiera que se me viera como una solista sino una colaboradora siempre . . . toda esa comunidad es la que nos hace sobrevivir" [I wouldn't want to be seen as a soloist, but always as a collaborator . . . it's that whole community that keeps us alive]. Rodríguez Lora's concept of motherhood includes care, collaboration, and survival, while community becomes a queer, anticapitalistic framework for mutual sustenance. These disrupt normative binaries and reclaim space and time through queer presence. In this way, she enacts what José Esteban Muñoz calls "concrete utopias"—collective hopes and decolonial possibilities (Muñoz 2009, 3).

Under the conceptual framework of motherhood, I analyze the ongoing performative project *La Mujer Maravilla* [Wonder Woman], first conceived in 2013.[3] This project is deeply informed by earlier works that significantly shaped its development, particularly the performances *I Wanted to Be a Cheerleader but My Cuntry Didn't Have It—La Tortillera* (2009),[4] and *Mamá Awilda: El duet* (2010). The second major work, the ongoing project *La Rosario,* initiated in 2014, serves as a conceptual bridge between motherhood and community. Guided by the notion of community, I then turn to Rodríguez Lora's daily video performance *Bailar todos los días* [Dancing every day], which began in 2015, and her ongoing project *Sustento* [Support], started in 2017. In these pieces, Rodríguez Lora reflects on the everyday labor and routines of queer artists—particularly queer women of color—highlighting the body in motion as essential to existence and survival. Through these works, performance emerges as a vital act of *sustento* [support] for the queer artistic community, rooted in daily creative practices.[5]

From Motherhood to Mothering: *La Mujer Maravilla*

A woman dances sensually to reggaetón, wearing a bikini patterned with the Puerto Rican flag. She moves in high heels, occasionally dons a wig and red lipstick, and wields a machete—undressing herself in public spaces until fully nude. Sometimes she wears a black t-shirt printed with a quote from French-Moroccan

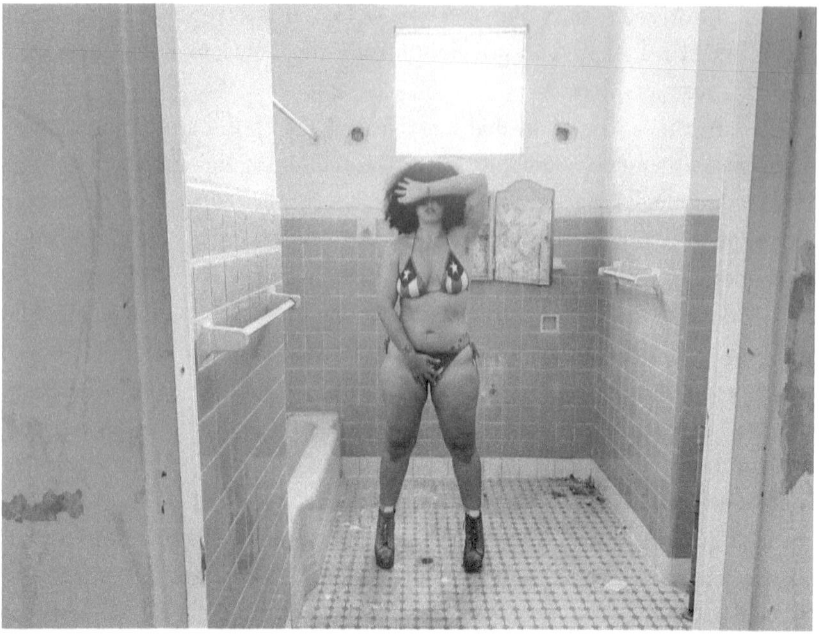

FIGURE 2.1. *La Mujer Maravilla.* Photo credit: Lara Medina Sepúlveda. Courtesy of Lara Medina Sepúlveda.

artist Yto Barrada: "I am not exotic, I am exhausted." In other performances, she pours a *malta* drink over herself and uses the American flag to clean up the spill—at times on a map of the Caribbean. She steps on the flag, writhes her body in sexualized positions suggestive of both consensual and nonconsensual acts, and invites the audience to help dress her. Her body bears red paint simulating physical violence; she leaves crimson footprints as she walks and stains her body and hands. On other occasions, she gathers mothers to breastfeed in a public plaza or poses as a warrior mother holding children and a machete.

These actions form part of Awilda Rodríguez Lora's ongoing performance project *La Mujer Maravilla,* begun in 2013. Drawing on the pop icon Wonder Woman—particularly the version portrayed by Lynda Carter[6] in the late 1970s—the project interrogates the social expectations imposed on women: beauty standards, heteronormative roles, motherhood, and obedience to patriarchal norms. Rodríguez Lora engages with these pressures through movement, improvisation, video, and sound, challenging dominant ideals of womanhood, sexuality, and bodily value in a colonial and capitalist geography like the Puerto Rican archipelago.

La Mujer Maravilla embraces disruption: its performances often feature repetitive movement, public wandering, unintelligible sound, and blurred or interrupted visual images. These strategies evoke what Jack Halberstam calls "the art of failure," a refusal of productive, gender-conforming linearity (2011, 25). Rather than offering polished narratives or neat conclusions, Rodríguez Lora's work affirms what it means to exist outside normative scripts of femininity. Her performances challenge capitalist and heteronormative logics, becoming spaces for rethinking the "economy of living" of the female body. In this way, the project is an "ethico-political practice of disorientation" (Halberstam and Nyong'o 2018, 572), a jolt to social order (Muñoz 2009, 6).

In interviews, Rodríguez Lora has explained that the project began as a reflection on her mother's caregiving and her own desire to become a mother. This autobiographical impetus led her to question what it means to be a woman within heteronormative frameworks of reproduction—as a queer, lesbian-identified woman. Her lived gendered experience resonates with the assertion that "there is nothing authentic about one's gender other than one's experience of it" (Saketopoulou and Pellegrini 2023, xxiii). For Rodríguez Lora, gender cannot be confirmed or disconfirmed but simply exists in lived experience. Through the figure of Wonder Woman, she explores alternative femininities—those deemed equally powerful and beautiful in their divergence. Moreover, given Wonder Woman's symbolic alignment with US nationalism, *La Mujer Maravilla* becomes a space for reframing femininity, motherhood, and womanhood from a decolonial, queer Puerto Rican standpoint.

Conceived during a 2013 residency at Patio Taller in Carolina, Puerto Rico, led by Las Nietas de Nonó,[7] *La Mujer Maravilla* has since grown through numerous explorations, each feeding into or emerging from Rodríguez Lora's wider body of work. Below, I provide a chronological list of these performances. This formatting choice—a break from standard prose—reflects both the challenges of reconstructing ephemeral performance and the disorder that *La Mujer Maravilla* deliberately nurtures. While the list offers an archive of sorts, it also stages a metaperformative gesture: it invites the reader into the chaos of the project, much like attending a live performance.

Selected explorations include:

Exploración #1 (Carolina, PR, 2013)
Exploración #2 (Bronx, NY, 2014)
Exploración #3 (Yellow Spring, OH, 2014)

Exploración #6 (Puerto de Tierra, *La Mujer Maravilla: Plaza de la mujer,* San Juan, PR, 2014)
Exploración #7 (Santiago, Chile, 2014), *#7.1* (Valdivia), *#7.2* (Puerto Montt)
INDIA$ (Miami, FL, 2015) and its variations in PR and Ann Arbor
La Mujer Maravilla: Somos Salvajes (Puerto Plata, Dominican Republic, 2015)
Río Piedras (Río Piedras, PR, 2015)
Exploración #8 (San Juan, PR, 2015)
Exploración #10 (2015)
La Mujer Maravilla: Guerreras (2016), *Cuerpa* (Brooklyn Museum, 2018), *Cuerpas* (Judson Church, NY, 2019)
La Mujer Maravilla: 4654 (2018)
Exploración #14 (2018)
Exploración #15 (2019)
LMM: Barbarie, Hidrante, San Juan, PR (2022)[8]

These performances engage recurring themes: motherhood, the female body, sexual violence, and the negotiation of women's presence in public and private spaces. For example, in *Exploración #14* (2018), Rodríguez Lora critiques the exoticized and sexualized representation of Caribbean women by dancing in a dress painted with an exaggerated white woman's bust. She evokes media tropes of female objectification in the Caribbean, preferred over sexualized women of certain skin complexions, and the racialized fantasies embedded in salsa and reggaetón.

In *Exploración #6* (2014), she invited mothers to breastfeed in public in San Juan's Puerta de Tierra, reframing maternal care as public performance. For this exploration Rodríguez Lora asked other women artists to perform while thinking of their own exploration of the concept of the "Wonder Woman." This is how performer Jomary Ortega, to artistically answer the question posed by Rodríguez Lora, started breastfeeding her daughter.[9]

In the explorations in Chile (#7, #7.1, and #7.2 in 2014) the artist wraps her naked body with several bras in different sizes, something that she also does in exploration #10 (2015). In *Exploración #10,* she wrapped her naked body in bras within her domestic space—a performance that collapses private and public spheres. As Jill Dolan and Rebecca Saunders have argued, such intimate performances render visible the constructed nature of desire and femininity in relation to space. This domestic staging also reflects José Esteban Muñoz's notion of queer time and Manalansan's call to consider the "wild measures

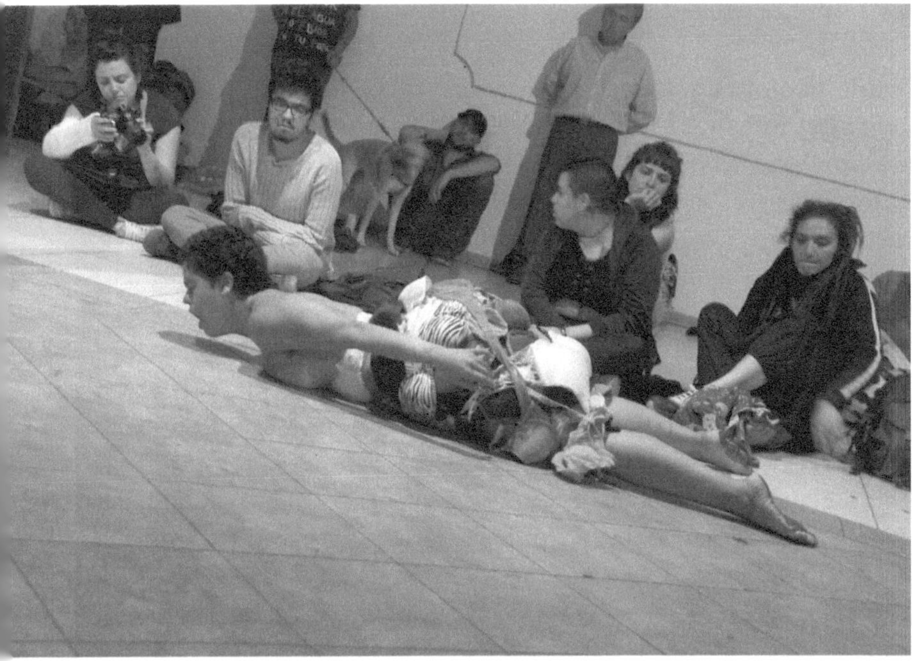

FIGURE 2.2. *La Mujer Maravilla: Exploración #7.* Photo credit: Dominique Wainstein M. Courtesy of Dominique Wainstein M.

and mess" of queer migrant life as openings for survival (Manalansan 2018, 495). Whether in public plazas or private homes, Rodríguez Lora's *La Mujer Maravilla* interrogates gender norms, challenges violence and feminicides, and reimagines the female body beyond colonial and patriarchal constraint.

In *La Mujer Maravilla: INDIA$* (2018), Awilda Rodríguez Lora explores the legacy of colonialism and its lasting impact on the treatment of female bodies. Referencing Christopher Columbus's arrival in the Caribbean—specifically to the Dominican Republic—the performance critiques how Indigenous women were labeled "Indias" and objectified from the outset of colonization. As the artist explains, "[O]ur bodies have been conquered violently and objectified through multiple colonizers and our current (more than 100 years) colonizer, the United States of America."[10] This critique materializes in performance through what Rodríguez Lora describes as "a sweet tropical pop experience" using her body, voice, and poetic imagery.[11]

In *INDIA$*, she wears a Puerto Rican flag bikini overlaid with the US flag, manipulating the latter in ways that evoke veiling, masking, and domination. The American flag becomes a metaphor for colonial power, visually layered atop

Puerto Rican identity. The performance culminates in Rodríguez Lora stepping on the flag, wielding a machete—a symbol of both resistance and sustenance—and removing her bikini to walk away nude. Here, nudity functions not as spectacle but as an act of liberation. The female body, the performance suggests, seeks to be free of nationalistic and patriarchal constraints alike.

In *La Mujer Maravilla: Cuerpa* (2018),[12] Rodríguez Lora confronts personal trauma by staging a performance based on her experience of sexual violence. Dressed only in underwear, she repositions her body into the very sexualized poses she was once forced to assume, thereby reclaiming her "cuerpa" through embodied memory. This act of bodily repossession draws from Saketopoulou and Pellegrini's notion that trauma demands psychic innovation, a "self-theorization" born from one's encounter with alterity (2023, viii–xxiii). For Rodríguez Lora, trauma does not define or invalidate her identity; instead, it becomes a means of articulating gendered experience.

The performance implicates the audience, positioning them as potential witnesses, consumers, or even voyeurs of sexualized violence. While responses may vary according to individual subjectivity, the performance destabilizes the binary between pleasure and violence, revealing how easily a female body may be objectified without consent. Viewers occupy what Cruz-Malavé calls a "condición porosa, 'traidora' de lo puertorriqueño"—a porous, even treasonous, position not to transcend but to authorize new modes of resistance (2023, 330). As Jacques Rancière suggests, this form of performance activates a "community rhythm" in which spectators are asked to move, reflect, and question alongside the performer (2011, 5).

In *La Mujer Maravilla: Guerreras* (2016), Rodríguez Lora critiques Puerto Rico's Bill 743—an attempt to penalize the wearing of face-covering masks in protests. She frames the bill not as a protection of civil order but as a tool of surveillance that threatens the identities of those fighting for social justice. In response, *Guerreras* imagines a counterimage: topless women using their shirts as face coverings while holding machetes, transforming themselves into symbols of both vulnerability and resistance. These warriors—mothers, daughters, fighters—stand against colonial, patriarchal, and state violence. A striking image from this performance depicts a mother holding a machete, flanked by her children, all bare-chested and wearing protest masks. They stand outdoors amid native plants, their gaze fierce and unwavering. This scene encapsulates *Guerreras:* a celebration of maternal strength rooted in land, love, and the readiness to fight. Through such performances, Rodríguez Lora channels the

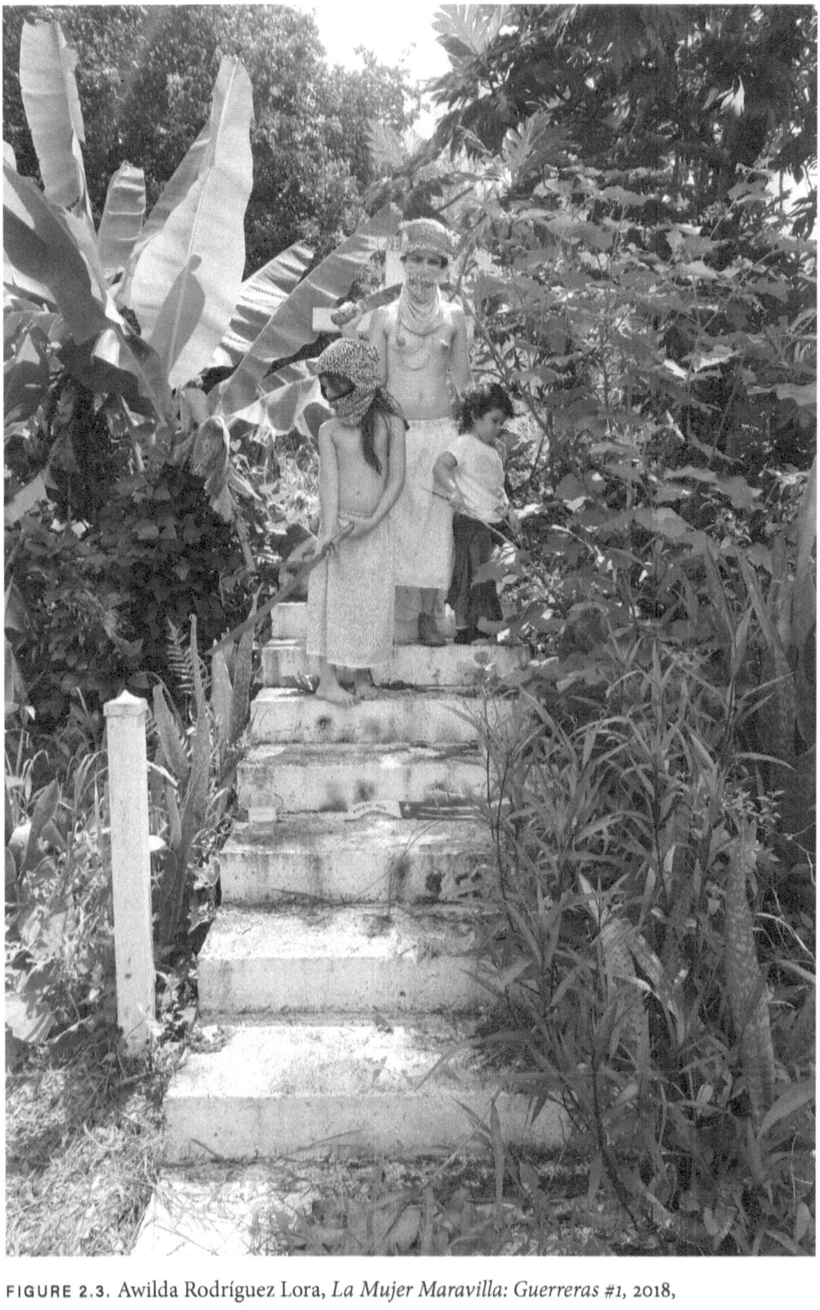

FIGURE 2.3. Awilda Rodríguez Lora, *La Mujer Maravilla: Guerreras #1*, 2018, Photograph, 24 by 36 inches. Courtesy of Awilda Rodríguez Lora.

contradictions of being a woman in a sexist, colonial society. Her nudity, often misread as mere provocation, instead underscores deprivation—an allegory of the political and material dispossession experienced in Puerto Rico.

Throughout *La Mujer Maravilla,* Rodríguez Lora consistently engages the audience in conversation, demystifying the artist and emphasizing shared vulnerability. Each performance becomes an occasion to "humanize each other," as she describes it, and to reflect collectively on what sustains us. This ethos of care and relationality later culminates in her 2019 project *Sustento* [Support], which grows directly out of the practices and philosophies developed in *La Mujer Maravilla.*

Indeed, Rodríguez Lora's artistic work forms a constellation of interconnected explorations. Prior to *La Mujer Maravilla,* she had already begun to articulate a queer, feminist performance practice in works like *La tortillera* (2009) and *Mamá Awilda: El duet (A Story in Tres Parts)* (2010). These earlier pieces laid the groundwork for her later inquiries into queerness, femininity, and motherhood. While *La Mujer Maravilla* marks a pivotal moment in her trajectory, it is both a continuation and a seedbed for what follows.

In her piece *La tortillera* (2009), part of the broader project *I Wanted to Be a Cheerleader but My Cuntry Didn't Have It,* Awilda Rodríguez Lora deploys an intentional misspelling of "country" as "cuntry" to recall the vulgar English term "cunt," drawing attention to the intersections of nationalism, gender, and sexuality. In the performance, the artist masturbates in a private space—identified in interviews as a closet in her New York apartment—claiming this intimate act as a form of political and queer resistance.[13]

The title and lyrics of the reggaetón-inspired video embrace the word *tortillera,* a reclaimed Spanish slur for lesbian, translated in English as "dyke." Dykeness is articulated through Rodríguez Lora's aesthetic choices, use of light and camera, and especially through sound and language. In this 3-minute, 53-second performance, she appropriates the vulgarity of "cunt" in a "cuntry" that marginalizes both her nation and her sexuality. By situating herself in a closet, masturbating with humor and candor, she reclaims lesbian pleasure and asserts an unapologetically queer presence. Her performance style emerges here as a form of embodied storytelling, where her body becomes a narrative medium. The performance enacts joy as a mode of resistance, opposing the shame and guilt instilled by heteronormative culture.

Visually, the video alternates between images of Rodríguez Lora dressed in a short apron-like dress reminiscent of both a doll and a maid and scenes of her naked or partially clothed body. Through doll-like movements, stilled frames,

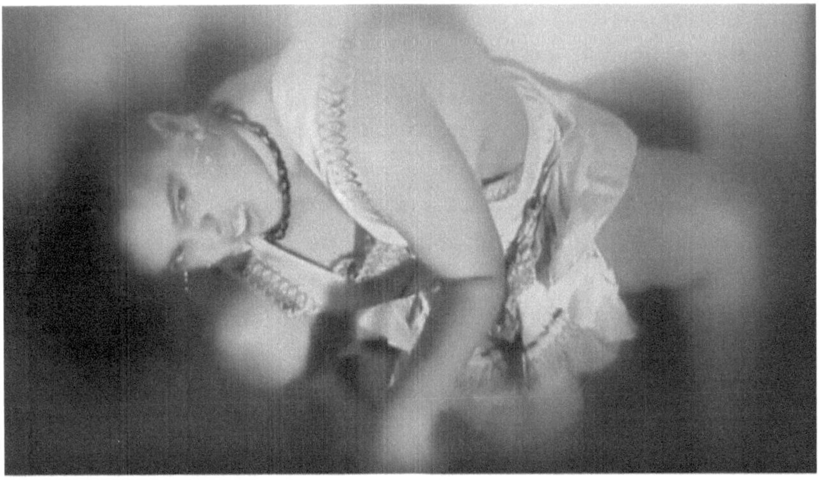

FIGURE 2.4. Still image of the video performance *Tortillera* by Awilda Rodríguez Lora. Courtesy of Awilda Rodríguez Lora.

and fragmented close-ups of her masturbating gestures, the video constructs a surreal, dreamlike narrative. Blurred motion, saturated lighting, and rhythmic editing produce a disorienting yet intimate portrayal of female sexual pleasure. This focus on masturbation invites reflection on the construction of desire and femininity, disrupting a psychoanalytic tradition that has historically framed femininity as lack (Irigaray 1977).

By embodying a Brown maid who exercises agency over her pleasure, Rodríguez Lora subverts the mainstream erotic economy and its objectification of racialized women. The maid figure—typically rendered voiceless—becomes a subject of autonomy, disrupting voyeuristic norms of the pornographic and erotic industries. Her direct gaze into the camera inverts the power dynamic of the gaze through a queer lens, exposing the viewer while reclaiming her right to look and to be seen on her own terms.

The song's lyrics, switching between Spanish and English, reflect a linguistic hybridity born from Puerto Rico's colonial history. This code-switching defies grammatical propriety and becomes a decolonial linguistic act, aligning with Gloria Anzaldúa's vision of language as a site of resistance (1987). Rodríguez Lora sings, "tortita de manteca" [little buttery cake] and later chants, "tortita tortita tortillera" [little dykey cake]—a chorus rendered deliberately off-key and sonically distorted. These sonic disruptions, layered with gasps, moans, vibrato, and whispering, create a soundscape that is simultaneously pleasurable and unsettling. The result is a complex audiovisual performance that constructs new forms of listening and intimacy, in line with what Przybylski calls "the sound of decolonization" (2023, 22).

The repetition of "la performera . . . una tortillera" [the performer . . . a dyke] (2:06–2:13) marks a pivotal moment of artistic becoming. The strategic pause between labels exorcises the insult and reclaims queer subjectivity. The final chant, "tortilleras unidas jamás serán vencidas" [dykes united will never be defeated], paired with explicit images of pleasure and affirmation, transforms the personal into the political.[14] The combative chant, paired up to images of the artist giving herself pleasure, opening her legs while looking at the camera, while calling herself "tortillera" is a declaration of queer collective happiness from a female perspective of intimate pleasure.

The personal pleasure becomes political because it comes from a body (the female body) that is treated and perceived constantly as a sociopolitical territory to institutionally control and contain. Awilda, then, disobeys and expresses her disobedience in this piece through irreverent movements. But also, she is disobedient and irreverent through the interruptions of the sound, the out of tone chorus, the vibrato and whispering, the repeated instrumental lines, the loops, the pitches and the gasps, the moans, and the almost nonhuman sounds.

The soundscape of *La tortillera* creates ruptures from the colonizing main Euro-American music industry and that, then, creates new possibilities of listening. This nonlinear sonic video performance draws new traditions of storytelling, and visits and revisits moments in a nonlinear way, creating a kind of freedom that, through sound, extends the territory that the artist can affect (Przybylski 2023, 19–20). This "kind of freedom" becomes the sound of decolonization and the attempt to create a space of possibility for decolonial practice. Also, she decolonizes her objectified body by dancing to rhythms and out-of-tune sounds that deconstruct "the implicit and explicit gender and racial bias [that] profoundly affects media-entertainment industries" (196). The intersection of gender, sexuality, race, language, and sexual desire establishes a cultural power expressed through "storytelling: in narrative, poetry, song, and in daily word choices" (220) or, as in the case of *La tortillera,* through performance. The stories are told through the body and the sounds, transmitting what needs to be told and to be heard in a constant negotiating dance with the listener (213, 215).

Live performances of *La tortillera* further intertwine personal history with queer eroticism. In one iteration, the artist discusses her tattooed name "Awilda" as a tribute to her mother's care and support, especially after leaving her father's home due to violence. She contrasts this maternal lineage—carried on her left arm—with the right hand that has taught her self-care and pleasure. Singing to her own hand and placing it inside her underwear, Rodríguez Lora draws a direct line between sexual autonomy and the reclaiming of personal narrative. This gesture, both intimate and political, breaks cycles of patriarchal violence and affirms queer selfhood. *La tortillera* becomes a space for envisioning lesbian pleasure not as marginal but as central, and for asserting that bodily sovereignty begins with reclaiming one's own desires. As Przybylski writes, "Gendered expectations . . . may not be readily apparent until disrupted" (224); this piece achieves such disruption through an embodied, audiovisual articulation of pleasure and resistance.

Rodríguez Lora's later piece, *Mamá Awilda: El duet (A Story in Tres Parts)* (2010), extends these explorations of womanhood and motherhood. This video performance trilogy, dedicated to her mother, blends Spanglish dialogue with fragmented editing and nonlinear storytelling. The artist juxtaposes domestic scenes—haircuts, conversations on a living room couch, outdoor strolls—with looped sounds, visual animations, and repeated phrases. Rather than presenting a coherent narrative, the performance demands what Przybylski calls "decolonial listening" (241), compelling the viewer to attend to silenced voices through disrupted, layered sonic experiences.

Here, the artist resists normative storytelling by privileging affective, sensory, and relational ways of knowing. The piece functions as a dialogic act of remembrance and repair, inviting the viewer into a collective, emancipated community of listeners and storytellers (Rancière 2011, 22). In this context, Rodríguez Lora's body, voice, and soundscape become the archive of untold stories, capable of disrupting hegemonic narratives of family, gender, and identity.

Awilda's mother, also named Awilda, narrates her fears and shares her traumatic experiences through subtle phrases, gestures, bodily movements, and laughter. She reflects on how strength is often a necessity, not a choice, for mothers—yet society frames it as a masculine trait. In an intimate moment with her daughter, the two discuss queerness, with the artist vulnerably recounting her own experiences. Mamá Awilda responds with candor and wit, declaring in her heavy Hispanic accent that she also is queer: "I am queer and so what? If you do not like it, do not take it!" (7:03–7:09). Her narration, both in the video performance and live renditions of the work, creates new modes of listening that disrupt the assumed clarity of familiar words. More than textual content, her voice is layered with sound, repetition, ellipses, pauses, and interruptions—each sonic element evoking individual memory and shared experience, contributing

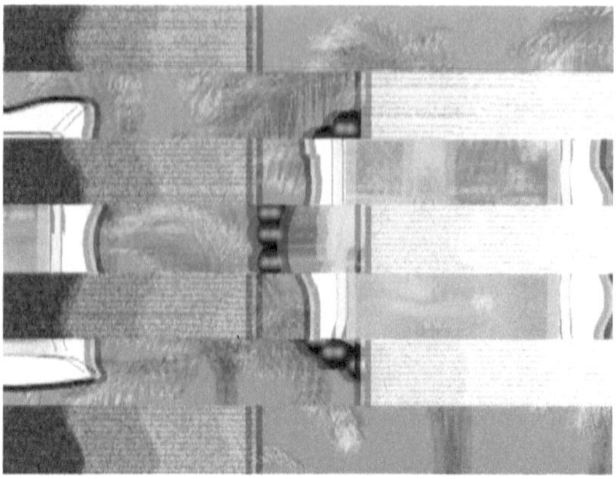

FIGURE 2.5. Example of the visual disruptions in the video. Still image of the video performance *Mamá Awilda: El duet* by Awilda Rodríguez Lora. Courtesy of Awilda Rodríguez Lora.

to what Liz Przybylski calls "memory, future hope, lived and relived experience" (2023, 242). This creates a shared, embodied encounter with sonic possibilities.

Mamá Awilda's fragmented visual and sonic storytelling reveals how society disciplines girls into performing femininities that do not align with their being, often requiring them to suppress their ambitions. As Saketopoulou and Pellegrini argue, the denial of psychic interiority to cisgender boys and the coercive regulation of gender norms show that "cisness is neither spontaneous nor the default" but rather maintained through violence and dissociation (2023, 81). Through her mother's voice, *la performera* exposes and resists these normalized violences, reimagining gender, motherhood, and womanhood.

The video performance defies colonial boundaries of form, resisting the logic of linear syntax and standardized grammar. As Saketopoulou and Pellegrini note, "[L]anguage changes, and so do gendered possibilities—though not always in sync with each other" (98). This dissonance enables what Przybylski describes as a practice of "sonic sovereignty," which links self-definition and collective determination outside the constraints of the nation-state and engages with alternative experiences of time (Przybylski 2023, 5). Thus, Rodríguez Lora's work functions decolonially, disrupting patriarchal and heteronormative expectations placed on women and mothers in Puerto Rico. Through sound, it constructs a Halberstamian queer temporality and space—one in which the artist asserts her agency by "choosing one's audience [. . .] and choosing when to be silent" (Przybylski 2023, 7). The sonic sovereignty she practices is inherently narrative: even as mainstream industries circulate colonialist and heteropatriarchal ideals, broadcasting and streaming create space for resistant storytelling (7).

In this work, Spanglish becomes a site of linguistic tension and identity assertion, while the looped, visually interrupted sequence of images and sounds metaphorically represents the fractured, cyclical nature of institutional, social, and domestic violence. The performance reclaims both language and sound to articulate a queer, feminist politics grounded in memory, resistance, and reimagined futures.

In *Mamá Awilda: El duet,* Awilda Rodríguez Lora uses visual and sonic disruptions—black screens, prolonged silences, technological references to 1980s television—as tools to deconstruct dominant narratives of womanhood and motherhood. These interruptions resist the linear storytelling expected of conventional video art, generating a critical tension that invites viewers to question societal norms surrounding family, maternal roles, and femininity. The piece enacts a queer, intergenerational gaze that reimagines motherhood in relation to agency, space, movement, and queerness. By breaking the formal expectations of the interview-performance video, Rodríguez Lora constructs a decolonial and intersectional femininity that, as Przybylski suggests, "refuses hierarchies and creates or re-creates alternative structures" (2023, 195).

Visual repetitions and interruptions further dismantle normative portrayals. In part one, the mother recounts how her father predetermined both the sex and name of her child, a moment that underscores patriarchal control (2:30–3:15). The editing—close-ups, repeated gestures, pauses—emphasizes the emotional toll of such control and frames the mother's narration as a site of unresolved trauma. Sound design also plays a critical role: electronic interference, reverberations, and repeated sonic fragments create a disjointed rhythm that unsettles the viewer, pushing them into what Halberstam might call a queer temporality of failure—an embodied refusal of capitalist, colonial, and heteronormative time. The fragmentation of both narrative and sound rejects traditional representational structures, embracing instead the "failure or refusal to domesticate, clean up, temper, and tame the unpredictable and immeasurable lives," which, as Manalansan writes, offers "a possible escape hatch" from oppressive frameworks (2018, 496). Echoing Butler's theory of gender as a "stylized repetition of acts," the performance reveals patriarchy itself as a system of damaging repetition—and one that the video critiques through its own performative excess and fracturing.

In another scene, the mother describes how "las madres . . . tienen que mostrarse fuertes" [mothers have to appear strong] (4:05–4:34), mocking the term "fuertes" with her expression. The scene is intercut with outdoor footage of mother and daughter laughing together—this juxtaposition is repeated multiple times. The repetition of joy and satire highlights both the absurdity of the societal expectation that mothers must always be strong and the shared complicity between the two women. As Consuelo Martínez Reyes (2021) points out, in Jack Halberstam's book *Female Masculinity,* Halberstam argues that society typically associates masculinity with men, linking it to traits like physical strength, financial independence, sexual power, and dominance in male-coded professions. When these traits are expressed by women, they disrupt conventional ideas about gender and reveal that masculinity itself is a constructed identity rather than an inherent one. In this sense, female masculinity exposes the mechanisms through which "true" masculinity maintains its authority by casting its alternatives as secondary or incomplete. Although Halberstam's analysis centers on masculine lesbians, the concept can extend beyond sexuality, since processes of masculinization also occur symbolically and socially, not just through the body (2021, 172). Female masculinity is then a productive concept to think about the "strength" expected by mothers that Mamá Awilda laughs about. In fact, this first part ends with mother and daughter dancing outdoors, heads shaved, adorned with large earrings—claiming femininity as queer, bodily, strong and vulnerable as much or as little anyone wants, and free.

In part two, Rodríguez Lora asks her mother to respond in English, and when she hesitates, the artist offers "Spanglish" (9:15–9:23). This exchange alludes, in my opinion, to Puerto Rico's colonial relationship with the United States and highlights Spanglish as a form of resistance. A trembling test pattern follows, recalling the artist's 1980s childhood and symbolizing narrative rupture. The story that ensues—of baby Awilda falling out of her carrier at the US embassy—becomes metaphorical: the helpless Puerto Rican body arriving at the feet of the empire. The image crystallizes the imposed, nonconsensual nature of Puerto Rican–US relations and the subaltern position of Puerto Rican subjects.

A pivotal moment arrives when the artist asks her mother, "Did you want to be a mom?" Her mother replies, "Not really" (15:20–16:14), unsettling heteronormative assumptions about maternal desire. This moment aligns with Halberstam's notion of queer time, suggesting alternative modes of relationality and subcultural existence (Halberstam 2005, 1). The mother's ambivalence positions her within a queer lineage, even as a cisgender heterosexual woman. The use of Spanglish, again, and disrupted visuals—such as palm trees overlapping a rainbow test pattern—evokes the layered colonial histories and fractured cultural identities of Puerto Rican women.

Later, Mamá Awilda reflects, "They [men] need to know sometimes you can have it, sometimes you cannot. Sometimes giving is wrong," a phrase repeated during a montage of family photos. This repeated phrase, paired with her dancing and laughter, visually dismantles the idealized heteronormative family and affirms a new model rooted in self-love, boundaries, and embodied liberation. As Victoria Pérez Royo argues, dance enables new understandings of space (2009, 30), and here, the mother's movements signal newfound autonomy.

Importantly, trauma operates not only as content but also as a liberatory method. Rodríguez Lora challenges the pathologization of queer identities as rooted in maternal failure—a trope historically upheld by psychoanalysis and psychiatry. As Saketopoulou and Pellegrini insist, trauma should not be framed as the cause of queerness but as a shared condition shaping all subjectivities (2023, 79). *Mamá Awilda* validates both the artist's queer identity and her mother's cisheterosexual identity through a shared narrative of pain—a pain that years later fueled the protests of summer 2019 and the *perreo combativo*—vulnerability, and resistance.

Part three visually layers close-ups of mother and daughter, aligning their gestures and expressions to emphasize both resemblance and divergence. As they dance to the 1982 salsa song *Awilda*[15] (28:32–31:21), they reclaim their shared name from the *machista* culture that once constrained them. The dance becomes an act of resistance, transforming a symbol of patriarchy into a marker of personal and political identity. In a later studio sequence, the mother speaks about the contradictions of being "strong"—a trait seen as masculine—while also being expected to embody feminine softness. Her voice-over accompanies the sound of dripping water (32:17–34:10), which evokes the cleansing, shifting, and liberating qualities of fluidity. Their dancing sheds imposed roles, exposing fears, dreams, and pain as sites of empowerment. The performance concludes with a looped sequence in which mother and daughter take turns receiving kisses. Their faces merge through soft fades, symbolizing a queer family legacy that honors the past, affirms the present, and imagines a freer future. The final moment—Mamá Awilda exclaiming "¡Qué rico!" [So good!]—cements joy as a radical gesture of survival and love.

In a 2010 live version, Rodríguez Lora enters the stage carrying a TV and videotape—symbols of 1980s domestic life—and sings the Cuban lullaby originally interpreted by Bola de Nieve[16] as "Duerme negrito," as her mother does in the film. As the lullaby plays, the artist wraps the TV cable around her neck and slowly sits beside the screen. This action invokes multilayered violence and intergenerational trauma: domestic, racial, colonial. The song's narrative—an enslaved mother leaving her child to labor—mirrors Puerto Rico's history of colonial extraction, enforced passivity, and multilayered gender and racial violence.[17] By staging this act of "choking" with a childhood object, Rodríguez Lora offers a cathartic confrontation with histories of maternal, colonial, and racial violence, but also evokes an umbilical cord that suffocates with intergenerational trauma and sustains and nurtures at the same time. Echoing René Marqués's idea of Puerto Rican obedience as "suicidal," this performance constructs a space for refusal and reimagines identity through disobedient movement.[18]

After her mother finishes singing in the video, the artist mimics a familiar comment about their physical resemblance, smiling and synchronizing her head movements with her mother's on screen. This overlapping of gestures and expressions marks a visual convergence between the two Awildas. In a sudden shift, the artist screams at the screen—"¡Pues, vete pal carajo, coño!" [Well, go to hell, damn it!]—and moves away from the TV. What follows is a visceral sequence of repeated actions: she slaps herself across the face and body, stomps heavily, collapses, rises, and begins again. With each fall, she manages to partially untangle a cable wrapped around her neck. Once free, she declares, "Let that be the first and last time that you ever do that to me" (4:52–4:56), before resuming the cycle of slapping and collapsing.

At one point, while falling and slapping herself, the artist's body appears to be dragged across the space—suggesting the physical and emotional weight of inherited violence. As this sequence ends, her mother's voice is heard echoing the artist's earlier words, now in Spanish: "Que sea la primera y la última vez que tú me haces eso" [Let that be the first and last time that you ever do that to me] (4:56–6:55). These words repeat as the artist gently hugs and caresses her body. She also caresses the TV screen, where her face continues to merge with her mother's. This moment, following the lullaby "Duerme negrito," reflects both a legacy of domestic and political violence and a movement toward healing. The artist shifts from involuntary, violence-induced gestures to deliberate movements of care and love—now possible once the cable is removed from her neck. She ends the sequence by sitting on the TV, legs open, evoking the posture of childbirth. This image becomes a powerful symbol of her cathartic rebirth—an act of resistance against the repetitive cycle of patriarchal violence (Halberstam 2005).

The live performance continues with the artist dancing to the salsa song "Awilda" in sync with the video. At the song's conclusion, she hugs herself as her mother, in the video, dances to the sound of dripping water. The two figures—mother in the video, daughter in live performance—move together across time and space, bound by the sound of water (12:07–15:37). The dance ends with her mother's voice offering reflections on how to be a good person (15:33–15:40). The artist then lifts the TV, which is still playing footage of her mother dancing, and embraces it. This gesture symbolizes a reconciliation with her roots—an acceptance of her history and a release of what she cannot control, coupled with an assertion of agency over what she can change.

In the final scene of the video, mother and daughter kiss and cuddle. The artist confesses her fear of becoming like her mother—of loving as her mother loved her father, the man who broke both their hearts. She admits to being afraid of becoming a woman, a lover, a mother, and a wife. Yet she reveals that she has learned to move and dance with these fears, and that her mother has been both her origin and her guide in learning to live with joy and strength. She closes the performance by affirming: "Mamá Awilda soy yo. Mamá Awilda somos nosotros." [Mamá Awilda is me. Mamá Awilda is us.] By claiming her name—shared with her mother—the artist embraces their shared vulnerabilities, imperfections, and histories. In doing so, she liberates herself to move in any direction. She asks for forgiveness, thanks her mother, and kisses the TV—mirroring the kiss playing on screen. The performance ends, like the video, with her mother exclaiming "¡Qué rico!" [How delicious!], reaffirming joy as a radical strategy for survival. The love and tenderness exchanged in these final moments lay the groundwork for a more loving intergenerational future—for women as mothers, daughters, and subjects capable of self-love and self-worth. As in the work of Macha Colón, joy and love emerge as radical tools through which women create spaces of freedom and embodiment.

Together, *La tortillera* (2009) and *Mamá Awilda: El duet* (2010) allowed Awilda Rodríguez Lora to deconstruct, explore, and reimagine femininity, womanhood, and queer identity. These performances opened an intimate and political dialogue about motherhood—with her mother, herself, and broader society. The themes explored in these early works resurface with renewed clarity in *La Mujer Maravilla,* where the artist continues to reflect on womanhood, queerness, femininity, and maternal desire. *La Mujer Maravilla* emerged at a moment when Rodríguez Lora was contemplating becoming a mother herself. Yet due to structural barriers—economic instability, lack of healthcare, and the absence of support for queer single women artists—she never became a biological mother. Her creative and personal experience thus shifted to a broader and more fluid practice of care, resistance, and embodied wisdom, and so her artistic and personal experience shifted—as the title of this section suggests—from *motherhood* to *mothering.*

From Motherhood to Mothering: *La Rosario*

La Rosario serves as a way for artist Awilda Rodríguez Lora to reimagine mothering and create space "to live [. . .] against erasure [. . .] into the settler colony we keep calling home" (Halberstam and Nyong'o 2018, 579). Upon her return to Puerto Rico in 2014, Rodríguez Lora, burdened by debt after completing her studies, transformed her apartment into a shared space—initially out of economic necessity, but increasingly as a deliberate act of community building. This shift paralleled her development of *La Mujer Maravilla*, marking a transition from using her domestic space for performance to opening it as a site for queer communal living.

Initially, she used platforms like Airbnb to share her home but quickly recognized their role in accelerating gentrification and displacing local communities. In response, she redefined her vision: *La Rosario* would not be a site of profit, but a refuge for marginalized queer artists, particularly those with limited resources and support systems. It became a queer collective, embracing "the mess of race, inequality, and other social debris" (Manalansan 2018, 492), and rejecting normative familial expectations.

This home evolved into an artistic and political project—a site where queer bodies could explore identity, performance, and solidarity. Weaving from the theoretical framework of thinkers like Saketopoulou and Pellegrini, Rodríguez Lora challenged the notion of a "true self" anchored in gender identity, instead creating a space where fluidity, vulnerability, and care became central. In this sense, *La Rosario* queers the very idea of domesticity, fostering a mode of mothering that defies patriarchal and heteronormative norms.

Rather than mothering in the traditional sense, Rodríguez Lora embraces "mothering" as a radical act of care, rooted in Afro-Caribbean feminist thought. The project reflects an alternative domesticity—one that does not reject family outright but instead reimagines it as a chosen queer collective grounded in mutual support and interdependence. As Halberstam writes, queer uses of space often exist in opposition to institutions of family and reproduction (1), yet *La Rosario* proposes a nuanced expansion of these concepts. Thus, it becomes a porous way to challenge the social understanding of the domestic space and of the private space. It does not exist "in opposition to the institution of family," but creates a queer home for a queer family where they can collectively and individually exist through their queer practices understood as artistic practices.

The dialectical tension between individuality and collectivity makes collective queer movements a possible practice that also becomes a practice of survival, of reciprocal support, and an act of solidarity in scarcity. This project, therefore, by including "these subjects who do not 'measure up'" (Halberstam and Nyong'o 2018, 493), becomes an ontological necessity. This way of revisiting the politics of mothering gave the artist permission to explore further the layers of sharing her own vulnerability and put her in the position of receiving and taking care of others' vulnerabilities. It also planted the seeds to create a space of rest that reframes "laziness" as a necessary strategy to resist the system. In performance and daily life, Rodríguez Lora uses *La Rosario* to explore how domestic labor, movement, and vulnerability can challenge colonial, capitalist structures. She plays with household architecture—sliding, crawling, improvising—to articulate embodied resistance, a sense of vulnerability, and of being suspended in complex political times.

La Rosario became the place from where the artist wanted to transform, to provoke change, to rethink the system, to mother her community, to be taken care of, and it is a place that she wants to use as a point of departure and of strength to make community. Awilda's human body interfacing with the architectural domestic space instructs on other possibilities of domesticity that can be nonconformist and socially disobedient (Halberstam and Nyong'o 2018). Her nudity in performance, for example, becomes a powerful gesture of shared vulnerability, asserting presence and agency in spaces where queer bodies are often erased.

Unfortunately, gentrification forced her to relocate *La Rosario*, underscoring the very systemic violence the project seeks to counter. Yet this displacement reaffirms the importance of such spaces: community homes that resist capitalist commodification, shelter queer individuals from public violence, and reclaim the domestic as a space of safety, art, and transformation.

Rodríguez Lora also uses *La Rosario* to foreground the value of domestic labor, critiquing how women's unpaid work often sustains economies that simultaneously oppress them. In this sense, *La Rosario* becomes a site of feminist critique, artistic experimentation, and communal survival.

La Rosario becomes a space for reflection on social and political issues that provoke violence against female and queer bodies. It is a place for artistic inspiration, for creation, for reinventing the ways to organize, move through, and live the domestic and the private space, and where to feel safe to move. On her website, Rodríguez Lora describes *La Rosario* as "a shared queer feminist collaborative home [. . .] to nourish creative practices [. . .] based on emergent strategies that embody trust, fluidity, interdependence and transformation."[19] Through this intentional framing, the project welcomes queer creators who prioritize feminist, inclusive practices—offering them a space of healing, freedom, and community. Ultimately, *La Rosario* queers motherhood itself. Rodríguez Lora moves from the desire to "be a mother" toward a practice of collective care that validates nonbiological, nonfemale forms of mothering. By opening her home and body to others, she challenges exclusionary norms and constructs a space where intersectional identities—marked by queerness, race, class, ability, and more—can be fully seen and held in their subaltern uniqueness.

Awilda, with the project of *La Rosario,* exposes her body and the private space of her household to tell her stories, to hear other stories from queer artists, and to build their own narratives together. Through their stories and their community they can potentially provoke a social change where to be together in difference, "[C]onstructing a place for solitude, an 'aesthetic' place [. . .] [where] The possibility to be apart [. . .] [connects] the link between the solitude of the artwork and human community [. . .] [as] a matter of transformed 'sensation'" (Rancière 2011, 53–56). *La Rosario* offers the space to revisit and reconnect with the importance of empathy and community, and to create individually while sharing emotions and vulnerabilities to become stronger. This is only possible when the body can move and can share freely any kind of taboo topic to resist a colonizing and capitalistic culture that classifies the worth of people based on their monetary income. Thus, the networking and support offered by the project of *La Rosario* is also a political act that analyzes and criticizes the economic measures taken against Puerto Rico, and so it metaphorically becomes a way to reject the political conversation on the Puerto Rican debt imposed by the United States. As a result, *La Rosario* offers a space in which queer folks own their space and have agency to dispute a colonizing system that subjugates and affects their everyday life. *La Rosario* becomes an opportunity to start a conversation with the country as queer subjects with agency, and from a feminist approach it allows the artists to draw boundaries with their bodies as a liberating act and as a statement of existence.

The queer bodies that share *La Rosario* compose a community that contributes to deconstructing the image of motherhood, the capitalistic approach to life, and the way the media projects the Afro-Caribbean female body in commercials, in TV, in the porn industry, and so on. These topics are all connected to the politics of the island and to the ways in which governments and laws want to control bodies. Thus, the artist's need to welcome in her domestic space, and to move freely and together in a private space that can be identified as home, aims toward an inclusion too often not represented in media and not lived in society. But also, it aims to deconstruct the idea that the private and the domestic spaces are the safest place, providing so a critique to the social neglect of domestic violence that particularly targets women and queer people. *La Rosario* wants to protect the domestic space and so becomes a place where new ways of living the private are possible and where nobody feels unsafe or as an outsider. These are the bodies of mothers, grandmothers, daughters, human beings who do not fit in their roles as they are socially expected because they are queer. So, *La Rosario* grants a domestic space where they can create their art, as well as a place they can share everyday moments, such as cooking, cleaning, hugging, and the like. This queer domesticity does not reject family, rather expands or reconfigures the family from a heteronormative institution to a queer one. The more the artist dreamed, planned, and practiced in *La Rosario,* the more Rodríguez Lora cultivated a sense of support that ultimately led to her future community-focused projects *Bailar todos los días* [Dancing every day, 2015] and *Sustento* [Support, 2019].[20]

Moving with the Community: The Life Project *Bailar todos los días*

"Bailar es soñar con los pies" [Dancing is dreaming with your feet] reads the tattoo inked on the back of Awilda Rodríguez Lora's calves. This inscription is more than decorative; it serves as a corporeal reminder of the expansive, unstandardized potential of dance—an art form that, contrary to popular perception, need not conform to institutionalized expectations of stage, form, or body. Traditional frameworks of dance—its venue, the dancer's appearance, age, audience, and motivations—have long shaped its perceived value. Awilda's tattoo challenges these norms, asserting through her body the possibility of alternative dances, alternative bodies, and alternative ways of moving through the world.

Her project *Bailar todos los días* [Dancing every day] exemplifies this reimagining. The teenage version of Awilda, once performing in high heels and tight clothing with bleached blonde hair on Puerto Rican television, encountered early on the tension between her aspirations as a dancer and the gaze she was subjected to. As her career evolved, she realized that her Afro-Caribbean female body often served to satisfy an audience that she had no desire to entertain. Around the age of twenty, Rodríguez Lora made a pivotal decision to shift from dancer to performance artist. This transition allowed her to disengage from the exoticization imposed on her body and to approach dance from a decolonial, liberatory perspective. Her practice became improvisational, site-specific, and

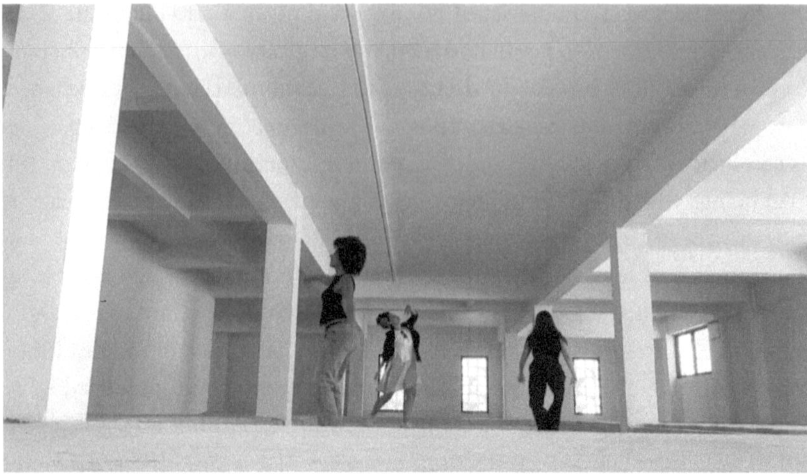

FIGURE 2.6. Moment of *Bailar todos los días*. Courtesy of Awilda Rodríguez Lora.

resistant to the discipline's rigid structures. It is in this context that *Bailar todos los días* emerged in 2015 as an ongoing dance project rooted in spontaneity, intimacy, and resistance.

Bailar todos los días is a self-sustained performance series comprising short, improvised dances shared through social media platforms such as Instagram, Facebook, Twitter, and Tumblr. The dances occur in a wide array of settings: urban streets, beaches, domestic interiors, natural landscapes, and temporary residences during artist residencies, both in Puerto Rico and abroad. Sometimes, others appear in the performances—friends, fellow queer artists, or curious passersby moved to dance alongside her. The project enacts a daily artistic ritual, wherein movement becomes a practice of community care, self-discipline, and healing. These dances, improvised and uploaded daily, interrupt the rhythms of capitalist productivity by affirming that the body—any body—deserves to move, to express, and to be witnessed.

Significantly, Rodríguez Lora foregrounds the changing, aging, and imperfect body as a site of creative potential. Her body, now in her forties, dances in a continuum that stretches back to her adolescent performances but now resists the ageism embedded in professional dance. Through *Bailar todos los días*, she asserts that all bodies can dance—regardless of shape, ability, or age—by choreographing her own daily presence in motion. These choreographies, or what André Lepecki calls *choreo-graphies*, inscribe her bodily presence in ephemeral acts of resistance (Lepecki 2004, 124).

In an interview with Emily Watlington in *Art in America*, choreographer Yvonne Rainer famously stated: "Everything is a performance if someone is watching" (60). Rainer's *Trio A*—a minimalist, 10-minute dance with no music, no climax, and performers in ordinary clothing—defied theatrical expectations and demanded that the dancer "lug [their] weight around" (61). As Rainer aged, her performances changed in pace and gesture, demonstrating that dance must adapt to the body rather than the reverse. She even created pieces from a hospital bed, moving only one hand, testifying that "dancing, like illness, results in knowing your own body intimately" (62). Rodríguez Lora's work resonates with this ethos. Her improvisations vary in intensity and scope—some days featuring large, sweeping movements, others focusing on the subtlest gestures from a bed, a couch, or a tabletop. Architecture and environment become prosthetic extensions of the body, enabling new "queer" spatial practices in both public and private spheres.

Ultimately, *Bailar todos los días* promotes self-love and joy as radical forms of survival. Joy, here, is not mere emotion—it is an act of daily defiance, a strategy to remain in motion despite fatigue, illness, or social marginalization. On days when her energy is low, Rodríguez Lora might dance from her bed, yet she still shows up. She honors the project's promise, and through it, creates a space where all bodies can reclaim movement as a fundamental right. These gestures, whether bold or barely perceptible, insist on the presence and persistence of queer life.

By uploading her dances to digital platforms, Rodríguez Lora builds an ephemeral yet enduring archive that defies traditional understandings of dance as an "irretrievable" and "non-translatable" art form (Lepecki 2004, 127). Lepecki argues that movement, by nature, "disappears," marking "the passing of time" and leaving only absence in its wake (127–28). However, *Bailar todos los días* makes queer presence visible precisely through this fleeting quality. The project enacts a choreographic trace—a Derridean notion that "undermines the weight of presence" by allowing absence to signify and circulate (Lepecki 2004, 132). Rodríguez Lora's dances are not performed for the permanence of the visual but for the affective resonance of fleeting contact. The artist does so by blurring the limits between body and text, dance and writing, as explicitly manifested—as Lepecki points out—in the word choreo-*graphy* (2004, 124). Awilda's improvised daily choreographies are present because they are ephemeral in the spaces and in the ways they happen. They reclaim public space, interrupt normative uses of the body, and make room for queer lives to be seen and felt, if only momentarily. In other words, they are present despite the social invisibility reserved to queer people by breaking daily (even if for a few seconds) the social purposes assigned to each public and social space.

The tension between presence and absence in *Bailar todos los días* mirrors the precarious visibility of queer existence. As Lepecki paraphrases Mark Franko, dance's ephemerality needs not be seen as a lack, but as a critical refusal of permanence (Lepecki 2004, 130). The project's daily dances constitute a "space of friction between body and text, movement and language" (124), staging queer existence not as a spectacle, but as a rhythmic trace. These dances do not serve the gaze. They do not seek to immortalize. Rather, their vitality lies in their disappearance, in their refusal to remain still. It is through the ephemerality of dance and the obsolescence of the digital medium that Awilda, through her ongoing project *Bailar todos los días,* promises queer existence and creates a circular appointment with a community that expects and shows up to watch the dances every day.

Rodríguez Lora's body becomes a "medium for temporal exchange" (Lepecki 2004, 126), telling stories without words, accompanied not by music but by ambient sounds: the call of *coquís,*[21] ocean waves, traffic, rustling trees, urban noise. She determines how she wants to be seen and heard. She breaks away from the expectations of choreography, scenography, and musical accompaniment, creating instead a poetics of motion that resists normative aesthetic conventions. By doing so, she redefines the function of dance as both individual and collective liberation. Her movements become acts of beauty in unexpected places, gesturing toward a world where movement is not dictated by formal training but by the desire to be free. Dancing becomes a poetic act that unveils beauty where it is not expected or noted.

Bailar todos los días deconstructs our conditioned perceptions of beauty and movement. It builds a collective memory through shared performances in urban, domestic, and natural spaces. These ephemeral archives serve as counterpoints to queer erasure, testifying that queer bodies exist, move, and persist. Even when society chooses not to see them, these dances insist on presence. When spectators follow the artist's terms, a decolonial soundscape emerges—one that reframes the ethical relationship between performer and audience (Przybylski 2023). When Rodríguez Lora dances to nature's sounds or the rhythms of the city, she expands the metaphors of movement, reimagining existence itself. She dances without a "proper" (according to heteronormative and Western standards) technique, without a "proper" stage, audience, soundtrack, or body. In doing so, she lives beyond and in spite of normative definitions of propriety. Her moving body becomes a space of queer resistance—a refusal to be fixed, categorized, or erased. The project critiques the dance industry's narrow ideals, which uphold standards of thinness, youth, and able-bodiedness. Instead, *Bailar todos los días* opens a space where Black, Brown, queer, trans, feminine, fat, disabled, and aging bodies can move freely and unapologetically.

This project is a call to movement, a celebration of bodies in flux. It invites us to discover new ways of being, dancing, and surviving. It is a daily act of accountability, an archive of persistence, and a testament to joy as resistance. *Bailar todos los días* shifts the meanings of space, personal space, and body functions in society. It also redefines the functions of the body in the public space and in the private space creating a new balanced environment and new possibilities for the body between choreography, geography, and space. So, it reveals more possibilities of being, and accepts that identity is not a monolithic and fixed aspect. Instead, it offers an opportunity for all identities to exist in its "own auto-poietic process [where] we do not (and cannot) control our own or another's gender-becoming" (Saketopoulou and Pellegrini 2023, xxv). Through *Bailar todos los días,* Rodríguez Lora transforms dance into a mode of life—a method for creating community, sustaining existence, and imagining more inclusive futures.

Moving with the Community: The Life Project *Sustento*

La Mujer Maravilla, La Rosario, and *Bailar todos los días* trace a trajectory in Awilda Rodríguez Lora's work that moves from a personal desire for motherhood to a broader practice of mothering community. This evolution culminates in her ongoing project *Sustento* [Support], which the artist initiated in 2017. *Sustento* carries forward elements from her previous performances, transforming them into a life-sustaining practice that engages affect, relation, and embodied resistance. In discussing *Sustento,* Rodríguez Lora reflects on how the project emerged from thinking about her own mother and how she provided sustenance. She frames the project as a space to ask, "What is SUSTE-NTO for us?"—a question that opens a collective reflection on care, survival, and relationality. The artist seeks to dismantle the traditional divide between performer and audience, emphasizing the importance of mutual recognition and vulnerability. For her, performance becomes a tool to process experiences that impact marginalized communities—particularly women of color and queer individuals—and to foster a sense of shared humanity. Ultimately, *Sustento,* she explains, is "what keeps us moving," offering a means to explore what sustains us individually and collectively.[22]

The central question Rodríguez Lora poses—"What is Sustento for *us?*" (emphasis mine)—is at once intimate and radically political. It encapsulates the queer, decolonial ethos that animates her artistic production in two key ways. First, the question challenges the normative assumptions of capitalist societies, where sustenance is often equated with financial capital, productivity, and accumulation. Instead, Rodríguez Lora opens space for a multiplicity of interpretations of what it means to be sustained. In doing so, she disrupts dominant logics of value, calling attention to affective, relational, and communal forms of care that are often dismissed or invisibilized. The very act of asking what sustains us reorients attention to embodied and collective needs—family, intimacy, interdependence, and the politics of communal survival.

Second, the use of *us* in the question implies the existence of a *them*—a normative subject or structure positioned in opposition to queer, racialized, and marginalized lives. Framing sustenance as a shared concern for a collective *us* politicizes the question itself. It becomes a declaration of queer existence and interdependence—a refusal of individualism, heteronormativity, and neoliberal self-sufficiency. Here, *queer* functions expansively, encompassing differences across sexual orientation, gender identity, race, class, age, ability, religion, and the many intersections among these social positions. To ask, "What is Sustento for us?" is to assert the right to define how one wants to live, love, move, and be supported—regardless of institutional sanction or recognition.

A central aim of *Sustento* is to gather a community that, through movement and shared reflection, can arrive at what Édouard Glissant calls a "poetics of relation." For Glissant, identity is not located in the singular, fixed root, but rather in the relational spaces between people—spaces activated by movement. He writes, "Relation exists in the totality of the elements put into contact with each other, and that totality does not exist without movement" (1990, 18). Movement, then, is not merely aesthetic; it is the condition of becoming and of entering relation. Similarly, Rodríguez Lora's movements in *Sustento* foreground this relational ontology. Through embodied wandering, public improvisation, and intimate questioning, she invokes a practice of relation that both reflects and produces the conditions for collective survival.

This relational movement also recalls Deleuze and Guattari's concept of the rhizome, where subjectivity and knowledge emerge through nonhierarchical, horizontal connections. In this view, movement leads to mutual transformation: participants in *Sustento,* whether passersby, viewers, or interlocutors, are invited into a dynamic exchange where vulnerability, care, and interdependence reconfigure the meaning of community. Relation, then, becomes a practice of constant negotiation—of balancing, shifting, and adapting. It is neither static nor teleological but always in motion. Through this lens, culture itself appears not as fixed heritage but as a process of becoming: unstable, plural, and evolving.

Sustento unfolds through Rodríguez Lora's physical and metaphorical wanderings—often in public streets—where she poses intimate questions such as "What sustains you?" to strangers and community members alike. This wandering initiates a performance of relational encounter. The question, unexpected and disarming, transforms the interaction from a casual moment into an act of cocreation. Even those not expecting to participate are drawn into an affective and reflective space, and in that encounter, community becomes possible. The project cultivates a public intimacy where vulnerability is not only permitted but honored. In so doing, it exposes the precarity of dominant social norms and reveals their instability.

In creating this space for reflection and relationality, *Sustento* challenges the "regime of measurement"—a set of technologies rooted in Western scientific rationality designed to manage and control bodies through hygiene, census, and anthropometry (Manalansan 2018, 494). These regimes seek to define value, normalcy, and life itself through quantitative metrics. *Sustento,* in contrast, opens with a deceptively simple, qualitative question that resists standardization. In that gesture, the performance reclaims the authority of the individual—and especially the marginalized subject—to name what matters, what nourishes, and what enables them to live.

In this way, *Sustento* aligns with Jack Halberstam's theory of the "queer art of failure," which posits that failure, messiness, and vulnerability offer alternatives to dominant narratives of success and power. *Sustento* affirms that being "messy"—being soft, unstable, unmeasured—is not only acceptable but vital to queer survival. It insists on the right to joy, to pleasure, to love, and to support—on one's own terms. As Halberstam writes, "There is a right to live life otherwise" (2). Rodríguez Lora's project enacts that right by blurring the line between art and life, between audience and performer, between the individual and the collective.

As previously noted, the performances of *Sustento*[23] take place in public spaces, most often on the street, where Awilda Rodríguez Lora walks among passersby carrying a glass bottle typically used for local rum—known as a *caneca*—filled with a mysterious transparent liquid. She asks people what *sustento* means to them, and then offers them a sip from her bottle, inviting them to receive some of her own *sustento*. In doing so, the traditional role of the spectator as a distant, protected observer is dismantled, allowing for direct engagement with the artist and the themes she brings forth. Through this exchange, Rodríguez Lora proposes an alternative to the isolation of contemporary social life, offering instead "a transformed sensation" experienced in the process of becoming through performance (Rancière 2011, 56). In this way, she lays the foundation for a temporary, yet intimate community formed in public space—a community built on trust, care, emotional openness, and the willingness to engage in vulnerable and profound conversations.

Rodríguez Lora seeks to share a form of vulnerability that becomes collective as it moves through public space, free of shame or taboo. As she states, support is "what keeps *us* [the queer community] moving" (emphasis mine). Movement, once again, becomes central—not only as a physical act but as a condition for emotional connection and shared existence. It is by moving through spaces, through emotions, and through social encounters that community becomes possible.

The act of drinking from the bottle without questioning becomes a symbolic gesture of trust and openness to receiving. The liquid inside is simply water, gathered from the local environment where each performance occurs. Water here is rich in symbolism: it evokes the fluid, ever-moving nature of queer and collective embodiment; it suggests cleansing and renewal; it reminds us of the essential role water plays in sustaining life; and how water in certain geographies becomes a luxury under colonial and capitalistic logics. By using water from the specific geographic location of each performance, Rodríguez Lora underscores the idea that communities are materially rooted in place yet constantly moving and transforming within that space. Although participants appear to drink the same water, they are in fact consuming different local waters—an embodied metaphor for the uniqueness of individual needs and experiences within a shared community. Water, as both a literal and symbolic substance, becomes *sustento* itself. It is through the offering of this *sustento*—and through her movement toward others—that Rodríguez Lora fosters relations and open spaces for geopolitical reflections, making space for a community to emerge.

Sustento is a project centered on recognizing, accepting, and embracing vulnerability. Rodríguez Lora proposes that only through vulnerability can new strategies for sustaining the arts in Puerto Rico emerge. Her work resonates with what Jack Halberstam describes as "alternative ways of knowing and being" (24). Through her performances, *la performera* enacts vulnerability as a form of

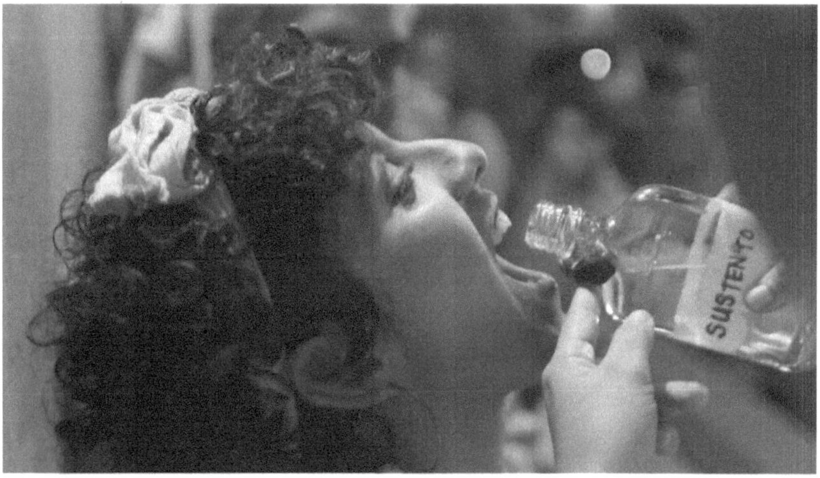

FIGURE 2.7. Still image of one exploration of the video performance *Sustento* (exploration titled *Sustento Capital*) by Awilda Rodríguez Lora. Photo credit: Juan Carlos Malavé. Courtesy of Juan Carlos Malavé and Awilda Rodríguez Lora.

power, teaching and inspiring audiences to embrace improvisation—not only onstage but in life. Her movements invite participants to consider how one might navigate uncertainty without a fixed destination, as both an introspective journey and a movement toward a community of outsiders.

Through *Sustento,* Rodríguez Lora has also been able to support her artistic work with *La Rosario,* shifting from decades of solo practice—largely imposed by economic constraints—to a model grounded in collaboration, mutual inspiration, and shared space. By foregrounding the often-silenced economic, mental, and emotional struggles of artists in Puerto Rico, she exposes and challenges the stigma and stereotypes surrounding the romanticized figure of the artist as endlessly inspired and content. She confronts the harsh realities of logistical and economic precarity, recognizing how these structural issues can stifle creativity. *Sustento* emerges precisely in response to these challenges, offering a platform for care, collectivity, and survival.

The project began in 2017, in the aftermath of hurricanes Irma and María, when Rodríguez Lora was confronted with the material consequences of colonialism in Puerto Rico. The devastation made it impossible to meet basic living needs, revealing how fragile and unstable the island's infrastructure was. In this moment, she recognized that being unable to support herself also meant being unable to sustain her home—and if the body is the first home, then its care is deeply entangled with economic systems. She began to reflect on the contradictions between self-care and the pressure to overwork in order to afford essentials like rent, food, and electricity.

In this context, overproduction as a means of survival left little room for joy. As a result, joy became a radical strategy: a way to question dominant economies of living, to resist the glorification of constant hustle, and to challenge the demand to thrive within conditions of permanent crisis. *Sustento* thus evolved into a method of cohabitation, recognition, and mutual support. It became a political act—a way for queer individuals to exist and to be, rooted in radical love and acceptance. It also became a space where people could choose how to love, whom to love, and how to practice self-love. Love and joy, in this context, require both physical and emotional space—a space to occupy, to be seen, and to be supported. *Sustento* offers just that: a shared environment for care, creativity, and collective existence.

In this sense, *Sustento* reconfigures the value of performative aesthetics. As Walter Mignolo and Rolando Vazquez argue, the project rejects the "colonized aestheTic" and instead promotes a "decolonial aestheSis" (Part II, fifth paragraph).[24] *Sustento* resists "the hegemonic normativity of modern aestheTics" by inviting participants to engage with performance through embodied perception, emphasizing the aesthetic practices of everyday life. The sensory and emotional experience of performance becomes a method for existing otherwise. By transforming the everyday struggles of life into performance, Rodríguez Lora makes visible what is often unseen while simultaneously challenging the untouchable aura of high art. As an artistic gesture, *Sustento* reflects on the transformative potential of the arts—not as isolated acts of creation but as tools for reimagining economies of care, community, and survival. It represents a commitment to exploring how artistic practices can be mobilized to support alternative forms of life rooted in mutual aid, creativity, and social justice. Through *Sustento,* Rodríguez Lora creates a safe space where individuals can express their identities in all their complexity and contradictions, regardless of what society demands or expects of them. The project reimagines the economy of living in ways that either nourish or deplete the body in the contemporary art world. *Sustento* thus becomes a maternal gesture toward queer bodies who, through *La Rosario,* find a physical and artistic home—a place to share, be inspired, and create.

In a 2021 interview with Larry La Fountain-Stokes, when asked how performance responds to the ongoing political, social, health, and environmental crises, Rodríguez Lora explained that for her it is about "performing the moment and performing the movement."[25] Her performances traverse geographies, histories, and realities, generating progressive dialogue around hemispheric colonial legacies and the instability of categories such as race, gender, sexuality, and class. Through movement, she challenges normative conceptions of womanhood, sexuality, and self-determination, drawing attention to how the economy of living shapes the body and its possibilities. For Rodríguez Lora, solidarity and celebration are fundamental strategies for sustaining community. During the COVID-19 pandemic, for example, she and fellow artists organized Zoom parties for the queer artistic community—virtual gatherings that provided joy, visibility, and mutual care during a time of extreme isolation.

Ultimately, *Sustento* is about connection: how we continue to move through life in the face of adversity, how we find support, how we remain present. The project intersects with all aspects of Rodríguez Lora's practice, from *La Mujer Maravilla* to *Bailar todos los días* and the programs at *La Rosario.* Its ethos also shapes her involvement in other community-based projects, such as Taller Comunidad La Goyco, where artists and neighbors have reclaimed a former elementary school in Santurce, transforming it into a cultural hub dedicated to sustaining and nourishing the local community. Through all of these efforts, *Sustento* becomes not only a performance but a living methodology of care.

The most recent exploration of *Sustento* took place in late 2023, when Awilda Rodríguez Lora premiered a video performance version of the project in collaboration with filmmaker Gisela Rosario Ramos. After a fundraising campaign, the video was first screened as part of the *Puerto Rico Negrx* exhibition at the Museum of Contemporary Art of Puerto Rico.[26] This 21-minute video experiments with movement in the context of digital technology and is closely linked to a shorter 3-minute, 25-second video titled *La performera BETA.*

La performera BETA serves as an early draft of the digital *Performera* figure that is later developed more fully in the longer video. Both works were featured in the museum installation: the shorter video was displayed on a wall at the entrance of a semienclosed screening space where viewers could sit and watch the longer piece. This arrangement allowed audiences to witness the creative evolution of the digital *Performera. La performera BETA* was made possible with the support of the Puerto Rican Arts Initiative, Northwestern University, the Andrew W. Mellon Foundation, the Wexner Center for the Arts, and *La Rosario.* The longer video performance *Sustento* was commissioned by the Wexner Center at The Ohio State University and also received support from the Puerto Rican Arts Initiative, Northwestern University, Mellon Foundation, *La Rosario,* and the Museum of Contemporary Art of Puerto Rico.

The final credits of both videos acknowledge numerous collaborators and supporters, including individuals and organizations also featured in this book—as either subjects of analysis or cited references—such as Macha Colón, Awilda Sterling-Duprey, *La Rosario,* nibia pastrana santiago, and Lío Villahermosa. While the complete list of acknowledgments is extensive, the inclusion of these particular figures highlights the dense web of interconnections between artists, projects, and initiatives. These works are not isolated acts of creativity; rather, they testify to how undisciplined artistic movements actively create, sustain, and make visible marginalized communities. They function as living archives of collective resistance.

La performera BETA is composed of 1 minute and 45 seconds of performance followed by an unusually long segment of end credits. Unlike most video works, where credits occupy only a brief moment, this piece redefines the visual hierarchy by sharing screen time between the performer and the community that enabled the work's creation. The extended credits become an integral part of the performance itself, shifting what may appear to be a solo piece into a collective one. In doing so, *La performera BETA* affirms an anticapitalist and decolonial ethic: it insists that movement—particularly free and creative movement—requires recognition and support from the collective. No individual success is possible without others.

The performance is entirely executed by a digital avatar of Rodríguez Lora, created through motion-capture technology using sensors placed on her body to digitally reproduce her movements and features. The avatar dances to an electronic disco track whose pulsating rhythm becomes repetitive and stuck toward the end of the piece (around 1:04). Yet, even before this moment, the performance is punctuated by intentional disruptions—through both movement and sound. The virtual *Performera,* nude on a vibrant, digital dance floor, subverts expectations associated with disco aesthetics. Rather than offering a polished, synchronized dance typical of club settings, the avatar engages in awkward, offbeat gestures—jumping, flipping, and making goofy moves. These choices break the illusion of sleek digital perfection and instead propose alternate modes of visual and bodily presence.

From the beginning, the soundtrack includes disembodied voices in English—one male and one female—speaking critically about immigration and queerness. The tone is disapproving, evoking the policing of identity. A third, feminine voice follows, affirming a deep connection to Puerto Rico and the ocean. Meanwhile, the avatar assumes a posture of exhaustion—a reference to the iconic *La Mujer Maravilla* t-shirt often worn by Rodríguez Lora, which

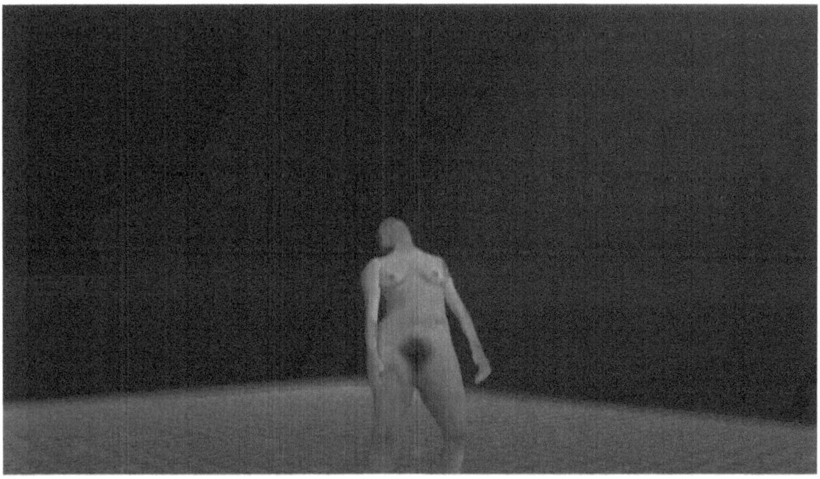

FIGURE 2.8. Still image of the video performance *La performera BETA* by Awilda Rodríguez Lora. Video. Courtesy of Awilda Rodríguez Lora.

features Moroccan-French artist Yto Barrada's phrase: "I am not exotic, I am exhausted." The piece concludes with the avatar running in circles, a gesture that embodies both fatigue and persistence.

The third voice continues singing out of sync, referencing her devotion to a place where there are "always hurricanes blowing . . . always the population growing . . . and the money owing nothing, and the sunlight [. . .] and the natives singing" (0:22–1:05). The audio of all the voices is either disrupted or difficult to fully discern, creating an unstable soundscape that metaphorically translates the socioeconomic and political instability of Puerto Rico into sonic form.

These overlapping narratives rearticulate in the virtual space the colonial condition and its consequences that Puerto Ricans confront daily in real life. These include the unregulated exploitation of tourism, the capitalist-driven privatization of public beaches, the gentrification displacing entire neighborhoods and causing housing insecurity for locals, and the exoticization of Puerto Ricans as perpetually joyful and musical—tropes commonly projected onto Caribbean subjects. These are recurrent themes in Rodríguez Lora's work.

As these layered voices unfold, virtual Awilda begins running in circles while the music transitions into a previously noted repetitive and distorted pattern (1:04–1:14). This shift from music to noise functions as a critique of the commodification of experience under contemporary capitalism, becoming what a "disturbing noise"—a sonic strategy that resists normative listening (Goddard, Halligan, and Hegarty 2012). The result is a dystopian, futuristic atmosphere that lays bare present-day crises while imagining a decolonial soundscape of possible futures.

Virtual Awilda intermittently pauses, moves in "inappropriate" ways, spins in circles, and eventually becomes frozen in a distorted, mid-running pose (1:14–1:45). Her nudity, erratic movements, and final deformation are all performative strategies that challenge normative expectations for Afro-Caribbean female bodies. Through awkward gestures and circular, nonproductive movement, Rodríguez Lora enacts a queer art of failure, rejecting capitalist metrics of success (Halberstam 2011). The avatar's final stillness and deformation represent alternative modes of existing amid disruption and offer new perspectives on beauty, embodiment, and the utopian potential of queer futurity (Muñoz 2009).

La performera BETA's raw and chaotic aesthetic embraces disobedience as an epistemological tool for survival (Halberstam and Nyong'o 2018), preparing the ground for its integration into *Sustento*, a longer video performance produced in late 2023 and also screened at the exhibit *Puerto Rico Negrx* at the Museum of Contemporary Art of Puerto Rico. This 21-minute, 7-second video, blending video game aesthetics, dance, and performance, serves as a retrospective cartography of Rodríguez Lora's work. In fact, the video performance recollects elements of *La Mujer Maravilla* (2013–on) and has scenes and gestures that recall first performances such as *La tortillera* (2009) and *Mamá Awilda: El duet* (2010).

Sustento reflects on the personal and professional pressures experienced by the artist, who, as this wonder woman figure, fears lacking sustenance and therefore overcommits to numerous projects to pay rent and buy food. The video critiques capitalist ideals of productivity and success, revisiting past performances and projecting into the future from the positionality of an Afro-Caribbean queer woman living under colonial conditions. The interplay between the real and virtual Awilda symbolizes a utopian framework for reimagining sustenance, community, and survival.

The appearance of *la performera 2.5*—the updated avatar—suggests a vision of queer futurity in which embodiment exceeds identity and becomes a medium of transformative politics. Their shared movements on screen propose possibilities for more inclusive and just worlds. As José Esteban Muñoz argues in *Cruising Utopia*, queer futurity offers a mode of resistance and hope. Similarly, in *Sustento*, Rodríguez Lora's choreography "cruises" through real and virtual spaces, unsettling patriarchal and heteronormative systems and reaffirming the need for fluid identities and collective change.

The two Awildas that gave life to the video performance *Mamá Awilda,* are now the two Awildas of *Sustento* the video performance, the avatar and the real one. Thus, just as *Mamá Awilda* was a reflection on the past to heal and exist in the present, the video performance *Sustento* uses the present to bridge past and future, offering a vision of queer social transformation. The video itself underscores this temporal and processual logic, showing both rehearsals and final sequences. In doing so, Rodríguez Lora enacts an anticapitalist performance strategy: giving equal value to process and product, to the unfinished and the complete (Halberstam 2011).

By incorporating material from earlier works such as *La Mujer Maravilla, La tortillera,* and *Mamá Awilda: El duet, Sustento* maps a trajectory of artistic and political consistency. It is a reflection on her solo practice, a growing awareness of community, a celebration of motherhood and ancestry, and a tribute to those lost during the COVID-19 pandemic—especially poignant given Puerto Rico's colonial status and the inadequate governmental response.

In a powerful scene, Rodríguez Lora calls for a minute of silence: "vamos a sostener un minuto de silencio" [let's sustain a minute of silence] (3:05). Here, silence becomes a strategy for preserving collective memory and connecting with ancestors. As she dances, the screen shows a younger, sexually objectified Awilda on television, evoking a transversal reflection across her career on what it means to be a colonial subject and what strategies—such as silence—enable resistance and community building.

Visual motifs from past works reappear—nakedness, aprons, blindfolds—evoking themes of domestic labor, feminicide, and female strength. Meanwhile, narration is often delivered in a robotic, glitchy voice that reinforces the speculative, futuristic tone. In one scene, Gisela Rosario Ramos's voice coaches Rodríguez Lora as she dances nude against a blue wall. The moment feels intimate, like a rehearsal, and transitions into a montage of joyful memories from the artist's life since 2020. The distorted voice returns, pleading "no se te olvide" [don't forget] (7:50–7:55), while an image of the *Sustento* bottle appears against a bright fuchsia screen—a reminder that sustenance arises through shared vulnerability. The use of the robotic voice guarantees a journey inside out, projected into a future beyond the borders of the body, where it will be possible to be vulnerable as a collective.

The final major sequence (8:15–13:00) shows Awilda on a small surface, her slow movements overlapping to form abstract, often contorted images. The

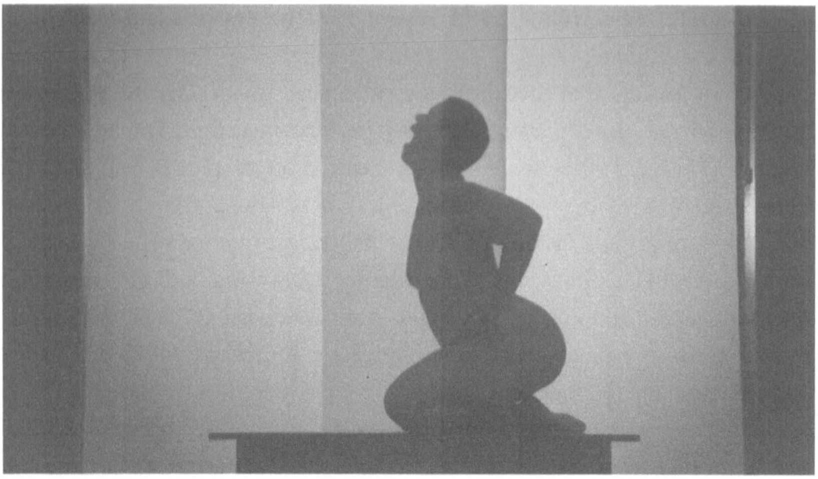

FIGURE 2.9. Still image of the video performance *Sustento* by Awilda Rodríguez Lora. Video. Courtesy of Awilda Rodríguez Lora.

sound of heavy rain muffles her voice, even as she screams. Eventually, she lies down, hands resting on her genitals, eyes closed. The gesture recalls a moment from *La tortillera,* but this time she remains motionless, almost meditative. Her uncomfortable stillness becomes a metaphor for the compounded crises—economic, ecological, political, and personal—that afflict Puerto Rico. Naked and silenced, the artist embodies the condition of being unheard and unseen yet still resisting.

The artist reminds the viewer that *sustento*—a term evoking sustenance and support—is more than a concept; it is an active, embodied, and communal force. She defines it as "a verb, an action, community, *la cuerpa, le cuerpe, el cuerpo* [the body in its queer gender variations in Spanish], *nosotras, nosotres* [us, first feminized, then queered in Spanish], bread, water, family, lovers, love, impulse, movement, energy, intangible," before pausing to breathe deeply, as though engaging in a meditative or relaxation exercise (13:20–14:27). This list functions as a kind of performative manifesto or living memorandum—an affective reminder of the stakes of the project and the reasons for its existence.

In the final segment of the video performance, the artist reflects on the endurance of Puerto Ricans through multiple pandemics and emphasizes that, despite these traumas, life has continued to produce beauty and possibilities for transformative justice. She encourages the viewer to practice self-love—"date cariño" [give love to yourself]—as the only sustainable mode of existence,

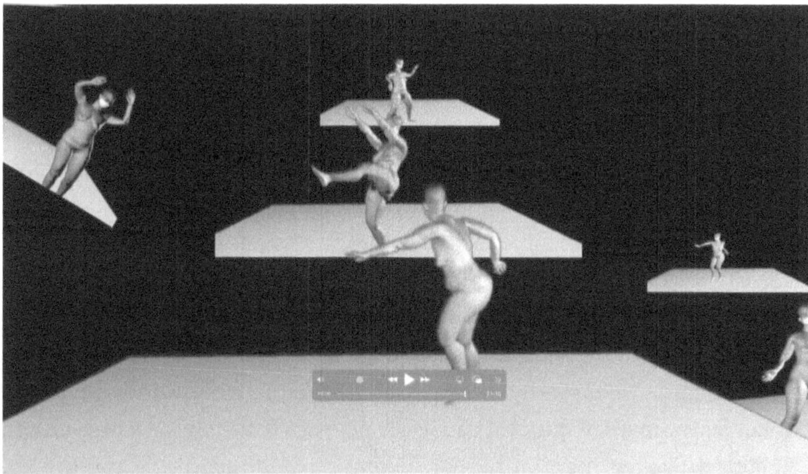

FIGURE 2.10. Still image of the video performance *Sustento* by Awilda Rodríguez Lora. Video. Courtesy of Awilda Rodríguez Lora.

insisting that "*la futura* es para vivirla" [the future—queering again the term in its grammatical genre in Spanish—is meant to be lived.] (Emphasis is mine; 14:53–15:40). By queering the word *futura,* she affirms the necessity of living toward a future shaped by queer care and resistance. She further urges: "Muevete con curiosidad y muevete con amor. Muevete confiando que eres parte del cambio." [Move with curiosity and move with love. Move trusting that you are part of the change] (16:05–16:12).

The performance concludes with an exhausted Awilda approaching her digital avatar. As they touch hands through the screen, the real and virtual selves acknowledge each other before parting ways, accompanied by nostalgic music. A futuristic Awilda, now 2,597 years old, is introduced through a distorted voice as a version who, after more than 3,500 performances, "will dance for you" (18:12–19:10). Multiple virtual Awildas then appear on screen, blending contemporary dance with movements reminiscent of bomba, a traditional Afro–Puerto Rican dance.

In these final sequences, *la performera 2.5* dances nude except for a mask, while Awilda is shown selecting and scrolling through personal photos, including moments of dancing bare-chested in a vibrant skirt. Both Awilda and her avatar embrace movement as a joyful, corporeal language—at times blindfolded, masked, or adorned with sunglasses—expressing vulnerability, pleasure, and power. Their gestures are not merely aesthetic but political: a way of imagining future modes of relationality, where the porous boundary between interior and exterior self becomes a site of connection, support, and queer collective survival.

Sustento is the life project of Awilda Rodríguez Lora, one that continues to evolve as the artist engages in ongoing investigation and creation. The significance of this project, in my view, lies particularly in its ability to offer a physical, public, or domestic space in which to gather and build community—a deeply necessary intervention for queer individuals who may lack safe spaces in their everyday lives. Another key value of *Sustento* is its capacity to normalize the everyday struggles of living, especially those often silenced or deemed taboo in mainstream discourse. By foregrounding life's challenges, Rodríguez Lora dismantles the myth of the artist as a figure exclusively sustained by passion and inspiration. She recenters the human dimension of the artist's life, performing an anticapitalist gesture and issuing a critique of the broader sociopolitical system, particularly within the colonized context of Puerto Rico.[27]

From Exhaustion to Existence: Dancing Toward Collective Survival

Awilda Rodríguez Lora transforms difficult life experiences into an artistic platform from which she creates, nurtures, and supports a community of queer artists. By embracing vulnerability and social discomfort as generative forces, she embodies the figure of Wonder Woman she envisions—imperfect, joyful, and radically present. Her daily practice of dance becomes a reclamation of space not only for pleasure but also for idleness and rest. These gestures actively subvert dominant narratives that equate productivity with value, challenging the capitalist and heteronormative frameworks that shape our understandings of time, labor, and worth.

In this way, Rodríguez Lora's movements are inherently political. As she asserts in a podcast recorded on March 7, 2024—quoted in the epigraph that opens this chapter—"[M]ovement is the cornerstone of my work. I feel that movement generates movement [. . .]. [I]t is about moving things, and things are moving within us even in stillness. This generates life, circulation, air, intestines, digestion . . . all of these are natural parts of us, part of our humanity, always observing movement as a generator of transformation." For Rodríguez Lora, movement is not confined to visible gestures but is deeply rooted in the internal rhythms of the body. Stillness, too, becomes movement—an embodied articulation of life itself. Through this lens, movement becomes the condition for transformation: of the self, the social body, and the institutions that shape everyday life.

Her artistic practice centers this philosophy by placing queer embodiment at its core. Movement becomes a form of sustenance, a mode of visibility, and a framework for collective care. In leading a community of queer artists through her performances and collaborations, Rodríguez Lora fosters a network of interconnected individuals who are invited to move, feel, and create together in reclaimed space. Her choreography functions not merely as artistic expression, but as an intimate, decolonial gesture—one that begins within the body and radiates outward, reimagining the places socially denied to queer people, artists of color, trans individuals, elders, disabled bodies, and all those at the margins.

Through her performances, A-*wild*-a[28] unleashes the *wild* she carries with her name, opening up political possibilities that invite her audiences to collectively envision wild, alternative futures for the queer community—futures marked not by constraint, but by freedom, mutual care, and imaginative reinvention. Throughout her body of work, Rodríguez Lora consistently interrogates how female and feminine bodies are expected to move through domestic, urban, and public environments. Through her embodied persona of *la performera,* she creates openings for political possibility, inviting audiences to collectively imagine wild, alternative futures for the queer community—futures grounded not in precarity and regulation but in freedom, mutual care, and creative reinvention (Halberstam and Nyong'o 2018). Her refusal to separate the personal from the political, or care from resistance, allows her to reframe performance as an act of survival rather than a spectacle.

Through *Sustento,* her broader artistic practice, and the living figure of *la performera,* Rodríguez Lora encourages us to inhabit discomfort as a generative site for queer futurities. Her work confronts everyday challenges—mental health, exhaustion, mothering, joy, and bodily exposure—while also claiming rest and sensuality as political acts. In doing so, she enacts a slow and deliberate undoing of the colonial and capitalist scripts that define how bodies should exist and move through space.[29]

By summoning avatars of the self, disrupting the temporal linearity of dance and labor, and centering community care over individualism, Rodríguez Lora expands the grammar of performance in Puerto Rico and its diaspora. She does not merely perform resistance; she inhabits it—through choreography, language, and relational practice. Her artistic labor does more than envision a decolonial queer future; it begins to materialize that future in the present, grounded in a queer feminine platform that extends openness and belonging to all—particularly to those who identify as women, or who carry, expose, and transform their femininity and vulnerability as sites of power. Here, Wonder Woman dances daily, not to escape exhaustion, but to transform it into radical motion. From exhaustion to existence, Rodríguez Lora moves with and for her queer community—dancing toward collective survival.

THREE

Entre Islas

Shifted Geographies, Displaced Borders, and the Queer Caribbean Movements of Helen Ceballos

Cada isla nos seduce, nos obliga a naufragar,
a llegar, llegar, llegar, a inventar un verbo nuevo.
[Every island seduces us, forces us to drown,
To arrive, arrive, arrive, to invent a new verb]
Manuel Ramos Otero, poem 6 in *Invitación al polvo*

When I arrived in Puerto Rico in the 90s, [. . .] clandestinely in a small boat,
[. . .] I entered Colegio de Diego [. . .] with a different name that was not mine.
They gave me the name Amy Solano [. . .]
Amy Solano is the first character I interpreted:
I had to soften my accent, not sound like a Dominican girl [. . .].
When the teacher introduced me to the group and I said, "teacher, I don't have a *macota*,"[1]
she asked, "*macota*, what is a *macota*?" and started making fun of me,
telling the other classmates, "don't make fun of her, she is *dominicaina*."
I remember that sea of laughter behind me, like being stabbed in the back,
as if that laughter was mockery, and I went silent and almost stopped speaking for a year,
engaging in such a deep listening exercise
that I learned and incorporated into my way of speaking the Puerto Rican accent.
Helen Ceballos / From the podcast recorded with the author on March 7, 2024

In 1993, a five-year-old girl and her mother crossed from the Dominican Republic to Puerto Rico on a *yola* (a small wooden boat).[2] This was the first time that Helen Ceballos (ella/elle; she/her/hers, they/them/theirs; b. 1986) moved *entre islas*—between (Caribbean) islands. This formative journey inaugurated a life in motion that deeply informs her artistic work. Through the lens of migration, Ceballos's transdisciplinary practice engages with broader narratives of displacement, marginality, identity, and border crossing. Her personal story, shared in both her performances and interviews, becomes a performative and fictionalized gesture that blurs the line between autobiography, fictionalized realities, and collective memory. As she recounts: "He vivido en 11 ciudades, 7 países y 35 casas, lo que significa que tengo casi tantas mudanzas en mi cuerpo como años en el mundo, y son precisamente estos traslados los que marcan una de las líneas temáticas más destacadas de mi trabajo: la migración" [I have lived in 11 cities, 7 countries, and 35 houses, which means that I have almost as many moves in my body as years in the world, and it is precisely these relocations that mark one of the most prominent thematic lines in my work: migration]. This statement encapsulates how her work transcends the singular self to speak from and to a community shaped by similar dislocations.

Migration—and everything it carries, from the risk of sinking to the desire for arrival—alongside memory, queerness, the body, gestures of remembrance, and shifting notions of belonging, form the backbone of Ceballos's artistic vision. Since that initial *yola* crossing, her practice has been shaped by a series of continuous, intersecting movements: surviving as undocumented; navigating physical spaces where she was not meant to belong; inhabiting multiple languages, jargons, and accents; and moving across countries, neighborhoods, and identities. These experiences animate her performances, which reflect a unique perspective as a Dominican raised in Puerto Rico—a group, as the artist addresses in the epigraph that opens this chapter, often marginalized and negatively portrayed in Puerto Rican society. As Yolanda Martínez-San Miguel has observed, Dominicans in Puerto Rico are frequently received with hostility, prejudice, and rejection, despite their long-standing contributions to the island's economy and society (1998). Jorge Duany further emphasizes that Dominican migration to Puerto Rico has helped forge transnational identities that reshape conventional understandings of citizenship and belonging (1990). In this context, the stories Ceballos tells through her body become essential in illuminating an often-overlooked facet of Puerto Rican reality.[3] Hence, her performative movements are made of those shifted Caribbean geographies, displaced borders, and queer ways of moving through life that she had to embody since a very young age in order to exist.

Ceballos is a transdisciplinary artist working within Puerto Rico's contemporary performance art scene. Her practice spans performance, installation, photography, and video, and she describes herself as transdisciplinary precisely because she merges diverse visual and conceptual languages. Her work explores identity, queerness, and cross-Caribbean connections through embodied practices that foreground diaspora, memory, and movement. Her performances are in direct dialogue with her lived experiences: if life provides the source, performance becomes the cathartic gesture that enables survival. Yet more than that, her work is animated by the physical and metaphorical movements that carry her from one piece to the next.

Recurring gestures across performances create a sense of fragmentation and incompleteness that not only connects her works but also affirms her existence as a queer artist. Following Halberstam's conception of queerness as incompleteness and failure, Ceballos embraces the queer refusal of capitalist logics that equate value with productivity and accumulation (Halberstam 2011, 2). In this sense, the "failure" inscribed in her work is not a lack, but a radical aesthetic and political strategy: one that sustains her right to exist and create on her own terms. If performance necessarily unfolds through the movement of the artist's body, in the case of Helen Ceballos, this movement frequently generates a sense of confusion or incompleteness. She often repeats gestures, phrases, or visual motifs across multiple works, creating continuity but also deliberately resisting linear narratives. For spectators familiar with her repertoire, this repetition may evoke disorientation—yet this very disorientation becomes the structure through which Ceballos blurs the boundaries between fiction and reality, between fragmented memories and their reinterpretations. These liminal zones become shared territories, populated by others who have lived through parallel forms of displacement, marginalization, and trauma. Her practice moves across performances as an embodied attempt to reconstruct memory through repetition—of movement, of words, of sounds—as a way to access what was once lost, to navigate identity through time, and to articulate that which exceeds language.

Ceballos tells her stories through fragments—images, sentences, sensations, and embodied memories—that invite the spectator to join her in navigating blocked or broken recollections. In doing so, reality is not simply reenacted but collectively reimagined. Performance becomes a space of refuge, a terrain where personal trauma is not only remembered but transformed. Chaos, in this context, is not a lack of structure but an aesthetic strategy that reflects the nonlinear, recursive process of memory-making in diasporic and queer lives.

As Paul Connerton argues, collective memory is often sustained through repeated bodily practices that form rituals and traditions. In contrast, Ceballos's repetitive gestures do not reinforce hegemonic narratives but dismantle them. Her bodily memory resists coherence, producing instead a shared fragmentation—an archive of loss, survival, and queer existence. These repetitions do not build monumental memory but validate fractured experiences common among the undocumented, the queer, the racialized, and the feminine. What might appear "unproductive" from a conventional perspective becomes a generative force: the consolidation of communal, embodied histories that have long been silenced or ignored.

Ceballos's performances reconstruct her lived experience—or, as she names it, her "fictional memory"—as a way to reclaim emotions and traumas she could not control as a child. In doing so, she invites a community to move with her, coconstructing a collective memory centered on the marginal, the illegal, and the queer. Personal trauma becomes, in the words of Avgi Saketopoulou and Ann Pellegrini, "more than misery"; it becomes a method of exploring memory's textures and accessing experiences that would otherwise remain unreachable (2023, viii, xxxv, 23). Her performances, thus, render visible the often marginalized stories of undocumented migration, fake identities, gendered violence, and institutional exclusion. Once shared, these stories not only become real for others with similar lived experiences but are validated and protected by the witnessing of the audience. In this sense, Ceballos's body in performance becomes a vessel through which marginal communities are recognized and affirmed. Her performative practice constitutes, following Nelson Maldonado-Torres, "a lasting material commitment to decolonization," one that detaches art from elite institutions and reconnects it to communities engaged in resistance (2023, 587). Through this lens, Ceballos's work is more than personal or aesthetic—it intervenes socially and politically, challenging how marginalized bodies are perceived and remembered.

This chapter focuses on the cultural impact of Ceballos's work as both a performer and a cultural manager within Puerto Rican society. It explores how her interventions challenge colonial and patriarchal aesthetics imposed on queer, immigrant, and racialized female bodies. Her artistic and managerial practices together stretch and disrupt spatial, institutional, and artistic boundaries, reimagining the Caribbean as a site of relationality rather than fragmentation. In this sense, Ceballos exemplifies what Nelson Maldonado-Torres describes as a "decolonial turn"—a process through which "modern/colonial hegemonic institutions become a problem—rather than the racialized and colonized individuals themselves"—and which opens up "a space of possibility for the generation of new views and practices of companionship and togetherness" (2023, 587). Ceballos enacts this shift by supporting local, independent cultural organizations and initiating projects that facilitate the movement of artists across Caribbean geographies. In doing so, she resists the logistical and economic constraints that often isolate the islands from one another. Through initiatives that provide visas, funding, and platforms, she enables otherwise impossible exchanges—allowing Caribbean bodies—and her Afro-Caribbean female body—to circulate across borders in acts of cultural solidarity.

Ceballos's works, then, show new possibilities of building and inhabiting the architecture of the Caribbean body in an interconnected public space. She does so through gestures that contain and free the body as she pleases, granting her a bodily freedom of movement that always had to be edited and contained when she was undocumented. Whether she ties her body, sets a skirt on fire, isolates a specific body part in performance, or renders fat and cellulite as aesthetic elements, Ceballos asserts bodily autonomy on her own terms. These gestures challenge heteronormative and patriarchal frameworks, opening new paths to understand diaspora, race, gender, femininity, womanhood, and sexuality. They also reclaim mobility and self-determination for a body long constrained by precarity, legal invisibility, and social surveillance.

As a transdisciplinary artist, Ceballos works across performance, video, photography, writing, installation, and cultural curation. This chapter examines how these multiple practices intersect, tracing the dialogue between her performance work and her role as a cultural manager, producer, and curator. Her artistic output from 2010 to 2023 includes a wide range of media, yet her central concerns remain consistent: the representation of Afro-Dominican/Puerto Rican queer womanhood, the aging body, motherhood, loss, belonging, and the ongoing negotiation of identity across borders. I argue that the concepts developed in her performances—such as migration, fragmentation, and queer embodiment—form the foundation of her curatorial and cultural management work. Together, these contributions constitute a significant body of decolonial praxis within and beyond Puerto Rico. As a result, Ceballos marks her presence in the field with an overwhelming number of diverse productions that also constituted the main challenge for the organization of this chapter.

As noted earlier, Helen Ceballos frequently revisits and reworks specific gestures, movements, sounds, and images across various media—performances, installations, photographs, and videos. Her performances often incorporate multimedia elements, creating layered, intertextual pieces that transcend traditional disciplinary boundaries. For this reason, I include two foundational works produced before the central time frame of this study (2013–23): *Sitiada* [Besieged] (2010) and *Lluvia/el destrence/el altar* [Rain/unbraiding/the altar] (2012). As I will elaborate later in the chapter, these early works serve as critical bridges that connect and anticipate the artist's later projects. This chapter thus focuses on performances created between 2010 and 2023 that recuperate and reformulate recurring themes, gestures, and images. Rather than following a strictly chronological approach, my analysis traces conceptual and formal continuities across her body of work, reflecting the nonlinear, recursive nature of Ceballos's creative process.

Ceballos's practice invites the spectator to move with her across time and space, artistic fields, and narrative fragments. Her movements are cyclical rather than linear; she returns to gestures and reimagines concepts from different angles, proposing alternative readings of the same stories. Her process—visceral, intuitive, and seemingly chaotic—mirrors the central themes she explores—fragmented memory, dislocated identity, and the body as a site of trauma, survival, and reinvention and as a vessel made of blood, flesh, and wounds. These performative reformulations are anchored in an Afro-Caribbean, queer, and feminine perspective, and consistently engage with themes such as migration, marginality, motherhood, mourning, and embodied resistance.

Among the works analyzed are two recent transdisciplinary projects: *Cerezas por papeles* [Cherries for papers] (2021) and *Rito de paso/comen de mí* [Rite of passage/eat out of me] (2022–23). These projects integrate diverse media—photo-essays, installations, video performances, music videos, and live performance—and synthesize images, gestures, and movements drawn from works spanning 2010 to 2023. As such, they function as both culmination and recapitulation of Ceballos's artistic trajectory. In mapping the continuities among these works, I focus on the evolution of recurring performative elements, which illuminate the logic of her practice.

This includes performances such as the aforementioned *Sitiada* (2010) and *Lluvia/el destrence/el altar* (2012), as well as *Estado de representación* [Representational state] (2013), *Sobrepliegues/torso habitado* [Fold on fold/inhabited torso] (2014), *Coito bucal* [Oral intercourse] (2014), *Desprendimiento* [Removal] (2015), *El cuerpo y la ruina* [The body and the ruin] (2018), *Golpe de agua*

[Water's impact] (2018), *No voy a pedirle a nadie que me crea* [I am not going to ask anyone to believe me] (2018), *Circuito* [Circuit] (2019), *Tener tus piernas* [Having your legs] (2019), *Hablar de la prole* [Speaking of the offspring] (2020), *Cuerpos fronterizos* [Border bodies] (2021), *Fue esa la vía* [That was the way] (2021), and *Memoria* [Memory] (2021), a music video by the Brooklyn-based experimental pop duo Combo Chimbita in which Ceballos is the sole performer.[4]

These performances, writings, and photographic works are inextricably tied to the artist's lived experiences—particularly her processes of mourning and loss; the recovery of familial and personal memory; and the navigation of geographic, political, social, and bodily borders. Far from discrete, these pieces exist in a dynamic network of mutual influence and iterative development. One work often leads to another or draws from the same performative gesture recontextualized in a new configuration. The interconnectedness of these pieces forms a metaphorical choreography through which Ceballos travels in time and within herself, enacting a cathartic experience that dissolves imposed borders and reassembles the fragmented Caribbean geographies of her queer life.

The performances examined here articulate the core concepts that shape Ceballos's artistic practice: undocumented migration, island geographies, water as metaphor and medium, mourning, the female and queer body, and the racialized subject.[5] These same concerns also inform her work as a cultural manager, producer, and curator, which I turn to next. In particular, I analyze her recent and ongoing projects *Plataforma Eje* [Pillar Platform] (2020–present) and *Cartografías del desplazamiento* [Cartographies of displacement] (2023). Though recent, these initiatives are grounded in over a decade of conceptual and organizational work, including the platform *Mezcolanza* [Mishmash] (2013–present), the artist residency *El cruce* [Crossroads] (since 2016), and the performance event *Mar de islas* [Sea of islands] (2021–present). These earlier efforts laid the groundwork for Ceballos's sustained engagement with transnational Caribbean cultural networks and continue to inform her present work.

Performing a Displaced Caribbean

When I met with Helen Ceballos during my UNCF/Mellon residency in Puerto Rico in the spring of 2024, we discussed the challenges of moving through the island: the urban planning that seems intentionally confusing for drivers, the near impossibility of walking anywhere, and how these spatial limitations reflect broader colonial legacies. We agreed that this immobility—structural, spatial, and symbolic—is the product of centuries of colonization designed to isolate and disempower Caribbean peoples, and it is pictured as "industrial progress" within its colonial and capitalistic context. We extended this reflection to the entire region: movement between Caribbean islands remains prohibitively expensive, producing a geography where only certain bodies—those with financial and legal privilege—can circulate freely.

Édouard Glissant, in *Poetics of Relation,* conceives the Caribbean as a space marked by shared historical conditions that carry both the pain of enduring colonial violence and the potential for unique, transformative forms of relation. For Glissant, this relationality—through acts of telling, listening, and connecting—is central to reshaping collective consciousness and building alternative social imaginaries. Ceballos's work echoes Glissant's poetics of relation. Her practice foregrounds the importance of movement and relation, even as it is rooted in a context of colonial immobility. In response to disconnected Caribbean geographies and intentionally disorienting urban landscapes, she transforms chaos into the generative core of her life, art, and performance.

The apparent chaos of her performances is sustained both by the recurrence of fragmented images and gestures across different works and by the unpredictable, often unruly presence of nature. The four classical elements—fire, water, air, and earth—frequently play a central role. At times, Ceballos performs amid a sea of candles or wears a skirt set aflame; in other instances, she submerges her body in a lake, river, or the ocean, or uses her wet hair to mop a stage. She might lie naked or seminaked on the ground, merging with the dirt, or allow the sounds of heavy breathing, wind through leaves, or ocean waves to dictate the rhythm of a piece. These elemental forces underscore the duality of nature: fire can warm or destroy; water and air sustain life but can also drown or suffocate; earth can nurture but also bury.

Through this interplay between elemental and bodily movement, Ceballos stages the chaos of life itself. Her performances refuse rehearsed perfection in favor of gestures that are alive—viscerally tied to the emotional and material conditions of the moment. The natural elements become conduits for embodied storytelling. Her body, marked by trauma and memory, functions as both archive and witness. The sensorial dimension of her work—its textures, sounds, and rhythms—allows her to share experiences that are deeply personal yet also collective.

In this way, the stories she tells no longer belong solely to her. The narratives of her mother, her relationship with her lineage, and her own queer, racialized experiences of womanhood become performative inquiries into how the female body inhabits and resists physical and metaphorical boundaries. The body in her work becomes a platform from which to interrogate religion, sexual abuse, ancestry, family, memory, grief, patriarchy, sexism, fatphobia, marginalization, migration, pleasure, queerness, belonging, and displacement. Womanhood, in its multiple and fluid dimensions, forms the connective tissue across her artistic oeuvre.[6] Ultimately, the wounds, cuts, and physical encounters with cold water, restricted breath, or scorched skin are not simply theatrical devices—they are embodied inscriptions of psychological trauma and fragmented memory. Through them, Ceballos crafts a poetics of corporeal resilience, transforming pain into presence and dislocation into relation.

THE BEGINNINGS: 2010–2012

Helen Ceballos began exploring themes of undocumented migration, uprootedness, and belonging in her 2010 performance *Sitiada.* In this piece, she retraces the struggles of those who choose—or are forced—to leave their homelands. Central to the performance is the notion of learning to carry "home" within oneself, of cultivating roots in reverse in a world where one no longer belongs anywhere—or, as Ceballos puts it, "la patria se hace portátil y es ilusorio el retorno" [homeland becomes portable and returning becomes delusional].[7] *Sitiada* marks an early turning point in Ceballos's artistic trajectory, where she begins to position her body not merely as subject but as narrative voice. Through movement, spatial occupation, and sound, her body articulates the affective and material experiences of undocumented life, while refusing dominant narratives that often reduce migration to statistics or legal statuses.

Rather than offering a straightforward story, Ceballos invites the audience to abandon preconceptions and instead follow her gestures—to be guided through a process of embodied knowing. One of the most arresting movements in *Sitiada* involves the artist soaking her hair in a bucket of water and then mopping the floor with it. This intimate and radical gesture initiates a larger reflection on domestic labor, a form of work often carried out by undocumented individuals, particularly women. Mopping the floor with her own hair becomes a metaphor for the invisibilized yet essential labor performed by those whose presence is frequently treated as a threat or problem within the workforce. In this context, hair and body become surfaces inscribed with unspoken histories and suppressed truths. Through this gesture, Ceballos implicates her audience—not merely as spectators, but as witnesses and potential accomplices—compelled to confront their own complicity in the systems that criminalize migrant labor.

This way, this performance is proposed as an opportunity to share a collective reflection that questions the social understanding and political categorizations of migrant bodies.

Sitiada serves as a foundational work in Ceballos's repertoire, laying the groundwork for her continued engagement with migration, corporeality, and the symbolic use of hair and water. In her 2012 video performance *Lluvia/el destrence/el altar*,[8] the artist revisits these themes through the simple yet potent act of unbraiding her hair. Lasting only 25 seconds, the video shows Ceballos slowly undoing her braids, a gesture rich with connotations of racial identity, Caribbean heritage, and belonging. At one moment, the camera shifts focus to a medicine cabinet in the background—an image that quietly gestures toward illness, caretaking, and the corporeal effects of displacement. The act of unbraiding, historically associated with resistance—particularly among enslaved African women who used braids to encode maps and messages—here becomes a way of recovering both personal and ancestral memory.

I propose reading Ceballos as a modern-day *cimarrona*, a maroon figure whose performative acts of bodily resistance challenge the constraints imposed by discriminatory immigration policies and capitalist structures that oppress racialized and marginalized bodies. Her use of hair in performance is not only political but also deeply personal: it becomes a vehicle through which she communicates with her mother, enacts a sense of origin, and attempts to reconcile a migration experience marked by silence and rupture. As Ceballos reflects in *Sitiada*, her roots are "upside down," suggesting a dislocation that is both bodily and genealogical. The image of braiding and unbraiding recurs throughout her work and personal archives, functioning as a tactile expression of intergenerational connection and healing where verbal language has failed.

The performance's tripartite title—*Lluvia/el destrence/el altar*—signals its layered structure: rain (*lluvia*), the unbraiding (*destrence*), and the altar (*altar*), each frame distinct but interrelated dimensions of the piece. While the act of unbraiding centers the body and gesture, the altar—typically associated with syncretic Caribbean spiritual practices blending African and Catholic elements—introduces a symbolic object of both personal and cultural resonance. However, in this performance, the altar is made not of candles or religious icons, but of medicine bottles. This substitution displaces the altar's traditional spiritual function and instead comments on the passage of time, bodily deterioration, and the commodification of health. The altar of medicines becomes a metaphor for a capitalist healthcare system where well-being is tethered to pharmaceutical industries and class status, highlighting the precarity of those living at the economic and medical margins. In this context, unbraiding becomes a metaphorical gesture that resists linear narratives. It performs temporal and corporeal undoing, revealing stories hidden in the strands—stories of resistance, illness, ancestry, and survival. Through such symbolic acts, Ceballos constructs a performance practice that is as much about personal healing as it is about collective memory and political reckoning.

DEVELOPING GESTURES: 2013-2019

Unbraiding hair becomes a metaphorical and performative gesture through which Ceballos unravels dominant narratives, reflects on the passage of time and bodily decay, and reveals hidden stories in need of telling. This gesture encapsulates themes of identity, belonging, migration, and motherhood—threads that resurface in her 2015 video performance *Desprende* [Release].[9]

In this 1-minute, 9-second piece, Ceballos revisits the act of unbraiding her hair, now set in an outdoor space under a torrential downpour. While the 2012 performance already referenced *lluvia* metaphorically, the 2015 iteration materializes it: the rain falls as she unbraids, suggesting both literal and symbolic acts of cleansing and release. The title, *Desprende,* signals not only the loosening of braids but also a letting go—of pain, memory, or identity. The gesture under the rain evokes an apocryphal baptism, marking a symbolic purification or transition into a new phase of life, a new way of moving through the world while reclaiming the past.

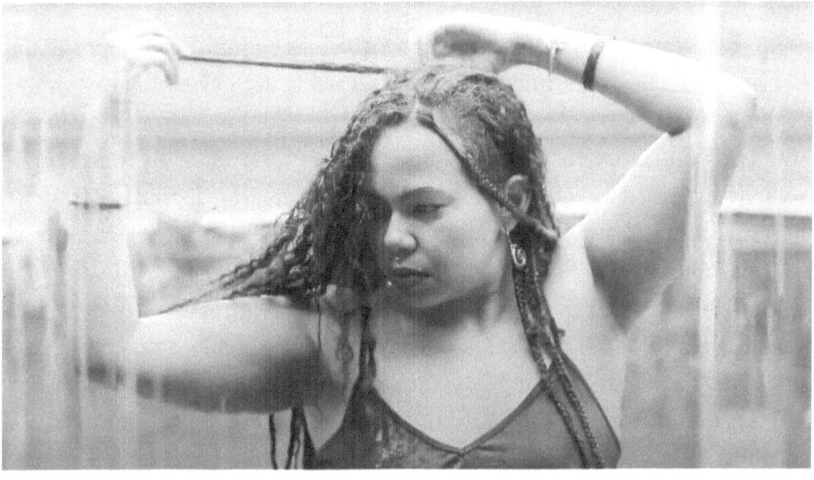

FIGURE 3.1. *Desprende,* Argentina, 2015. Photo credit: Matías Kedak. Courtesy of Matías Kedak and Helen Ceballos.

The altar—introduced through her mother as a central object of domestic and spiritual life—reappears in her 2013 photographic series *Estado de representación.*[10] In these images, Ceballos stages herself as an Afro-Caribbean Virgin on an altar. By embodying this sacred figure, she challenges the Eurocentric aesthetics of holiness and femininity, confronting the cultural norms that idealize whiteness and purity. Her depiction of an Afro-Caribbean woman with natural hair dismantles religious and patriarchal ideals of virginity and sanctity, while also celebrating the altar as a syncretic site of African and Catholic traditions in the Caribbean. Through this visual intervention, she asserts the female body's autonomy, defying sexist narratives and asserting the right to define and represent oneself.

Ceballos deepens this exploration of bodily agency in her 2014 video performances *Sobrepliegues/torso habitado*[11] and *Coito bucal.*[12] In *Sobrepliegues,* the artist frames her naked torso and belly, manipulating her breasts with her hands until they resemble eyes, while the folds of her belly suggest a mouth. This act constructs a puppet-like face, humorously defamiliarizing the hypersexualized female body. Through this manipulation, she asserts control over her image, reclaiming her body as a site of self-representation rather than objectification. Similarly, in *Coito bucal,* a close-up of her face captures her tongue simulating oral sex. The gesture—alternating between tension and softness—deconstructs the phallus while emphasizing female sexual pleasure and the right to express it. The presence of saliva becomes a powerful symbol of bodily fluidity and intimacy, undermining societal taboos around the female orgasm and challenging heteronormative sexual scripts.

Both performances are grounded in Ceballos's commitment to presenting her body—its fat, folds, and cellulitis—as a living archive of identity and resistance. These works dismantle rigid gender expectations, reconfigure beauty standards, and claim visual and sexual autonomy for women. By transfiguring socially expected movements and aesthetics, Ceballos disrupts patriarchal narratives about how women's bodies should look, behave, and express desire.

This emphasis on fluidity—literal and symbolic—reappears in *Golpe de agua* (2018),[13] a performance rooted in water's purifying and violent potential. In one version, staged during a residency in Spain, Ceballos immerses herself in a river, naked and holding branches. She begins by soaking her hair, then striking herself and the water with the branches—echoing the title's malleable meaning, as *golpe* in Spanish means both "blow," "strike," and "hit." In other iterations, she brings a bucket of water onstage. The performance concludes with

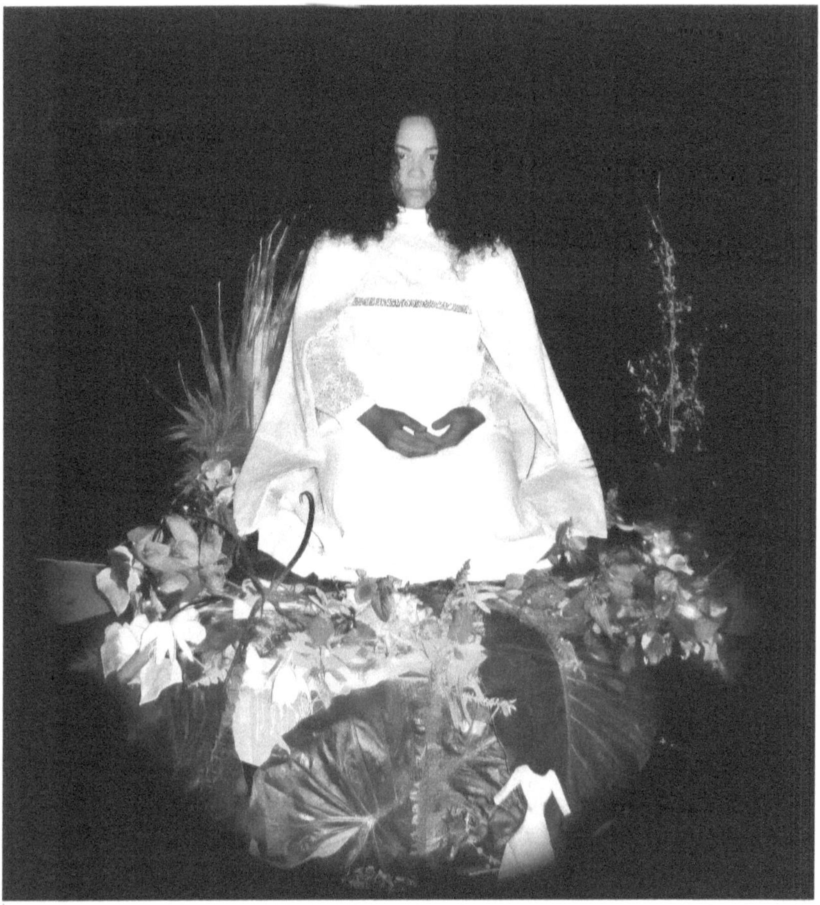

FIGURE 3.2. *Estado de representación.* Photo: "La Virgen," Argentina, 2015. Photo credit: Ina Morales. Courtesy of Ina Morales and Helen Ceballos.

her wet hair covering her face, symbolically erasing her identity and merging her presence with that of all undocumented migrant women.

If the earlier unbraiding gestures functioned as rites of passage or baptism, *Golpe de agua* suggests an act of cleansing—an attempt to purge unprocessed emotional pain tied to childhood memories of migration. The soaked hair, first introduced in *Sitiada* (2010) as a reflection on undocumented domestic labor, now broadens to encompass the broader migrant experience. Water, in this context, becomes both healing and dangerous—an element capable of sustaining life or taking it, especially during migration journeys.

Water functions as a potent symbol in Ceballos's work, drawing from Afro-Caribbean spiritualities where it represents rebirth, resilience, and feminine power. Her performances invoke the Yoruba orisha Oshun, the deity of sweet waters, femininity, fertility, and love.[14] Through Oshun, water becomes a medium for survival and resistance—a space where memory, migration, and emotional labor converge. Ceballos's invocation of Oshun not only resists Eurocentric and patriarchal systems that devalue Black and Brown women's bodies and desires but also reclaims an Afro-Caribbean epistemology where femininity is sacred, not shameful. Her work thus articulates an embodied, decolonial politics that foregrounds softness, erotic power, and survival as radical acts.

In her work, Helen Ceballos reclaims water as more than a site of trauma or death—it becomes a sacred, feminine, and healing space, a conduit for ancestral memory and spiritual resilience. While scholars like Moreno have emphasized the sea as a militarized space of surveillance, in Ceballos's performances it transforms into a site of divine presence and embodied connection with past, present, and future, where the orisha Oshun presides (Hey-Colón 2023).[15] Ceballos aligns her body with the qualities of Oshun, embracing vulnerability, pleasure, and fluidity as forms of resistance—channeling through movement an existence that defies capitalist ideals of perfection and productivity.

The low-resolution, grainy quality of the video performance *Golpe de agua* (2018)—with its blurred, decentered frames—mirrors the imperfect, marginal, and fragmented narratives Ceballos chooses to tell. Her aesthetic embraces the poor-quality image, visually enacting a politics of imperfection aligned with her decolonial and antinormative practice. Migration as lived and embodied experience—particularly as an undocumented subject—becomes the central theme in another 2018 performance, *No voy a pedirle a nadie que me crea.*[16] Here, for the first time in her work, Ceballos introduces the symbolic use of fire and candles—elements that will return in later performances. In a meta-performative gesture, she projects *Golpe de agua* on a wall while embodying a Virgin figure—an image previously explored in *Estado de representación* (2013)—thus interweaving earlier religious iconographies with new explorations of identity, memory, and pain. Candles surround her, some arranged to resemble the three main islands of the Spanish Caribbean (Cuba, the Dominican Republic, and Puerto Rico), others shaped like *yolas,* and still others framing the Virgin-performer as if on an altar. Through the element of fire, she symbolically burns away sociopolitical stereotypes around undocumented migration, telling intimate and collective stories—including likely references to her mother's own memories. At one point, a voice recalls: "yo no sé porque tú me estás preguntando de esta vaina, de verdad que . . . yo lo único que le he pedido a Dios durante estos últimos años fue que me hiciera olvidar esta vaina" [I don't know why you are asking me about this stuff, really . . . the only thing I've asked God these past years is to help me forget it] (2:33–2:41). For Ceballos's mother, forgetting becomes a survival mechanism. In contrast, Ceballos seeks to recover fragmented memories as a decolonial strategy to reconstruct self and collective identity beyond capitalist logics of productivity and coherence.

Ceballos's repeated performative gestures across works enact what Paul Connerton describes as bodily memory—even in its fragmented state. The tension between remembering and forgetting becomes central to her practice: memory and its absences are not oppositional but mutually constitutive forces in a process of survival, healing, and resistance. Her choreographies hold both memory and its limits. When memory becomes too painful, forgetting is embodied as a protective gesture. Her movements synthesize this dialectic between remembrance and erasure, making it both visible and visceral.

In a pivotal moment of *No voy a pedirle a nadie que me crea,* Ceballos informs the audience that every land border in the world has witnessed bloodshed—excluding those lost daily at sea. Attempting to pass through a metallic grill, she repeats: "me he pasado toda la vida moviéndome, migrando, perdiendo el aire, buscando un sitio donde pueda respirar" [I've spent my whole life moving, migrating, losing my breath, searching for a place where I can breathe] (4:33–4:47). She concludes the performance by returning to the candlelit altar surrounded by Caribbean Island silhouettes and boat-shaped candles.

The physical intensity of the performance—walking barefoot over candles, forcing her body through metal grates—manifests shared and scattered memories on the skin. Her body becomes both archive and map, inviting the audience on a journey not as passive observers but as participants sharing proximity to her breath, burns, sweat, and fatigue. This corporeal closeness enables what Rancière terms a "transformed sensation"—a moment of shared vulnerability that bridges individual subjectivity and communal experience (2011, 56). Ceballos's work enacts this transformation, gesturing toward possible new communities forged through embodied empathy.

The sensorial nature of the piece exceeds visual or linguistic meaning. As Ceballos rattles the grill, surrounded by overwhelming candlelight, her breath shifts with each movement. There is no separation between performer and audience; they follow her from space to space, physically and emotionally engaged. Smells, sounds, lighting, and bodily rhythms engulf the spectators, dissolving

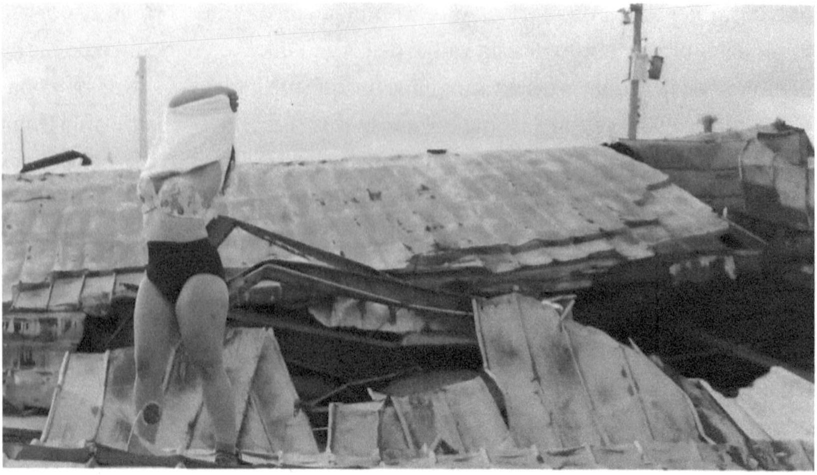

FIGURE 3.3. Photo from the photo series *El cuerpo y la ruina*, 2016. Photo credit: Amarilis Torres Carrasquillo. Courtesy of Amarilis Torres Carrasquillo and Helen Ceballos.

distinctions between human and nonhuman elements. As noted by Przybylski, these nonhuman sounds unsettle traditional modes of perception and open a space for reconsidering the value assigned to undocumented lives (2023, 7). Through this immersive performance, Ceballos invites viewers to embody—however momentarily—the precarious existence of the undocumented subject, traveling through metaphorical islands—*entre islas*—and colonial geographies.

The theme of bodily decadence is central to Ceballos's decolonial aesthetic. As Analola Santana argues, Latin American identity has historically been constructed through the figure of the "freak"—a grotesque embodiment of colonial trauma (2018, 9). By engaging these figures, Ceballos's work contests normative ideals of beauty, ability, and national identity. Her performances transform marginal, undocumented, and "freak" bodies into sites of resistance that challenge dominant ideologies and expose the violent logics of racialized and gendered othering.

This aesthetic is vividly present in her 2018 photo series *El cuerpo y la ruina*, produced in the aftermath of Hurricane María. Amid devastation, Ceballos's body traverses ruined landscapes, embodying the coexistence of survival and collapse. With little aid from the US despite Puerto Rico's colonial status, the island faced months without power, clean water, or basic necessities. Ceballos's images capture life amid ruin, making chaos not only a theme but a condition of being. Movement through chaos becomes the very sign of continued existence.

Ruins establish an unconventional stage where individuals can experience a theatrical sense of presence—spaces where, much like in the theater, "reality" can be reshaped, affording a sense of agency. Francine Masiello describes ruins as a performative and liminal space that conveys power through its symbolic and material ambiguity. She asserts that "ruins stage an in-betweenness: on the one hand, a connection between past and present, between life and death; on the other, the transitory nature of all human progress, a subtle movement in time in which nature comes back to reign over the works of human creation" (2009, 30). In Helen Ceballos's photographic series *El cuerpo y la ruina*, ruins become the landscape of her bodily endurance, a terrain navigated through movement. Her embodied performance within these spaces enacts tensions between life and death, resistance and erasure, articulating what Lazzara and Unruh describe as an "'ecology of everyday experience' that might unmask the mechanism of modern 'progress' that spawn the debris" (2009, 2). Through these gestures, the series empowers both the marginalized body and the colonized space—entities often neglected, labeled as freaks, and rendered "in ruin"—positioning them as "an allegory of otherness" (Santana 2018, 13).

The temporal suspension evoked by ruins—between past and future—mirrors the sociopolitical rift between state and citizenry, questioning who is designated as the "other" while also underscoring the vulnerability of built structures. Architectural decay becomes a metaphor for both historical amnesia and futurity in crisis. Within this framework, memory must actively reconstruct a resistant, reinvented space. Ceballos's body, entwined with and inserted into these ruins, offers a multiplicity of perspectives that embrace decay and fragility. Her corporeality functions as a reclamation of absence, attempting to inhabit the gaps left by structural collapse. This embodied interaction aligns with Gilles Deleuze and Félix Guattari's notion of the "body without organs"—a body stripped of institutional support, yet capable of becoming a vehicle for rereading complex pasts and navigating colonized presents while imagining a future that is plural, divergent, and fundamentally uncertain.[17]

This theme of the body in ruin recurs in Ceballos's live performance *Circuito* (2019), which featured other queer Puerto Rican performers such as Lionel Villahermosa, Pó Rodil, and Edrimael Delgado. In this piece, Ceballos reintroduces the motif of candles—previously used in *No voy a pedirle a nadie que me crea* (2018) to trace the geographies of the Dominican Republic, Cuba, and Puerto Rico. In *Circuito,* however, the candles delineate the perimeter of a human brain, symbolizing its fundamental cognitive functions. Fire thus serves to map both the artists' spatial trajectories and the internal geographies of the body. Each performer embodied a single basic human activity—eating, sleeping, walking—until a pivotal moment when the brain is declared to have suffered a "derrame" [hemorrhage]. The performance charts a metaphysical journey from the external world to the interior self, exploring how life under economic austerity and colonial marginalization erodes essential life functions. Ultimately, *Circuito* articulates the fragmentation of memory and ability in a context of historical trauma, sociopolitical precarity, and uncertain futurity.

Ceballos continues this exploration of bodily memory and origin in the photographic series *Tener tus piernas* (2019).[18] Here, she juxtaposes her body with those of her mother and sister to examine the deterioration and transformation of the body through the lens of motherhood and inheritance. The maternal body—both biological and symbolic—becomes a point of origin, of displacement and return, grounding Ceballos's practice in an axis of instability and resilience. In these images, the artist connects feminine embodiment and ancestral temporality, articulating a queer reimagining of womanhood and maternity. By doing so, she dismantles normative expectations of femininity, motherhood, and bodily purpose, proposing a radical reinterpretation of female genealogies and corporeal knowledge.

LATEST PRODUCTIONS: 2020-2023

Helen Ceballos's performances are deeply rooted in an autobiographical exploration of memory, particularly as it relates to her mother and early experiences of displacement. This thematic thread is powerfully sustained in the video performance *Hablar de la prole* (2020),[19] which opens with a striking declaration: "Hay ciertos recuerdos que sí me gustaría sacar de raíz" [There are some memories that I would like to eradicate from the root]. With this statement, Ceballos foregrounds memory—its erasures, its ruptures, and its affective weight—as the central concern of the piece. She signals a desire to unearth and articulate fragments of a past obscured by childhood trauma, and her mother's reticence to recall or transmit certain experiences.

Rather than following a linear narrative structure, *Hablar de la prole* unfolds through a collage-like layering of audio tracks—some recycled from earlier performances, others representing personal reflections or reenacted conversations. The effect is a nonchronological, fragmentary narrative that resists coherence, mirroring the disjointed nature of traumatic memory itself. For instance, Ceballos repeats the evocative phrase "cargo más mudanzas en el cuerpo que años en el mundo" [I carry more moves in the body than years in the world] (0:08–0:12), a motif that recurs across her body of work and

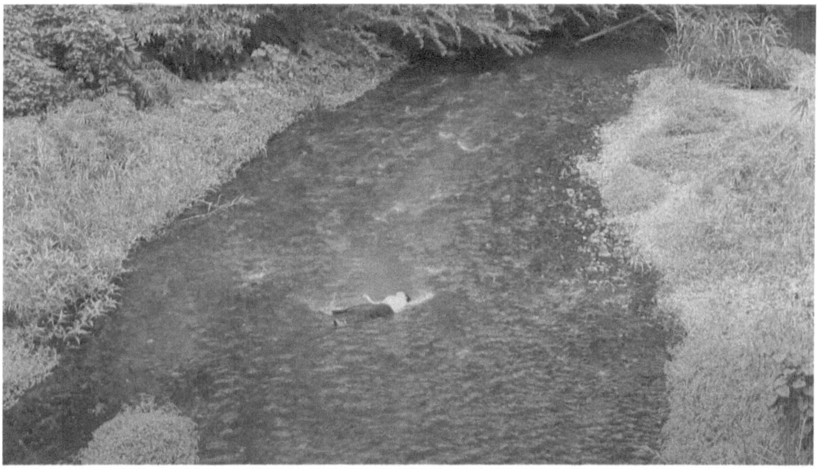

FIGURE 3.4. *Hablar de la prole*, 2020. Concept and execution: Helen Ceballos. Photo credit: Ali Petru Gerena. Courtesy of Ali Petru Gerena and Helen Ceballos.

signals a life marked by constant migration and instability. She also returns to the formative memory of crossing the sea with her mother in a *yola* in 1993—a moment that functions as both personal and geopolitical origin story.

The disjointed structure is further exemplified through a reconstructed dialogue with her father. At one point, she imitates his voice, asking, "¿y los novios cómo están los novios?" [And the boyfriends, how are they doing?] (0:19–0:22), shortly after recounting, "Todavía sigues preguntándome por los novios" [You are still asking me about the boyfriends] (0:12–0:14). Later, in an interior monologue, she silently responds: "No papi, yo tengo ocho años en una relación con una mujer" [No dad, I have been in a relationship with a woman for eight years] (0:32–0:35). These disjunctive moments—unmoored from temporal sequence or narrative causality—expose the tensions between familial expectations and queer identity, as well as the limits of intergenerational understanding.

Toward the end of the video, Ceballos confronts the difficulty of articulating the performance's central message. She admits: "me gustaría explicar de manera sintética de qué carajo quiero hablar en esta pieza" [I would like to explain, briefly, what the hell I want to talk about in this piece] (1:59–2:03), just as she revisits the story of her clandestine journey to Puerto Rico as a child. She then reflects: "yo lo tengo claro a nivel conceptual, lo difícil es bajarlo a tierra" [Conceptually, it is clear to me; the difficult part is how to bring it down to earth] (2:14–2:18). This metacommentary acknowledges the challenges of translating deeply personal, complex memories—particularly those shaped by trauma, migration, and queerness—into a coherent artistic discourse. In embracing fragmentation and uncertainty, *Hablar de la prole* enacts a poetics of memory that resists closure, offering instead an intimate and disjointed archive of diasporic life.

Hablar de la prole culminates in a sonic crescendo, as overlapping audio tracks merge into an indistinguishable cacophony of voices and memories. This auditory collapse mirrors the fragmentation and simultaneity of traumatic recollection, where individual memories blur into a larger, affective landscape. The final image of the performance depicts Ceballos lying motionless in a river, surrendered to the current. Her passive, almost lifeless posture evokes the spectral presence of those who have perished at sea while migrating in search of a better life, transforming her body into a haunting emblem of diasporic loss.

Structurally, the performance mirrors the process through which Ceballos herself recalls her past: discontinuous, layered, and emotionally charged. In this sense, *Hablar de la prole* operates as a reciprocal mechanism—Ceballos's scattered memories sustain the performance, just as the performance serves as a vessel through which she accesses her history, her origins, and her queer identity. The work becomes a cathartic praxis of memory, where art and personal narrative are inextricably linked.

This intimate engagement with memory continues in Ceballos's 2021 appearance in the music video *Memoria* by Combo Chimbita, a first-generation Brooklyn-based experimental pop duo whose backgrounds are Colombian.[20] The song's lyrics invoke the four classical elements—tears (water), sun (fire), breath (air), and walking (earth)—as metaphors for emotional and ancestral presence, aligning closely with the thematic and symbolic language of Ceballos's performance work. The chorus emphasizes the dialectic of remembering and forgetting:

> Eres lo que haces y lo que haces olvidar [repeated 3x]
> Así y recuerda, bien clarito
> Sin miedo
> Sin miedo, acá te espero
> [You are what you do and what you make others forget
> So, and remember, very clearly
> With no fear
> With no fear, here I will be waiting for you]

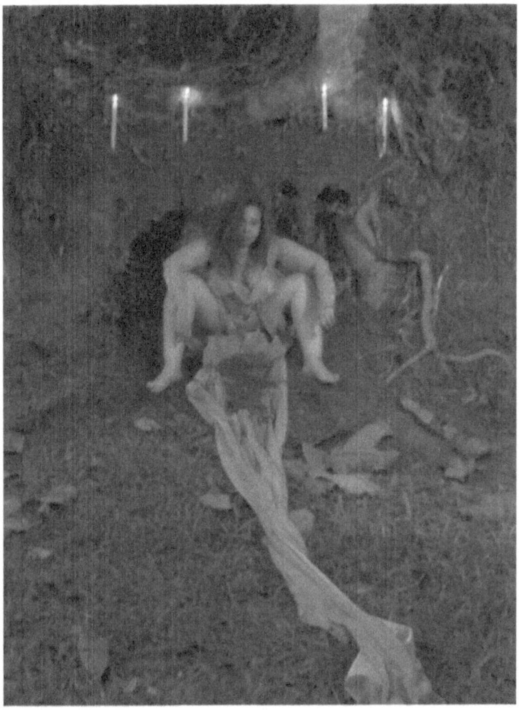

FIGURE 3.5. *Memoria*. Combo Chimbita. 2021. Helen Ceballos. Photo credit: Ali Petru Gerena. Courtesy of Ali Petru Gerena.

This lyrical emphasis on the interplay between memory and erasure resonates deeply with Ceballos's artistic ethos, where remembering is not only a personal act but a political gesture of survival and resistance.

In the video, Ceballos appears in a highly symbolic and visually arresting performance. Emerging from a golden veil in a cave nestled within the forest floor, she evokes the Yoruba orisha Oshun, goddess of love, rivers, and fertility.[21] The space around her is charged with ritual significance: exposed roots surround the cave, and candles illuminate the earth, creating an atmosphere of sacred emergence. As she crawls out, her body is covered in dirt, which also clings to her veil and hair, signifying a visceral connection to land and ancestry. She eventually settles into a seated position with her legs spread open, the golden fabric pooling between her legs in the form of a womb or vagina filled with soil—an evocative image of birth, regeneration, and embodied memory.

Through this performance, Ceballos stages a rebirth that is simultaneously queer, diasporic, and decolonial. As she is moving in a sequence of scenes that simulate a woman giving birth, the connection between her Oshun-looking laboring body in contact with the ground, surrounded by roots, goes back to her own work on motherhood, belonging, and memory. In later sequences Helen comes out of a sack almost as a silkworm, wearing an Afro hairstyle. As she works her way out of the sack, this image metaphorically communicates rebirthing by maintaining and remembering origins and ancestors even when "la luz se apagó" [the light was turned off] (1:55–2:05), symbolizing a state in which remembering is impossible and memories are swallowed by the darkness of existence.[22] The invocation of Oshun and the elemental forces, along with the cyclical interplay of remembering and forgetting, position her body as both archive and oracle—an affective site through which ancestral knowledge, migration, and queer identity converge.

Midway through the song in Combo Chimbita's *Memoria*, a shift occurs from a meditative, new-age tone to a more energetic, electronic cumbia rhythm. This transformation signals what Przybylski calls "multiple possibilities at once" in listening practices, disrupting linear perception and evoking multiplicity and simultaneity (2023, 16). In the video's second half, Helen Ceballos emerges wearing a wig constructed from long, entangled roots while ascending a stone staircase that evokes an altar—an image that recalls her earlier photographic series *Estado de representación* (2013). However, this Virgin figure is not bound by traditional religiosity. The root wig, which references earlier works such as *Lluvia/el destrence/el altar* (2012) and *Desprendimiento* (2015), functions simultaneously as a prosthetic, a symbol of maternal embodiment, and a resignified gesture of queer resistance.

This embodiment of motherhood challenges patriarchal norms by reclaiming maternal symbolism from within a decolonial and queer feminist framework. The motif of birth reappears in the dirt-stained train of the veil, shaped into a womb as Ceballos positions her legs in an open seated pose. In this moment, she performs a ritual that both conjures and critiques memory, labor, and gendered embodiment. The warrior-goddess figure reaches the top of the altar, removes the root wig, and repeats a movement previously seen in *Golpe de agua* (2018), ultimately leaning into the camera's gaze while the lyrics "sin miedo" [without fear] resonate. In doing so, Ceballos declares her readiness to confront memory from multiple angles—rhythmically, corporeally, and politically.

In the same year, Ceballos developed *Cerezas por papeles,* one of the most comprehensive projects of her career. This transdisciplinary work includes a live performance and installation, a video performance, and a photo-essay. It revisits themes present since *Sitiada* (2010)—namely undocumented migration, memory, and belonging—while expanding them into a multilayered meditation on diaspora and identity. The performance-installation took place at El Cuadrado Gris, a contemporary art space in San Juan, Puerto Rico. Ceballos transformed the gallery into the domestic interior of a fictional middle-aged Dominican woman named Eduviges, situated in the working-class neighborhood of Barrio Obrero. The space functioned as both a metaphorical uterus and a site of diasporic memory.

Unlike conventional gallery performances, *Cerezas por papeles* incorporated outdoor interventions and neighborhood walks, inviting embodied participation from local residents. This situated aesthetic offered a rare opportunity to walk in a Puerto Rican neighborhood that resembles a Dominican barrio—an act of spatial and cultural reterritorialization. The walk began at Plaza Barceló, a known drop-off point for undocumented Dominican immigrants, and the very place where five-year-old Helen and her mother first arrived in 1993. Through this gesture, Ceballos grounds her own migratory experience in a collective history of displacement, invoking a feminist politics of location.

Inside the installation, domestic and religious iconographies—such as syncretic altars blending Catholic and Santería elements, a rooster (central to Afro-Caribbean traditions), and familiar furnishings—become narrative devices.[23] These objects narrate a story of migration, labor, and mourning. Of particular significance is the recurring motif of the candle. Fire, since *No voy a pedirle a nadie que me crea* (2018), has symbolized destruction, purification, and rebirth. In *Cerezas por papeles,* candles modulate sensory experience, altering the room's light, temperature, and scent and thereby engaging the audience in a ritual of affective transformation. The flame becomes a living guide—symbolic of ancestral presence and spectral survival.

The central figure, Eduviges, has a son, Francisquito, who arrived in Puerto Rico at a young age—mirroring Helen's own experience. The performance thus becomes both a reenactment and an exorcism, bridging Ceballos's autobiographical narrative with broader histories of Caribbean migration and marginalization. The piece also highlights her dual role as performer and cultural manager, transforming art into a community-engaged praxis.

Complementing the live work is a photo-essay (2021), formally linked to her video performance *Hablar de la prole* (2020). The essay interweaves photography and prose into nine fragmented sections, each separated by one of eight images taken in 2020. Its nonlinear format mimics the erratic processes of memory and trauma. The text navigates themes of illegality, displacement, domesticity, and queer survival. The first section ends with the following reflection: "Accedemos a la memoria con detalles difusos teñidos de espantorecuerdos a largo plazo. Somos cuerpos en una atmósfera ligera. Invisibles y reflejados, fuimos otros para poder existir. Cuando uno llega vivo, queda claro que el premio no iba a llegar." [We access the memory with diffuse details tinged with fright—long-term memories. We are bodies in a light atmosphere. Invisible and mirrored, we were others to be able to exist. When one arrives alive, it becomes clear that the prize was not to arrive.][24] This is a reference to her arrival as a five-year-old, separated from her mother right after jumping in the water for the last swim toward the beach, and arriving on the shore alone and in the dark with no sight of what was going on in the water or around her. She did not know if her mother could swim or if she would ever see her mother again. It was immediately clear that the "prize was not going to arrive."

This reflection dissects the brutal disillusionment of migration: the act of arriving alive does not guarantee freedom, stability, or belonging. Rather than reward, arrival often exposes migrants to systemic violence, economic precarity, and social invisibility. The phrase "el premio no iba a llegar" functions as a direct critique of the American Dream, demystifying its imperial promise of social mobility. For Afro-Caribbean migrants like Ceballos, the destination—Puerto Rico—is not the mainland United States but a colonial borderland shaped by its own exclusions. Dominican migrants arriving in Puerto Rico often face discrimination from both Puerto Rican society and US institutions, revealing the multilayered nature of imperial marginalization.

Ceballos's work confronts the myth of arrival as liberation. Through the migrant body, she exposes how borders—geographic, psychic, and symbolic—continue to operate long after the journey. Puerto Rico, as a US territory, embodies this paradox: it is both part of the empire and subjugated by it. Migrants arriving there confront a deferred dream, where the fantasy of inclusion collapses against colonial and racial hierarchies. In *Cerezas por papeles,* Ceballos reclaims this broken narrative through a poetics of resistance. Memory, forgetfulness, embodiment, and ritual become tools to rewrite the story—not as a story of failure, but as one of radical survival and refusal.

Cerezas por papeles [Cherries for papers] intricately weaves photography, performance, and autobiographical narrative to interrogate themes of migration, gendered violence, and the fluidity of identity. Through a nonlinear, fragmented structure, Ceballos invites viewers to engage with the embodied experiences of Afro-Caribbean women, particularly those navigating the precarity of undocumented migration. The photo-essay opens with a picture titled *Período* (Period), depicting Ceballos's nude body from an aerial perspective, lying atop a red circular flotation device in a river. The location reminds the viewer of the one in the video performance *Hablar de la prole* (2020), which highlights once more the connections between these two works of the artist. The vivid red hue and the title evoke menstruation, referencing a traumatic memory from her childhood migration journey. At five years old, Ceballos witnessed a menstruating woman being cast into the sea by a fellow migrant, who justified his action by claiming that blood would attract sharks, endangering the group. This harrowing incident underscores the compounded vulnerabilities faced by women during such perilous crossings.

Subsequent images delve deeper into themes of identity and displacement. A photograph of a fabricated Puerto Rican birth certificate under the alias "Amy Solano" reflects the lengths to which migrants must go to navigate bureaucratic systems. In *Torniquete* (Tourniquet), Ceballos appears nude with her face enveloped in golden fabric beside a river, symbolizing the erasure and reconstruction of identity. This motif continues in *El premio no fue llegar* [The reward was not to arrive], where she reenacts her first memory of her mother upon arriving in Puerto Rico, capturing the uncertainty and emotional turmoil of familial separation and reunion.

The narrative's nonlinear progression mirrors the disjointed nature of memory and trauma. In *Sin permiso* [Without permission], a black-and-white photograph of her teenage sister applying lipstick preludes a recounting of Ceballos's adolescence, marked by early independence and a harrowing experience of attempted sexual assault by her sister's father. These personal histories are not isolated anecdotes but are emblematic of broader systemic issues affecting marginalized communities.

Ceballos's work consistently centers the corporeal as a site of resistance and resilience. Through these narratives, the artist opens a space to address generational trauma, sexual abuse, and sexism. Ceballos writes and performs these stories to demonstrate how resilience and disobedience become essential tools for navigating life and ensuring survival. In *En tránsito* [In transit], the image of two nude legs wading through water encapsulates the perpetual state of movement and the search for belonging inherent in the migrant experience. *Ponerle cara* [Facing it] juxtaposes the dehumanizing aspects of immigration with intimate domestic scenes, such as her mother and sister braiding her hair—a recurring motif in Ceballos's oeuvre symbolizing heritage, identity, and connection since her early performances, such as *Sitiada* in 2010, *Lluvia/el destrence/el altar* in 2012, *Desprende* in 2015, or *Golpe de agua* in 2018, just to mention a few. In Helen's work, hair is always presented as roots, as family connection, as racial identity, and as home. *Ponerle cara* becomes in the essay a visual shield between the cruelty of immigration laws (which Helen always exposes in her work) and the small stories that portray her mom as a person with her own personal and intimate identity. This identity was denied and devalued, and needed to be manipulated and forgotten in order to have the right to "lawfully" exist.

The culmination of the photo-essay is an untitled black-and-white image of Ceballos nude amid foliage, her face partially obscured by braids. The absence of a title and the concealment of her face speak to the complexities of self-identification and the agency in choosing when and how to reveal oneself. This image is accompanied by a narrative reflecting on her early experiences with labor and the metaphorical and literal implications of "selling cherries," a term laden with connotations of innocence, sexuality—since *cherrie* can also refer to the vulva or virginity—and commodification.[25] Ceballos recounts an incident from her childhood in Santo Domingo Este, where, at four years old, she attempted to sell cherries:

> The first time I tried to earn a few coins, I was four years old and was selling cherries from my house in Cachón de la Rubia in Santo Domingo Este. I picked a couple and sat in the street before the door, yelling *Veeeeeeendo cereeezas, veeeeeendo cherriiiees.* A man approached smiling, took three, and left without paying. I decided that day that I would never sell my cherries to anyone who did not understand their value.[26]

This anecdote encapsulates the intersection of economic precarity, bodily autonomy, and the exploitation of women within patriarchal and capitalist structures. *Cerezas por papeles,* then, becomes an essay about the common struggles of Afro-Caribbean women, as well as a platform from which Helen Ceballos has been symbolically selling her cherries for her papers to establish her identity and agency, and to reclaim her right to occupy her space, her stage, and her breathing air.

The trilogy concludes with the video performance *Fue esa la vía* [That was the way] (2021), a 7-minute, 18-second piece reenacting the treacherous journey of undocumented migrants by sea. Opening with an aerial shot of an empty *yola,* the video employs visceral imagery and sound to immerse viewers in the migrants' experience. The red stains on the boat's floor evoke both the bloodshed associated with such voyages and the earlier motif of menstruation, linking personal trauma to collective memory. The performance eschews linear

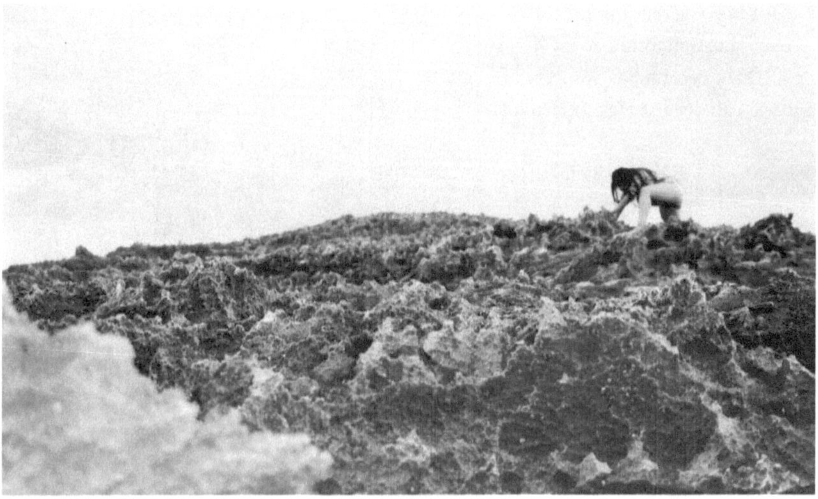

FIGURE 3.6. *Fue esa la vía.* 2020. Concept and action: Helen Ceballos. Photo credit: Ali Petru Gerena. Courtesy of Ali Petru Gerena and Helen Ceballos.

temporality, instead oscillating between scenes of swimming, running, and hiding, reflecting the disorientation and fragmentation inherent in the migrant experience. The concluding scene features individuals running toward the *yola,* interspersed with images of bodies floating in the sea, culminating in the poignant refrain: "no moriré extranjera" [I won't die as a foreigner].

The title *Fue esa la vía* appears at both the beginning and end of the video, framing the piece as a closed, cyclical reflection. The video oscillates between sensorial, immersive experiences and a more installation-like aesthetic. This alternation embodies how Ceballos's performative gestures function as a form of catharsis—not only allowing her to process personal traumas and reclaim her story and memories but also inviting the viewer to inhabit the experience from an alternative perspective. The spectator of *Fue esa la vía* is metaphorically submerged in the waters of the performance, yet offered a chance to come up for air, to take a transformative breath and reconsider the realities of undocumented migration, particularly as experienced by women. The song's final lyrics refuse the label of outsider or foreigner, asserting instead a fundamental human drive for movement, connection, and belonging. Even when geography dictates exclusion, *Fue esa la vía* insists on the persistence of relationality and community.

Cerezas por papeles is a complex, multilayered project that takes various forms—performance, installation, video performance, writing, and photogra-

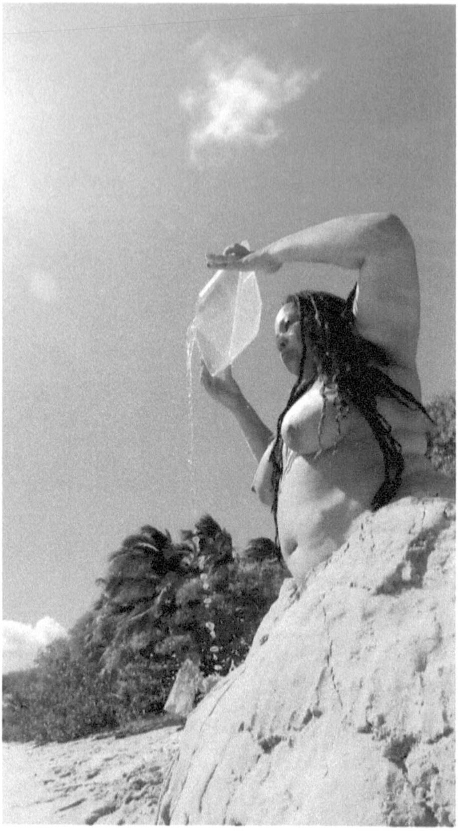

FIGURE 3.7. *Cuerpos fronterizos*, Martinique, Artindince 2022. Photo credit: Fabrice Paimba. Courtesy of Fabrice Paimba and Helen Ceballos.

phy. These diverse media collectively trace Ceballos's artistic and conceptual evolution. Her gestures and performative movements evoke her earlier works, inviting the audience to engage in an exercise of memory and to experience the stories she shares in a deeply embodied way. *Cerezas por papeles* thus becomes an opportunity to forge bonds with a visible or invisible audience, one that exists across the multiple platforms she employs. Much like the subjects she centers—particularly undocumented migrants and women—this invisible audience holds significance in the empathetic space forged between the spectator's gaze and the images or texts they encounter. That space—fragmented, chaotic, and beyond the control of artist or viewer—mirrors the structure of Ceballos's memories as they are performed and narrated. In this apparent disorder, *Cerezas por papeles* creates a sense of community that emerges in the moment of encounter. The audience is invited to surrender to the queer possibility of existing beyond binaries and linear temporalities.

Between 2021 and 2022, Ceballos produced another significant work: *Cuerpos fronterizos* [Border bodies], a live performance recorded during her residency in Martinique.[27] In it, the artist positions herself at the shoreline, bare-chested and adorned with blue braided hair. She wears what appears to be a long skirt made entirely of sand and holds a small, *yola*-shaped triangular glass filled with water. Throughout the 7-minute performance, Ceballos recites a poetic text three times—twice in full and once partially.

The poem honors the endurance of border bodies, especially migrant women, in phrases such as:

> Cuerpos fronterizos / que se peinan y se visten pa la guerra / cuerpas[28] que resisten / que se pelan / cuerpas que son cruces de caminos . . . vamos a tomar el trono por haber sobrevivido / hoy vamos a celebrarnos / porque llevamos [. . .] un cuerpo que ha resistido.
>
> [Border bodies / that comb their hair and dress for war / bodies that resist / that are stripped bare / bodies that are crossroads / platinum bodies / let's build a statue for those thrown into the river / for those launched, glittering / let's light a fire so they can find their way / let's claim the throne for having survived / today we celebrate ourselves / because we carry [. . .] a body that has endured.]

These words resonate with the imagery of the performance. As Ceballos struggles under the weight of the sand skirt, she moves in circular motions until she ultimately frees herself and bathes in the sea. The camera lingers on intimate parts of her body: areas where sand clings to skin, where sunburn is visible, where body fat resists concealment. This attention to corporeality underscores a politics of visibility and embodiment, reinforcing the performance's core message: survival itself is an act of resistance and a call to collective memory.

This piece revisits the theme of undocumented maritime migration that Helen Ceballos has addressed in previous works, but with a heightened focus on the experiences of undocumented women. As is characteristic of her artistic practice, this performance is intertextually linked to earlier visual and performative motifs. In particular, *Cuerpos Fronterizos* (2021–22) can be read as an extension of the imagery found in *Estado de representación* (2012), where the iconography of the Virgin on an altar was already being critically reworked. In the more recent piece, the altar and the Virgin figure are rendered apocryphal, deconsecrating their symbolic authority and drawing attention to the displaced, abused, and marginalized realities of female migrant bodies.

Cuerpos Fronterizos also marks the first significant exploration of the skirt as both a performative object and a conceptual device in Ceballos's work. The skirt, traditionally a symbol of femininity and often implicated in patriarchal, misogynistic, and sexually abusive dynamics, here becomes a heavy sculptural element made of sand—physically weighing down and immobilizing the performer. Ceballos's physical struggle to move and liberate herself from the sand skirt becomes a metaphor for the generational labor of survival under patriarchy—a labor shared by her mother, the women in her family, and herself. This embodied struggle is not only individual but collective and historical.

The performance also incorporates the four classical elements—air (wind), fire (sun), earth (sand), and water (sea)—which serve dual roles. On the one hand, they symbolize endurance and survival; on the other, they represent forces that threaten life, reinforcing the precarity and resilience of migrant and gendered existence. Another recurring visual motif in the piece is braided hair, which Ceballos uses symbolically to signify belonging, cultural lineage, and identity. At the same time, the braids function as a form of armor—a visual declaration of resistance and readiness for battle. In *Cuerpos Fronterizos,* the artist's female body exists in a liminal space: between the shore and the ocean, between immobility and movement, between visibility and erasure. The sand skirt becomes a material frontier that both defines and confines her, just as gendered social norms do. Her body, as a border itself, marks the tension between origin and displacement, memory and forgetting, constraint and liberation. It marks where to end and where to begin in a suspended space that is made of violence and invisibility hidden under a skirt that Helen in this piece destroys with the movements of her body.

The symbolic and performative significance of the skirt is further developed in her most recent project, *Rito de paso/comen de mí* (2023). This dual-titled work consists of a live performance (*Rito de paso*) and a video piece (*Comen de mí*), which are conceptually interconnected. As with much of Ceballos's practice, this piece builds upon previous explorations, revisiting key gestures, images, and materials. The skirt reappears—this time not as a fragile sand structure but as a metallic garment that is eventually set on fire. The transformation of the skirt from earthbound weight to fiery spectacle underscores the evolving symbolic register of Ceballos's performances.

Rito de paso/comen de mí also reflects a processual and research-driven methodology. The project was developed while Ceballos traveled through the Caribbean, during which she conducted interviews with women and engaged with local communities. The opportunity to perform across different island con-

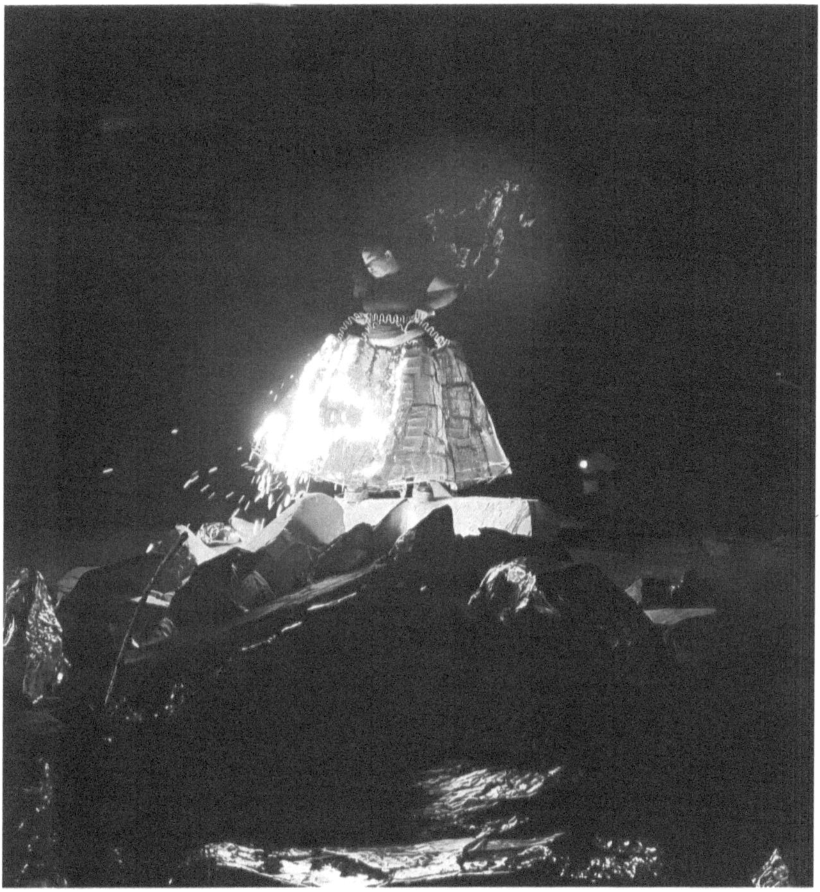

FIGURE 3.8. *Rito de paso*, Boston, 2023. Photo credit: Analola Santana. Figure Courtesy of Analola Santana and Helen Ceballos.

texts allowed her to refine her movements and deepen her engagement with the material. As such, the work is not only a performance but also a cartography—a mapping of a decade-long artistic inquiry into the displacement of the female body. This trajectory, as the chapter will later explore, also informs Ceballos's work as a curator and cultural manager, revealing the expansive scope of her decolonial and intersectional praxis.

Helen Ceballos's *Rito de paso/comen de mí* extends the artist's long-standing engagement with undocumented migration, gendered violence, and the symbolic weight of the female body in transit. In *Rito de paso*, the live performance centers on the artist's bodily struggle to wear and set fire to a metallic skirt—an act that places her at real risk of physical harm. This dangerous garment, difficult to manipulate and potentially injurious, reactivates the recurring motif of the skirt in Ceballos's work. As in *Cuerpos fronterizos* (2021), where a skirt made of sand immobilizes the body, in *Rito de paso* the metallic skirt becomes a symbol of the oppressive weight of patriarchal and heteronormative norms imposed on female bodies. The performative risk—burns, cuts, immobilization—renders literal the metaphorical violence of gendered and racialized social constraints. The artist's body becomes a site where symbolic and physical abuse converge.

This performance also marks a return to the Virgin-like imagery introduced in *Estado de representación* (2012). If in earlier work the Virgin was brought down from the altar to critique religious control over women's bodies, in *Rito de paso* Ceballos escalates this gesture by setting the symbolic skirt on fire while wearing it, enacting rebellion through an artifact that dynamically moves with her pain and movement. As Consuelo Martínez Reyes addresses, female characters function as decolonial tools of affect by disrupting normative gender expectations and offering alternative ways of being. Further following Martínez Reyes's argument, the author sees how women's characters are constructed as epistemic and cultural artifacts—objects that both embody and resist the colonial order (2021). She uses "artifact" not in the sense of inert or museum-like objects, but as repositories of memory, language, and affect that carry the traces of colonial violence while also enacting resistance. In her reading, these characters' bodies, gestures, and narratives become living artifacts that mediate between past and present, personal and collective history. Similarly, if we understand Ceballos's whole performance *Rito de paso* through the artifact of the metallic skirt on fire, it becomes a materialized performative trace of resistance. The object—being the metallic skirt on fire—carries affect, history, and relational meaning when in movement with the body of the performer. The artifact, then, beyond the object, becomes the scene, the embodied practice, the whole meaning of the performance, and thus, ultimately, a site of agency. The artifact in movement in *Rito de paso* materializes and holds visible those alternative modes of being as preserved, remembered, refused, or performed. They can challenge norms by their very presence. This trajectory—from still image to bodily action—traces a transformative arc in Ceballos's performance practice, one where the skirt evolves from icon to incendiary artifact, a decolonial device that is a place of memory and resistance.

The second component of the title, *Comen de mí* [They eat out of me], refers to a 3-minute, 59-second video performance that is still in postproduction.[29] Aesthetically distinct from her previous work, this video omits the artist's physical presence entirely. Instead, Ceballos constructs a narrative around her absence—her stories are told, but her body remains offscreen. This absence becomes a powerful metaphor: a critique of how society consumes women like her—undocumented, racialized, and marginalized—while rendering them invisible. In choosing not to appear, Ceballos asserts a form of agency, reclaiming the right to escape surveillance and asserting control over spatial and visual boundaries. Her refusal to be framed is itself a refusal of sociopolitical constraint.

Visually, *Comen de mí* uses a surreal aesthetic of cold blues, grays, greens, and sandy hues that evoke a dystopian coastal landscape. The recurring image of worms trapped in a glass bottle suggests both entrapment and migration. Abstracted, these worms resemble swimmers viewed from above—perhaps referencing migrants struggling to reach shore. Their writhing mass within the confined space speaks to the dehumanizing experience of forced proximity and constrained mobility under systems of racial capitalism. The beach scenes, the fish-eye perspectives, and the sound of heavy breathing layer the video with somatic urgency. The dystopic imagery serves not only as metaphor but as visual language for the often-invisible trauma of undocumented life.

Despite its visual and formal divergence from *Rito de paso, Comen de mí* is deeply connected in theme and intention. Both works reflect on the exploitation and consumption of female migrant bodies. Through a surrealist and experimental vocabulary, *Comen de mí* articulates a reality both intimate and collective, known yet unspoken, close yet unseen. It renders visible the mechanisms of gendered violence and systemic erasure that condition undocumented women's lives.

The development of *Rito de paso/comen de mí* was deeply research driven. As Ceballos recounts in interviews such as her conversation on the podcast *Latinx Visions*,[30] she engaged in ethnographic interviews with sex workers across the Caribbean—including in the Dominican Republic, Martinique, and Cuba—as well as with women in her own family who had engaged in sex work as undocumented migrants. These testimonies inform the emotional and political register of her performances, turning them into cross-Caribbean reflections on mobility, survival, and embodied memory.

Ceballos's focus on sex work finds critical resonance in scholarship by figures such as Lorgia García Peña and Juana María Rodríguez. García Peña's work on Black and Brown migrant women underscores how they are criminalized and hypersexualized under racial capitalism and state violence. While not focused solely on sex work, García Peña highlights the structural conditions—

colonialism, displacement, and border regimes—that push women into informal and precarious economies. Rodríguez, in contrast, directly engages sex work through a queer-of-color feminist lens. In *Sexual Futures, Queer Gestures, and Other Latina Longings*, Rodríguez refuses reductive readings of sex work as mere exploitation, instead framing it as a space of agency, negotiation, and embodied knowledge. Ceballos's performances emerge from these intersecting critical paradigms. Her work often begins from the invisibility García Peña theorizes—statelessness, precarity, marginality—and transforms it into a space of radical presence. Her use of the body as medium confronts audiences with the contradictions of survival under postcolonial and neoliberal conditions. Like Rodríguez's "queer gestures," Ceballos's performances disrupt dominant narratives of shame and silence, offering instead embodied narratives of resilience and complexity. Ceballos does this not only through content but through form: her fragmented narratives, shifting personae, and invocation of Afro-Caribbean spiritualities (e.g., Yemayá, Oshun) position her art within a long tradition of embodied resistance and diasporic memory. Her aesthetic practice—fragmented, nonlinear, spiritually infused—aligns with García Peña's call for epistemic justice and Rodríguez's insistence on the political significance of pleasure, pain, and sexuality in the lives of queer Afro-Caribbean and Latinx subjects.

Rito de paso/comen de mí thus emerges as a trans-Caribbean performance that interrogates and resignifies the racialized, sexualized body. Moving between Martinique, the Dominican Republic, and Cuba, Ceballos maps a cartography of embodied resistance, one that foregrounds Afro-Caribbean women's labor, memory, and struggle. These works not only summarize a decade of performative practice but also signal a shift in her career as she deepens her roles as curator, producer, and cultural manager.

Indeed, *Rito de paso/comen de mí* bridges Ceballos's performance work with her broader cultural practice. These pieces trace a Caribbean cartography of the migrating female body and lay the groundwork for her curatorial and managerial projects. Her identity as a queer Caribbean woman of color informs a practice grounded in empathy, solidarity, and communal care. These ethics counter the dystopic survival narratives often inscribed onto undocumented migrants, reimagining performance as a space for collective healing and political agency.

Both *Cerezas por papeles* (2021–22) and *Rito de paso/comen de mí* (2023) represent the culmination of Ceballos's poetics over the past decade. As the following section will explore, these works also mark a conceptual and methodological shift that informs her work as cultural producer. Projects such as *Mezcolanza* (2013–present), *El cruce* (2016–present), *Plataforma Eje* (2020), *Mar de islas* (2021–present), and *Cartografías del desplazamiento* (2023) reveal the depth of her engagement as a cultural manager. Through these initiatives, Ceballos continues to center diasporic, queer, and Afro-Caribbean voices while building sustainable artistic and community-based infrastructures across the Caribbean.

Managing the Borders of Culture

In the preceding section, we examined how Helen Ceballos's performances chart a cartography of movement—both physical and symbolic—through which she narrates her personal history. Initially centered on her own experiences, Ceballos soon recognized that her story was inextricably linked to those of the women in her family and others who endure similar struggles. She came to understand that her artistic practice was not solely a means of personal catharsis or memory recovery but also a vehicle for recuperating marginalized narratives. Her performances evolved into acts imbued with anticapitalist, anticolonial, and decolonial energies, aiming to amplify the voices of the invisible and to foster communities grounded in empathy and mutual support across lines of race, class, gender identity, sexuality, age, ability, religion, and geography.

This section explores how performance became the impetus for Ceballos to venture into other professional realms—production, cultural management, and curatorial work—without abandoning her identity as a performer. Rather than compartmentalizing these roles, she interweaves them, creating a holistic practice where each facet informs and sustains the others. Through merging these practices Ceballos realized that her identity as a performer needed to expand into the territories of production, cultural managing, and curatorial activities to manage, push, deconstruct, and transform—from an anticolonial and decolonial perspective—the borders of culture.

Through this integrated approach, Ceballos has established platforms that uplift a diverse array of Caribbean artists who might otherwise lack access to resources such as funding or visas. By stepping off the stage to organize events, process paperwork, secure funding, and curate exhibitions, she challenges the myth of the solitary, self-sufficient artist, revealing instead the often-invisible labor that sustains artistic production. This perspective is particularly poignant given her position as a queer woman of color from a colonized and economically challenged territory like Puerto Rico. Consequently, Ceballos's movements in all her professional activities offer a necessary decolonial, anticolonial, and anticapitalistic journey that defies the borders of current politics, immigration laws, social marginalization, and patriarchy.

To illustrate the breadth and impact of Ceballos's work, I focus on five key initiatives from the decade spanning 2013 to 2023: *Mezcolanza* (producer, 2013–present), *El cruce* (producer, since 2016), *Plataforma Eje* (cultural manager, 2020–present), *Mar de islas* (producer and curator, 2021–present), and *Cartografías del desplazamiento* (curator, December 2023).

Plataforma Eje serves as the umbrella organization for Ceballos's various projects, formalizing her role as a cultural manager. The platform supports community-based organizations, promoting economic autonomy through decentralized programs managed within the Caribbean. As Ceballos explained in the *Latinx Visions* podcast, *Plataforma Eje* emerged during a period when she sought a stable foundation for her professional growth. It provided the structure to offer workshops on mental health, alternative medicine, and LGBTQ+ support, as well as educational activities highlighting the island's resources. Through *Plataforma Eje,* Ceballos not only engaged with her community but also increased the visibility of a Dominican, queer, Afro-descendant, immigrant woman artist. Simultaneously, the platform became a pillar for the LGBTQ+ community, affirming their right to community and support.

Although *Plataforma Eje* was formally established in 2020, it consolidated preexisting initiatives, such as *Mezcolanza,* which began in 2013 while Ceballos was pursuing her master's degree in Argentina. Invited to perform at a queer bar in Buenos Aires, she curated a two-hour program featuring a diverse array of artists and art forms, effectively becoming the event's organizer, producer, cultural manager, and curator. *Mezcolanza,* meaning "mishmash," evolved into an itinerant festival that returned with her to Puerto Rico in 2016. The festival maintains its core characteristics: showcasing various art forms—from puppetry to video, performance to circus—and featuring artists from around the world. Even when visa issues prevent physical attendance, artists contribute via video. *Mezcolanza* provides a platform for experimental and diverse works, including activities for children, challenging conventional artistic boundaries and fostering creativity and community. Rooted in queerness, the festival originated in a queer space and continues to prioritize queer artistic expression.

In 2016, Ceballos initiated *El cruce,* a pedagogical program facilitating the exchange of performative practices among artists across the Caribbean. Comprising workshops, residencies, conferences, research, and presentations, *El cruce* aims to amplify Caribbean arts and foster dialogue with global practices. By providing visas and travel support, the program counters historical and political barriers that have hindered inter-island connections, asserting a decolonial and anticolonial presence. *El cruce* has convened in the Dominican Republic and Cuba, offering to artists, and to Ceballos, a supportive environment to develop their own work in an environment that is comfortable and that speaks directly to Helen's way of producing art.

Mar de islas (2021–), another initiative under *Plataforma Eje*, convenes artists in Puerto Rico for ten-day workshops to reconceptualize the Caribbean from a decolonial perspective. Participants receive support to focus exclusively on their work, resisting capitalist production pressures and allowing for creation at one's own pace. As Halberstam notes, such endeavors offer a "queer adjustment in the way in which we think about time" and engender "new conceptions of space" (Halberstam 2005, 6). Located in the island's southern region—where Ceballos arrived with her mother in the 1990s and where undocumented Dominican immigrants often settle—*Mar de islas* embodies the Caribbean's diversity and resilience. It illuminates marginalized geographies and fosters free movement and thought.

This event is deeply connected to Ceballos's exploration of elements central to her artistic practice: the ocean, the body, borders, and sociopolitical constraints. *Mar de islas* extends an invitation to other Caribbean artists to engage with her decolonial vision. The Caribbean becomes a space to explore the complex dynamics of identity, cultures, and history that determine the relationships between individuals. As Glissant argues, Caribbean identities are best understood through a "poetics of relation," emphasizing interactions and exchanges that celebrate cultural hybridity and resilience. *Mar de islas* creates a space to recall alternative histories and supports the construction of a collective queer memory and artistic community. The ocean, a repository of Caribbean history and memory, becomes a metaphorical and literal conduit for these explorations. *Mar de islas* is an invitation to navigate that body of water that is the blood that keeps Caribbean identities alive. And water and migrating movements across the Caribbean are the backbone of Ceballos's performative work.

In December 2023, Ceballos cocurated *Cartografías del desplazamiento* with Abdiel D. Segarra Ríos for Art Basel Miami Beach, assembling seventeen Puerto Rican artists to examine displacement—a condition historically shaping Caribbean realities. The curators' statement highlights how displacement, coloniality, and gentrification affect daily life in Puerto Rico, reconfiguring communities and challenging identities, and defines the show as "a bet on the right to remain."[31] "The right to remain," to occupy the space where one exists, and the right to movement have been cardinal points in Ceballos's artistic work. Thus, as in the case of the previously analyzed initiatives, once more her performances inform and expand into her other activities, and they are all connected by the same conceptual thread. The exhibition sought to illuminate the knowledge and experiences arising from these movements, exploring changes in landscape, memory construction, and conceptions of geography and relationships. By including performance and video art, the exhibition not only reflected Ceballos's curatorial identity but also provided a platform for artists to interrogate hegemonic cultures and question official histories, particularly amid widespread emigration and displacement. Consequently, through curatorship, Ceballos managed to open a space for questioning official history, especially when most of the Puerto Rican population is forced to emigrate and is pushed away from their homes and neighborhoods. The art included offered a tool to recognize and think about the contradictions and challenges of life nowadays in Puerto Rico and in the diaspora, from a queer perspective, and during an art event in the United States.

Collectively, initiatives like *Mezcolanza* (2013–present), *El cruce* (2016–present), *Plataforma Eje* (2020–present), *Mar de islas* (2021–present), and *Cartografías del desplazamiento* (2023) exemplify how Ceballos navigates and redefines cultural borders. Her extensive engagement with the queer Caribbean community of color is evident in the myriad workshops, conferences, residencies, exhibits, events, fellowships, and collaborations listed on *Plataforma Eje*'s website.[32] Through her work, she has cultivated an inclusive community for those compelled to invent new modes of existence, traverse borders, dismantle sociopolitical and cultural barriers, and reclaim their spaces. As Halberstam suggests, embracing failure and unmaking can offer more creative and cooperative ways of being. By validating the "failed" and the marginalized, Ceballos's work affirms queer legitimacy, transforming her home into a welcoming space of everyday resistance—where people regularly gather to cook, share, and imagine future endeavors, as I have personally witnessed on numerous occasions.

Ultimately, Ceballos's performative practice and her roles as cultural manager, curator, and producer are deeply rooted in her lived experiences. As she expresses in her performances, art can be both suffocating and salvific, compelling her to delve into her history and share her narratives. Her work embodies a decolonial, anticapitalist, and anticolonial existence as a Caribbean queer woman of color. Through her movements—geographic, literal, and symbolic—she exposes systemic injustices and centers her body as a vessel of fragmented memories and life experiences. Her interdisciplinary practices forge a common grammar of resistance across islands, *entre islas,* shifting geographies, and displacing borders to reimagine a queer Caribbean life in perpetual motion.

"Inventar un verbo nuevo": Queer Cartographies of Arrival and Resistance

I began this chapter with an epigraph drawn from Manuel Ramos Otero's *Poema 6* in *Invitación al polvo,* a piece that captures the island's seductive power—a seduction that is both irresistible and perilous, because "nos obliga a naufragar" [it forces us to drown].[33] Yet within that shipwreck lies a generative paradox: the poem compels us to invent "un verbo nuevo" [a new verb]. Drowning, then, is not solely a sign of despair but a precondition for surrendering and transformation. It is through this necessary rupture that we are driven to create new forms of existence—embodied in the act of "llegar" [to arrive]—as a gesture of creative survival and reinvention.

Helen Ceballos's transdisciplinary practice materializes what Manuel Ramos Otero evokes in his verses: the island as both seduction and compulsion, a geography that demands shipwreck and reinvention. "Inventar un verbo nuevo" [Inventing a new verb] becomes not just a poetic imperative but an epistemological and aesthetic strategy through which Ceballos articulates a decolonial, queer, and Afro-Caribbean grammar of presence. Her work inhabits the interstices of migration, racialization, and gendered violence, transforming personal and collective memory into performative counterarchives. Drawing on the quotidian—her kitchen, her body, her voice—she unsettles the colonial logics of legibility and legitimacy, offering instead relational modes of knowing, creating, and surviving. In doing so, Ceballos redefines arrival not as assimilation but as a continuous, embodied act of resistance, care, and radical imagination.

This logic of wreckage and reinvention is at the heart of Helen Ceballos's transdisciplinary work, which emerges from the fragmented geographies of migration, dispossession, and precarity. Her performances, curatorial practices, and autobiographical narratives embrace the shipwreck not as finality, but as origin point: a place from which to arrive otherwise. In embodying the verb *llegar*—as movement, resistance, and refusal—Ceballos invents a "new verb."

Through this act, she constructs a poetics of queer Afro-Caribbean becoming grounded in womanhood, femininity, and female existence. Her vision is inclusive—through a queer lens—of all feminine, female, and women's bodies that insist on memory, collectivity, and the radical possibility of inventing life anew amid collapse.

FOUR

Artistic Articulations

The Visual Movements of Awilda Sterling-Duprey

> I have always been here.
>
> Awilda Sterling-Duprey / Interview with the author, January 11, 2024

> [F]rom a young age, I began establishing a relationship with myself,
> but it had to be in silence for me to be able to listen to myself [. . .]
> silence gives a lot of definition to my work;
> it is very much connected to those experiences from my childhood
> because they heal me, bring back memories,
> and also because it is part of an aesthetic
> that is not usually expressed here in Puerto Rico.
>
> Awilda Sterling-Duprey / From the podcast recorded with the author on March 7, 2024

One of the primary questions I asked myself when first engaging with the work of Awilda Sterling-Duprey (she/her/hers, b. 1947) was, Why does such a foundational artist in Puerto Rico's experimental art scene still lack substantial scholarly attention? Sterling-Duprey has been a pioneer of experimental dance in Puerto Rico, forging a groundbreaking interdisciplinary practice that integrates visual arts, dance, choreography, installation, and performance. Central to her work is a persistent engagement with Black identity and ancestral memory.

In a conversation with the artist about the scarcity of academic work on her oeuvre, she responded with a mix of humility and pride: "Siempre he estado aquí" [I've always been here], underscoring her continuous presence as an artist despite the lack of formal recognition. This quiet insistence on presence is emblematic of Sterling-Duprey's ethos. She does not simply produce art; rather, she translates lived experience and reflection into movement and image. Through this translation, she embodies a *cimarrona*[1] sensibility—a rebellious, self-liberated force—transforming her bodily gestures into acts of resistance that challenge conventional norms, academic invisibility, and aesthetic boundaries.

As Sterling-Duprey explains in a 2022 interview with the Joan Mitchell Foundation:

> My installations and performances intertwine marginalities of self-representation and resistance, confronting the silencing and invisibilizing of Afro-Caribbean women. Drawing from Yoruba-Caribbean traditions and working across disciplines, I transgress the boundaries between drawing, painting, and performance through a decolonizing practice that challenges the conventions of Puerto Rican fine arts.

This transgressive, decolonial impulse has shaped her life and art from childhood. Sterling-Duprey often recounts being considered a "strange" child, one who would hide in nature to observe life from the shadows. Her connection to the Caribbean landscape—the movement of waves, the rustling of palm leaves—later informed her kinetic vocabulary as a performer.

This tendency to hide was also a strategy of resistance against a strict domestic upbringing rooted in gendered and racial discipline. She was taught how a girl "ought" to sit, laugh, move, and wear her hair. Race and discrimination, she was told, were not proper topics for a future wife. Her body, subjected to this regime of discipline, became an uncomfortable space—one she later reclaimed and transformed into the central medium of her artistic practice.

The linear, patriarchal structure imposed on her as a child clashed with what she calls the "cosmic natural order"—a dynamic, spiraling, and chaotic force that mirrors Puerto Rico's own colonial condition.[2] The discomfort she felt in navigating that imposed order became a generative tension, fueling her exploration of movement as resistance. As she observes, the linearity of colonialism parallels the expectations placed on young women in her family. The similarities between her linear education and the colonial state of the island refer, in a metaphorical sense, to the ways in which colonialism also imposes a linear order in the space of a colonized island. Sterling-Duprey opposes through an artistic language that defies categorization and traditions, and that embraces chaos as a creative principle.

This rejection of discipline—both artistic and social—is central to Sterling-Duprey's evolution as an interdisciplinary artist. Long before terms like "intermedia" or "transdisciplinary" became widespread in the art world, she was dissolving the boundaries between genres. Audiences and critics often expressed surprise at her work across media, asking how she transitioned from visual art to experimental dance and performance. But as she clarifies: "Yo no hago distinción entre una y la otra porque [. . .] el movimiento es el elemento principal en mi trabajo, tanto visual como corporal" [I don't distinguish between one or the other because . . . movement is the principal element in both my visual and corporeal work] (Homar and pastrana santiago 2022, 293). This chapter explores the work of an Afro–Puerto Rican artist whose visual and performative language centers on what I define as *undisciplined movements*—movements that challenge rigid conventions around race, gender, age, and embodiment. Sterling-Duprey uses dance, performance, and visual art not as separate disciplines but as interwoven strategies to articulate complex social, political, and aesthetic critiques.

The prolific and chronologically expansive nature of Awilda Sterling-Duprey's artistic career provides a foundation for focusing on works created within the temporal scope of this book (2013–23). However, I also include select pieces produced just prior to 2013, as they establish key conceptual and aesthetic pillars that continue to shape her later work. This chapter draws from a diverse selection of projects that exemplify Sterling-Duprey's interdisciplinary practice and her sustained engagement with movement and visualities, Blackness, gender, ageism, and decolonial aesthetics. These include *Reggaetón lento* (2010), *Toque de tambor para las diosas* (2011–12), and a series of projects centered on the legendary Afro–Puerto Rican singer Ismael Rivera ("Maelo"), such as *Maelo en el cuerpo* (2015), *De Maelo al hip-hop* (2015), and *Al son de Maelo* (2023). Other notable works include *Transparente desnudez/transparencia, no desnudez* (2015), *en-cierro* (2015–17), *Soy la reencarnación de un alma esclavizada* (2021), *Lacks Criticality* (2018–23), and *. . . blindfolded* (2019–23).

Through these works, I trace the intricate tapestry of Sterling-Duprey's artistic journey as a dancer, visual artist, and performer. Her movements—visual, kinetic, and conceptual—constitute an ongoing statement of presence. Despite the scarcity of academic writing on her, Sterling-Duprey—as indicated in the epigraph that opens this chapter—has always been here: doing, being, pausing, and reimagining the conditions of artistic expression through a decolonial and Black feminist lens.

Visual Emotions, Unpredictable Movements: The Performances of Awilda Sterling

In a September 2022 interview with Miguel Trelles, Awilda Sterling-Duprey affirmed that the place where she feels most free is onstage while performing (10:49–10:53).[3] For her, working with the body is "a way to stay alive" [con el cuerpo es una manera de seguir estando viva] (10:44–10:48). In another conversation, this time with performer and choreographer Merián Soto, Sterling-Duprey explained that her movements onstage allow her to externalize what lies within—her emotions, fears, pain, and inner experiences (7:11–9:55).[4] In the same interview, she reflected on the role of silence in her performances, describing it as a fundamental element that allows her body to fully inhabit presence: "When I am in stillness, I am in presence" (33:58–35:22). Silence, she suggests, facilitates a solitary state that contrasts the overwhelming noise of social life. In this state, a link is forged between silence and collective experience.

While silence is often seen as discomforting or commodified in the post-industrial era (Goddard, Halligan, and Hegarty 2012, 4), in Sterling-Duprey's work it becomes an invisible bridge—connecting her internal world with the affective responses of those who witness her performances (Trelles interview, 52:52–54:17). This connection enables a shared language of expression; a common sensory experience grounded in presence and vulnerability (Rancière 2011, 56).

Sterling-Duprey's sense of freedom onstage is mirrored in her academic, artistic, and personal trajectory. Born in 1947, she was raised primarily in Barrio Obrero, a working-class neighborhood in Santurce, San Juan, Puerto Rico. She earned her first bachelor's degree in humanities at the University of Puerto Rico, Río Piedras (1963–67), followed by a second degree in painting at the Escuela de Artes Plásticas de Puerto Rico (1968–71). Later, she pursued an MFA in Studio Art and Painting at the Pratt Institute in Brooklyn (1977–79). During her undergraduate years at UPR, she trained in Caribbean dance with poet and activist Sylvia del Villard Gilbert, who emphasized the recovery of African heritage in Puerto Rican dance. Reflecting on that formative period, Sterling-Duprey stated:

> Back then, in Puerto Rico, it was very difficult to acknowledge being of African descent. There is a fallacy that we came from three cultural components: Spanish—always first—Taíno second, and African, always the third and the last. Gilbert pioneered the first interdisciplinary African-

> based dance theater in Puerto Rico, connecting the island within a larger Afro-Caribbean context. Her presence is a constant essence in my life. (Estrada 2018)

Since then, Sterling-Duprey has continued her studies through workshops across the Caribbean, including Cuba, Trinidad, Barbados, St. Lucia, and St. Croix. In 1982, she became a founding member of Pisotón, Puerto Rico's first experimental dance collective. In 1985, she was awarded a National Endowment for the Arts Choreographers Fellowship. Her work has since been presented throughout Latin America, the United States, Europe, Puerto Rico, and the Caribbean.

She is the recipient of numerous prestigious awards and residencies, including the United States Artists Fellowship (2010), the Tree of Life Artist Grant (2019), Beta-Local's El Serrucho grant (2019), the Joan Mitchell Fellowship (2022), and residencies at the MASS MoCA (2023). Sterling-Duprey's career spans a wide range of mediums including painting, drawing, mixed media, installation, dance, and performance. Her practice integrates musical forms ranging from Afro–Puerto Rican folk music to salsa, jazz, urban sounds, reggaetón, and silence. Both music and silence function as essential elements—not only in her dance but also in her visual and performative works, as will be explored in the following sections.

Audible Gestures, Silent Archives: The Soundscapes of *Reggaetón lento* and Other Works Inspired by the Figure of Ismael "Maelo" Rivera

Sterling-Duprey's choreographic language is deeply intertwined with sound—its rhythms, disruptions, absences, and echoes. Her performances unfold within sonic landscapes shaped as much by silence as by music, drawing from Afro-Caribbean percussion, jazz improvisation, reggaetón, silence, and the environmental noise of everyday life. In these works, sound is never merely accompaniment; it is a generative force that moves through the body, shaping gesture and presence. At the same time, silence in her practice becomes an equally active material—one that creates space for interiority, vulnerability, and ancestral resonance. These performances—in this section and in the following ones—illustrate how Sterling-Duprey's work constructs affective, embodied soundscapes that challenge disciplinary boundaries and reimagine Afro–Puerto Rican aesthetic memory through audible gestures and silent archives.

REGGAETÓN LENTO

One compelling example of how Awilda Sterling-Duprey bridges dance and performance art to interrogate and deconstruct musical genres through a racial and gender lens—foregrounding urban soundscapes and silence—is her piece *Reggaetón lento* [Slow reggaetón] (2009–10).[5] Sterling-Duprey first performed this work at the University of Puerto Rico, Río Piedras, in 2009, during the closing event of *Parti-Dos* at the independent cultural space Nueva Sala Beckett PACA. The performance centered on her interpretive dance to "Loíza" by Afro–Puerto Rican rapper Tego Calderón (b. 1972), a track from his influential 2002 album *El abayarde,* which blends reggaetón with salsa influences inspired by Ismael Rivera and socially grounded lyrics.

In *Reggaetón lento,* Sterling-Duprey dances slowly—as the title implies—to Calderón's song. She deliberately reinterprets traditional reggaetón dance movements by performing them asynchronously with the music. This disjunction invites a reexamination of gestures often associated with hypersexualized representations of the body—especially the breasts, hips, and buttocks—when performed at reggaetón's typical tempo. By decelerating the movement, Sterling-Duprey shifts focus to the African diasporic origins of these gestures. Her body, inclined toward the earth, evokes ancestral communication, recalling grounding movements common in many African-derived dance traditions.

Throughout the performance, Sterling-Duprey stylizes her gestures, dances with her own shadow, and playfully emphasizes certain body parts—most notably her buttocks—eliciting laughter and excitement from the audience.[6] However, the performance undergoes a sudden shift: the music stops abruptly, yet she continues to dance. This moment of silence dramatically alters the audience's perception of her movements. The absence of music creates a soundscape in which listeners are prompted to move beyond passive hearing and become active, attentive witnesses. As Przybylski explains, "[T]he absence of music requires the hearer to become a listener—someone who attends not only to music but to the sounds of nature, the environment, and the artist's body" (2023, 237–38).

In this second half of the piece, the same movements are repeated but take on new meanings. Sterling-Duprey intermittently calls out "¡oye!" [listen!] as she slowly exits the stage. This auditory rupture—transitioning from musical accompaniment to ambient sound—compels the audience to imagine the rhythm of the dancer's body in the absence of music. That imagined rhythm becomes a shared, collective experience, forming what Connerton describes as a collective memory (1989). The deceleration of movement and the prominence of ambient sounds—such as the characteristic calls of Puerto Rican *coquís* and the slaps of the artist's hands against her own body—reveal background noises typically overshadowed by musical foreground.

As LaBelle asserts, background noise "does not merely go unnoticed; rather, it contains the very material through which the foreground gains meaning." He adds, "[T]he background embodies the weight and potential of surroundings . . . to make audible the very promise of noise to deliver the unknowable" (LaBelle 2015, xx). Sterling-Duprey's sonic intervention thus invites the audience to engage with other ways of listening that include marginal, silenced, or invisible sounds. In this sense, the absence of reggaetón in a piece titled *Reggaetón lento* becomes a symbolic provocation: a call to pause and attend to what is usually ignored—the sounds, bodies, and histories rendered inaudible or invisible by dominant structures (Przybylski 2023, 237).

The slow, unaccompanied movements of Sterling-Duprey's aging female body further underscore the visual dissonance between heteronormative expectations of reggaetón's hypersexualized performances and the lived realities of Black women's bodies. Her presence disrupts those expectations and critiques how the music industry objectifies Black femininity, marginalizes aging, and upholds rigid beauty and gender norms.

Sterling-Duprey's repeated call—"¡oye!" [listen!]—resonates on multiple levels. On one hand, it evokes a decolonial imperative to attend to the voices of the marginalized—the elderly, the racialized, the invisible—whose experiences are often excluded from mainstream discourse. Listening becomes a radical, collective political act: a decentering of dominant narratives. On the other hand, the exclamation echoes Tego Calderón's own lyrical refrain, establishing an intertextual and sonic dialogue between performer and musician.

As noted, the piece is set to Calderón's "Loíza," a song that foregrounds Black Puerto Rican identity by referencing the historically Afro-descendant town of Loíza. The song opens with the same exhortation—"¡oye!"—used by Sterling-Duprey during the silent portion of the performance. Calderón's lyrics express both love for Loíza and frustration at systemic neglect: "Ando sin prisa, pero tu lentitud me encoleriza / Y es que no bregan con Loíza" [I'm not in a rush, but your slowness infuriates me / They don't deal with Loíza]. He also critiques the racial ideology that denies structural inequality, noting how Blackness continues to be erased under the myth of racial harmony: "Me quieren hacer pensar que soy parte de una trilogía racial / Donde to' el mundo es igual, sin trato especial" [They want me to think I'm part of a racial trilogy / Where everyone is equal, with no special treatment].

Calderón addresses the legacies of slavery and contemporary anti-Black racism, particularly the mass incarceration of Afro-descendants: "Cambiaste las cadenas por esposas / Ah no, todos somos iguales en términos legales / Y eso está probado en los tribunales" [You exchanged chains for handcuffs / Oh no, we are not all equal under the law / And that has been proven in court]. He calls for Black pride and denounces those who internalize Eurocentric ideals: "Yo soy niche, orgulloso de mis raíces / De tener mucha bemba y de grandes narices" [I am Black, proud of my roots / Proud of my big lips and large nose].[7]

In the performance, the music cuts off immediately after Calderón proclaims: "Yo soy niche, orgulloso de mis raíces." Sterling-Duprey steps back, slaps her buttocks, and continues dancing in silence, rhythmically calling out "¡oye!" This moment marks a powerful shift, emphasizing the rhythm of the body as a communicative force. As Massumi notes, "Rhythm is the most perceptually salient dimension of language—it carries the force of the phrase, beyond its structure and meaning" (2012, 42). Sterling-Duprey's choreographic language persists beyond musical accompaniment, carried by rhythm itself and the body's resonance with ambient sound and silence. Her gestures communicate messages that transcend verbal language—urging listeners to attend to the silences that contain histories, traumas, and embodied knowledges excluded from dominant discourse.

Rhythm outside of the socially accepted parameters of sound, when music is absent, it is the fuel that makes her feel alive, that allows her to think about herself and her materiality in the space, while she keeps calling the masses' attention by asking them to listen (to themselves, to her, to the marginalized, to the unknowable—outside of hegemonic, capitalistic, and patriarchal social structures). The last words of the song that both the performer and the audience hear are "Yo soy niche, orgulloso de mis raíces." The artist translates that pride and historical pain into movement, while only the command to "listen!" interrupts the silence that she has created and the background noises of this *Reggaetón lento* to stress what can no longer be ignored.

By embracing reggaetón and slowing it down, Sterling-Duprey invites us to reflect on the histories of Black Puerto Rican communities and to reconsider the aesthetic and political implications of genre, race, and embodiment. By slowing down the frenetic dance, Sterling-Duprey shapes a rhythm that creates a "visual analogue of human language" (Massumi 2012, 42) through which she is extending an invitation to listen to one's body, to move slower to relate to the experiences of others, to take the time to think about and acknowledge racial injustices, not to be afraid of aging as society would like women to be, and to pay attention to a history that has been distorted and manipulated for centuries. Her choreography offers a critical dialogue with reggaetón—a genre that often objectifies Black female bodies—reclaiming it as a site of resistance. Thus, with this piece, while she establishes a connection with younger generations that mostly consume this music, she is using the stage to shed light on racial injustices and Puerto Rican Black institutionalized invisibility intertwined with sexism and ageism. She offers a critique of the oversexualization of the Black female body in the music industry and in pop culture for a heterosexual male-gaze consumption. In doing so, she forges intergenerational connections with younger audiences while also challenging the music industry's marginalization of Black artists and genres.

Silence, in this context, becomes a decolonial strategy—an opening for other sounds and other voices to emerge. The rhythmic presence of the *coquí,* the body's movement, and the call to "listen" become part of a sonic landscape that resists colonial, capitalist, and patriarchal frameworks. As Przybylski writes, *Reggaetón lento* produces a form of "sonic sovereignty" that fosters relationality and transformation:

> Listening builds the archive of the body: the listener can transform as she listens; she becomes a witness and changes through the witnessing. What she carries forward, then, is her experience and the experiences of others whose narratives fold together through musical storytelling. And through music listening . . . she changes with each iteration, over time, as her archive of bodily knowledge expands with each experience. (2023, 237)

Reggaetón lento creates a powerful oxymoron: a slow reggaetón. In doing so, it generates a space for rethinking embodiment, memory, race, and justice. Through the bodily archive of sound, silence, and movement, Sterling-Duprey invites us to slow down, to listen, and to remember.

MAELO EN EL CUERPO

As previously mentioned, in *Reggaetón lento,* Awilda Sterling-Duprey incorporated Tego Calderón's song *Loíza,* a track from an album infused with salsa elements inspired by the legendary Black Puerto Rican composer and singer Ismael "Maelo" Rivera (1931–1987). This indirect reference to Rivera later resurfaced more explicitly in Sterling-Duprey's work, particularly through her performance *Maelo en el cuerpo* (2015), her workshop *De Maelo al hip-hop* (2015), and her participation in the music festival *Al son de Maelo* (2023), dedicated to the artist's legacy. Tego Calderón's invocation of Maelo catalyzed

Sterling-Duprey's desire to further explore Rivera's influence—this time through her own body. Thus, in 2015, *Maelo en el cuerpo* was conceived.

Ismael Rivera, affectionately known as Maelo, was a prolific salsa artist who hailed from the neighborhood of Santurce—formerly known as San Mateo de Cangrejos—in San Juan, Puerto Rico. This is the same community where Awilda Sterling-Duprey was raised and where she currently resides. Established in the late nineteenth century, San Mateo de Cangrejos was historically a peripheral zone of the capital, inhabited primarily by Black Puerto Ricans and, occasionally, by upper-class families during the summer. As Edwin Quiles Rodríguez explains in *San Juan tras la fachada,* the convergence of these two social groups in a marginalized area, once a refuge for escaped enslaved, allowed San Mateo de Cangrejos to "negotiate existential spaces of resistance and survival" (2003, 108–9). According to Quiles Rodríguez, Santurce developed largely independent of governmental intervention, emerging as a site marked by architectural, infrastructural, and demographic diversity—a "porous" and hybrid space of identity (121).

From the 1970s through the 1990s, Santurce became institutionally stigmatized as a dangerous area, where the *cimarrones* that historically populated the neighborhood became undocumented immigrants, sex workers, or drug traffickers. Yet despite such criminalizing discourses, the neighborhood has remained a stronghold of cultural and social diversity, continually shaped by working-class Afro-Caribbean communities. If Cangrejos was historically a refuge for runaways and outcasts, it was also a site of rebellion and cultural resilience. Today, Santurce preserves this spirit through what could be termed an *artistic cimarronaje,* with Awilda Sterling-Duprey's work on Maelo serving as a compelling example.

Rivera himself was Black, working-class, and from Santurce. He began his career as a carpenter and was later incarcerated for drug possession. *Maelo en el cuerpo* reflects on these biographical elements through embodied performance, connecting Sterling-Duprey's body to the architecture of the neighborhood—particularly Rivera's childhood home—its urban fabric, and its community. By inhabiting and moving through the space, she renders visible an affective history of Santurce through her corporeal memory, allowing Maelo's legacy to resonate anew.

The performance featured collaborations with other artists and cultural practitioners, including Teresa Hernández and Windy Cosme, and involved Rivera's family, the Fundación Ismael Rivera, sculptor Melquiades Rosario

Sastre, architect Carlos Castrillo, and the Ballets de San Juan. Supported by the Museo de Arte Contemporáneo de Puerto Rico (MACPR), the project wove together multiple artistic disciplines. As Afro–Puerto Rican painter Edwin Velázquez Collazo observed in *Puerto Rico Art News*, Sterling-Duprey's gestures and rhythmic movements, set against a soundscape of Rivera's music and compositions by artists like Miguel Zenón and DJ Velcro, created a "sea of gestures" infused with construction tools—cement sacks, a shovel, soil, cinder blocks, and a cement mixer. These tools evoked Rivera's early years as a construction worker and revealed a more intimate, vulnerable side of the artist: "the man who cried and suffered for love, the one of lament, of sobbing, of the Nazarene's wail." Sterling-Duprey's movement, laughter, and gaze, suffused with the grace of contemporary dance, brought Maelo back to his neighborhood and allowed the audience to witness a "magical reunion" made possible only through the power of art and the presence of a great artist (Velázquez Collazo 2015).

At one moment in the performance, Sterling-Duprey applies imaginary cement to her body using a mason's trowel, a poetic gesture that suggests both the limitations imposed on Maelo—by labor, race, or geography—and his capacity to shape material and meaning alike. The performance foregrounds Rivera's humble beginnings while also honoring the labor, art, and social history embedded in the physical and symbolic architecture of Santurce. In this way, *Maelo en el cuerpo* invites spectators to reimagine the figure of Rivera, the *barrio*, and their intertwined histories through embodied narrative. Ultimately, the performance becomes a meditation on Black resilience, joy, and community. It suggests that Rivera's story is not singular—any "Maelo" could overcome barriers of race and class through cultural expression and collective memory.

Importantly, Sterling-Duprey does all this through her Black, female Caribbean body. In embodying a popular male icon, she reclaims and reconfigures the cultural legacy of Maelo through a feminist, decolonial lens. In the Afro-Caribbean—and evidently Puerto Rican—context, Black women often occupy a contradictory position within the social fabric: central as caregivers and moral anchors, yet marginalized and erased in public discourse and official historiography, often reduced to stereotypes of hypersexuality, strength without vulnerability, or invisibility altogether. Their emotional and reproductive labor is essential to community survival under the strains of colonialism, racism, and poverty, but is seldom recognized as political or creative work.

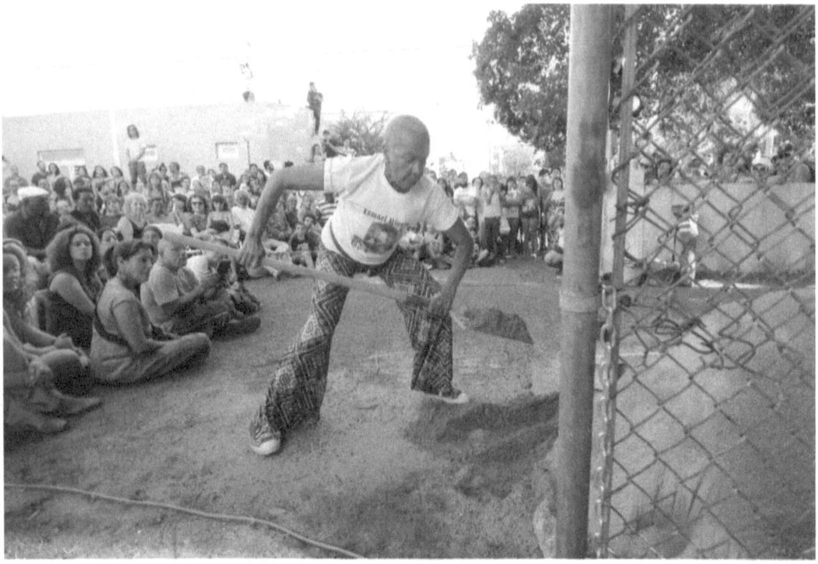

FIGURE 4.1. Awilda Sterling-Duprey holding a shovel in front of a crowd during the performance *Maelo en el cuerpo*. Awilda Sterling-Duprey, *Maelo en el cuerpo*, 2015. Project commissioned by the Museum of Contemporary Art of Puerto Rico as part of its program MAC en el Barrio. Photo credit: Ricardo Alcaraz. Courtesy of Awilda Sterling-Duprey and Ricardo Alcaraz.

Ismael Rivera has long represented *el pueblo*, the people: a figure of patriarchal tenderness, resistance, and masculinity. His music is imbued with longing, devotion, and a deep identification with community. But, while women are often present in his music as muses or caregivers, they are rarely positioned as authors or archivists of culture. Sterling-Duprey's performance unsettles this logic. Rather than mimic Rivera, she *translates* him—activating her own mature, Black, female body as a living archive of sounds, gestures, and memory. This act shifts the axis of representation: she makes visible the often-erased presence of Black women as interpreters and carriers of culture, while also asserting the body itself as a site of resistance and reimagination, repositioning women not only as preservers but also as producers of cultural memory. Her translation of Rivera is therefore deeply political. It dismantles masculinist assumptions about artistic genius and affirms the central role of Black women in shaping the Puerto Rican imaginary. Through this act, she disrupts both familial and national narratives that depend on patriarchal genealogies, asserting that Black women are foundational not just to kinship structures but to the archive, the stage, and the future of Puerto Rican identity itself.

In a 2018 public conversation with Yanila R. Rivera, later published in *Habitar lo imposible* (edited by Susan Homar and nibia pastrana santiago), Sterling Duprey reflected on this dynamic by emphasizing the role of contemporary art: it "taught me to defy" ("me enseñó a desafiar"; 303).[8] Indeed, *Maelo en el cuerpo* brings to the surface structural issues often rendered invisible—then and now—including patriarchy, racism, and classism. Through a language of gesture and spatial memory, the piece challenges the dominant ideologies that sustain discrimination, ageism, and sexism. Sterling-Duprey's body becomes not only a vessel of memory but a mode of resistance, reminding us that performance can be both archive and act of insurgency.

DE MAELO AL HIP-HOP

The pedagogical potential of *Maelo en el cuerpo* led to the development of a related community project: the workshop *De Maelo al hip-hop* (2015), created in collaboration with Afro–Puerto Rican DJ and rapper Velcro. Designed for residents of Santurce, the workshop aimed to inspire participants—particularly younger generations—to articulate their emotions and perceptions of reality through music and movement. Drawing on the figure of Ismael "Maelo" Rivera and the socially conscious themes in his music, the workshop invited participants to write their own lyrics under Velcro's guidance, using hip-hop as a contemporary vehicle for self-expression.

The second phase of the workshop, led by Awilda Sterling-Duprey, focused on transforming the participants' original compositions into embodied performances. Through movement-based exercises, Sterling-Duprey guided attendees in developing choreographies that reflected the emotional and narrative content of their songs. Supported by the Instituto de Cultura Puertorriqueña, the workshop was offered free of charge and culminated in a public performance held in front of Rivera's childhood home in Santurce.

This project exemplifies the powerful intersection of music, memory, and embodiment. By engaging both the emotional and physical body, the workshop allowed participants—and, by extension, their families and broader community—to experience the transformative potential of art. The performative process not only honored a local cultural icon but also activated a collective memory rooted in place and experience. In doing so, *De Maelo al hip-hop* created a space where participants could reconnect with their neighborhood's history while also envisioning its future. Through artistic practice, the workshop affirmed the centrality of community and positioned its members as active protagonists in shaping a more hopeful and self-defined Santurce.

AL SON DE MAELO

Between 2018 and 2023, Awilda Sterling-Duprey revisited the figure of Ismael Rivera, reactivating her performance *Maelo en el cuerpo* during the fourth edition of the music festival *Al son de Maelo* (To the rhythm of Maelo), sponsored by the Instituto de Cultura Puertorriqueña, the Museo de Arte Contemporáneo (MAC), and the Fundación Ismael Rivera. While Rivera's cultural legacy in Puerto Rico is indisputable, Sterling-Duprey's embodied interpretation of his persona—staged across three distinct performances—offers a unique lens through which to engage his memory.[9] Through movement situated in specific, often historically charged spaces, her performance renders memory not as a fixed narrative but as a sensorial, affective force capable of linking individual experiences to collective histories.

Sterling-Duprey's work makes visible what she describes as an *ancestral memory*—a form of embodied knowledge that responds to the music of an Afro–Puerto Rican icon while simultaneously recovering shared memories, particularly for Black Puerto Ricans. Her performances cultivate a dialogic relationship with the audience, where meaning emerges not from direct representation but from the viewers' own interpretive frameworks—their personal histories, affective responses, and social positioning. In this way, her choreographic interventions reconfigure structures of memory and propose alternative forms of communal knowledge.

Staged in Rivera's neighborhood—one historically neglected by state institutions and increasingly threatened by gentrification—*Maelo en el cuerpo* acquires a powerful spatial and political dimension. Sterling-Duprey's work, both conceptually and architecturally grounded in place, unleashes what can be described as a decolonial aesthetic: one that challenges dominant historical narratives and offers alternative imaginaries rooted in Black Puerto Rican life. Her performance not only critiques the colonial entanglements between Puerto Rico and the United States but also centers Afro-Caribbean subjectivity, reimagined through a gendered and feminist lens.

Rather than framing Puerto Rico solely as an object of colonial controversy, Sterling-Duprey's work asserts Puerto Rican subjectivity as generative and transformative. In doing so, this piece highlights "how imperial methods sustain nations and dismantle bodies [. . .] while simultaneously revealing how practices of the Empire surpass the annexation of land" (Ruiz 2019, 1–2). Through her choreography, Sterling-Duprey redirects attention toward the endurance and resistance of the Afro–Puerto Rican body, which becomes a site for registering pain, violence, marginalization, and resilience and for shifting the political contours of existence (Ruiz 2019, 3). Her performances operate through silence, rupture, noise, and the unpredictable movement of a Black female body, disturbing conventional narrative structures and resisting capitalist demands for coherence and productivity (11).

In *Maelo en el cuerpo*, salsa functions not merely as a musical genre but as a sonic archive of Afro-Caribbean memory, resistance, and embodied history. Specifically, the sonority of Maelo's salsa becomes a terrain where political histories and cultural identities converge with bodily expression. Sterling-Duprey transforms these sounds into choreographic language, allowing her body to listen, translate, and resignify the affective power embedded in Maelo's vocal textures—his phrasing, breath, and timbre. As Juan Carlos Quintero Herencia asserts in *La máquina de la salsa*, salsa is a machine for the production of meaning, capable of generating potent social imaginaries rooted in working-class *barrios*, racialized geographies, and collective memories. Sterling-Duprey's choreography materializes this capacity through an intimate corporeal engagement with Maelo's recordings, inviting the audience to perceive salsa's temporal, diasporic, and emotional layers as embodied knowledge—simultaneously mourning and celebrating, grieving and surviving.

Licia Fiol-Matta's *The Great Woman Singer* provides a critical framework for understanding the gendered stakes of this work. Although her study focuses on female vocalists in Latin American music, Fiol-Matta emphasizes that voice operates as a site of racial and gender formation. Sterling-Duprey's performance builds on this insight by queering the traditionally masculine figure of Maelo. Channeling his voice through her Afro-Caribbean, feminine, and queer body, she performs a radical act of revoicing that unsettles patriarchal and heteronormative narratives often associated with iconic male salsa artists. In doing so, she expands the affective and political horizons through which Maelo can be heard and felt.

In this sense, *Maelo en el cuerpo* offers a powerful instance of decolonial memory work. Salsa, here, is not deployed as nostalgia but as a living archive—a site where unresolved legacies of colonialism, displacement, and racial exclusion are choreographically activated. Sterling-Duprey's performance turns the sonic residue of salsa into a terrain for testimony, where bodies move not only in rhythm but in resistance. Her aesthetic strategies allow for an embodied reckoning with the historical and political weight of the Black Puerto Rican body, proposing alternative modes of being, remembering, and imagining from a feminist, decolonial, and Afro-Caribbean perspective.

The Recuperation of the Black Puerto Rican and Caribbean Culture: *Toque de tambor para las diosas* and *Soy la reencarnación de un alma esclavizada*

Blackness and the reclamation of Afro–Puerto Rican and Afro-Caribbean cultural memory are central pillars in the artistic practice of Awilda Sterling-Duprey. Her performances *Toque de tambor para las diosas* [Drumbeat to the goddesses] (2011–12) and the video performance *Soy la reencarnación de un alma esclavizada* [I am the reincarnation of an enslaved soul] (2021) exemplify this commitment. These works stand out for foregrounding a racialized Caribbean perspective that is often marginalized or erased in dominant historical and cultural narratives. At the same time, they refine this perspective through a distinctly feminist and spiritual lens.

In both performances, Sterling-Duprey engages in a dual process: she revives silenced histories by reclaiming gestures, movements, and embodied traditions, and rearticulates them through a contemporary performative language. Crucially, this process is mediated through her own Black, female, Caribbean body, which becomes both a conduit and a witness to these ancestral memories. By doing so, Sterling-Duprey not only recuperates suppressed narratives but also reimagines them through the lived experience and epistemological standpoint of a Black Caribbean woman. Her work challenges colonial and patriarchal frameworks, offering instead a decolonial aesthetic rooted in embodied knowledge, spiritual resilience, and cultural continuity.

TOQUE DE TAMBOR PARA LAS DIOSAS

Toque de tambor para las diosas [Drumbeat to the goddesses] was conceived as a hybrid artist talk and performance by Awilda Sterling-Duprey, first presented at Casa de América in Madrid, Spain, in 2011.[10] The performance opened with Sterling-Duprey dancing with a machete in hand, accompanied by live drumming by Afro-Cuban musician Jesús Catalá.[11] Following the initial performance, Sterling-Duprey explained that the work aimed to foreground the histories of enslaved Yoruba people who were forcibly brought to Cuba, contributing significantly to the island's cultural and spiritual fabric. Her performance sought to recover and honor these erased histories by emphasizing the diversity among enslaved Africans—diversity embodied in their distinct physicality, customs, musical traditions, foodways, and languages.

Central to the piece is the influence of *la Regla de Ocha,* or Santería, an Afro-Cuban religious tradition in which Sterling-Duprey is initiated.[12] During the talk, she described Santería not only as a religion but also as a philosophy of survival—an epistemology grounded in ancestral memory. Through Santería, enslaved communities developed mechanisms of cultural cohesion that transcended tribal and linguistic differences. The artist then elaborated on the deity she embodied in the performance: Oyá, a powerful orisha associated with transformation, war, and the whirlwind.

Sterling-Duprey noted that orishas are understood in Santería as energies with masculine or feminine attributes but without fixed gender identities. Oyá, while recognized as a feminine force, exhibits traits often coded as masculine—physical strength, leadership, determination—and is the deity who incites her consort, Changó, to battle. Sterling-Duprey interpreted Oyá's force as a symbol of necessary upheaval and change—a metaphor for social transformation through unity in difference. She explicitly linked this call for change to the condition of Puerto Rico, inviting her Spanish audience to consider her performance as a gesture of hope for a more sovereign and unified Puerto Rican future. The performance's emphasis on movement mirrored Oyá's own whirlwind energy, embodying both constant flux and the potential for renewal. Through subsequent performative segments, Sterling-Duprey staged a call for solidarity among Afro-descendant Caribbean communities, highlighting embodied knowledge as a site for diasporic memory and resistance.

While *Toque de tambor para las diosas* draws from Yoruba spiritual cosmologies, it also offers a critical meditation on gender. Sterling-Duprey centers Oyá's feminine force to challenge the male-dominated hierarchies often present in Afro-Caribbean religions. Her interpretation reclaims the centrality of women within these traditions and affirms that spiritual knowledge is dynamic and evolving. She explicitly frames her performance as a reinterpretation of ancestral stories, aligned with the intellectual and spiritual development of contemporary practitioners. In this way, the piece queers the Yoruba tradition by reimagining it through the lens of a Black Caribbean woman's body, creating space for new forms of understanding and belonging.

The performance also acquires layered significance through its geographic and historical context. Staged in Spain—the former imperial center of both Puerto Rico and Cuba—Sterling-Duprey's presence in that space is charged with symbolic weight. Throughout the talk, she referenced Puerto Rico's colonial status under US control since 1898, pointing to the ongoing political subjugation of the island. By performing in Spain, the original colonizer, Sterling-Duprey creates a complex site of embodied memory and critique. Her body, channeling an Afro-Caribbean deity, confronts a colonial legacy on its own historical terrain. Thus, *Toque de tambor para las diosas* becomes more than a performance of religious or folkloric tradition—it becomes a decolonial intervention that reframes official histories and affirms queer, Black, feminist presence in cultural institutions traditionally shaped by empire.

By inserting Afro-Caribbean ritual performance into the institutional space of Casa de América in Spain, Sterling-Duprey disrupts dominant narratives and reclaims intellectual and cultural authority. What is often dismissed as "folklore"—and what was erased under Spanish colonial rule in order to impose Catholicism—is instead recontextualized as critical knowledge, articulated by an Afro–Puerto Rican woman within the symbolic center of colonial power. In this way, *Toque de tambor para las diosas* functions as both a performance and a political statement: an embodied archive, a spiritual invocation, and a radical act of cultural and historical reclamation.

SOY LA REENCARNACIÓN DE UN ALMA ESCLAVIZADA

The second performance that engages with the racial history of Puerto Rico from a feminine and embodied perspective is the video performance *Soy la reencarnación de un alma esclavizada* [I am the reincarnation of an enslaved soul] (2021). This 4-minute piece was commissioned by Slavicult (Slavery and Visual Culture) for the digital curatorial project *Visualizing/Performing Blackness in the Afterlives of Slavery: An Archive* at the University of Chicago. The video opens with a dedication to the memory of Ángela María Dávila—Afro–Puerto Rican poet, visual artist, and Afro-feminist—who considered her Black Puerto Ricanness to be central to both her identity and creative practice. Dávila passed away in 2003 at the age of fifty-nine due to complications related to Alzheimer's disease.

The performance, as clarified in the final credits, is a "texto visual basado en el poema *Déjenme sola* de Ángela María Dávila" [visual text based on the poem *Leave Me Alone* by Ángela María Dávila] (3:19).[13] Since the poem serves as the foundation for the video performance, I begin by analyzing the literary text before addressing the visual components.[14]

Déjenme sola is a poetic plea for solitude amid suffering, in which the speaker demands to be left alone with her bodily and emotional pain.

The speaker demands solitude in the most intimate domestic spaces—such as the bathroom or bedroom—and during mundane tasks like cooking. She describes herself as infected, wounded, and hallucinatory, evoking the image of a sick, abject body. The juxtaposition of this decaying body with nourishing acts like preparing traditional Puerto Rican meals becomes a potent metaphor for a decaying national body. This tension poetically constructs a counternarrative to hegemonic imaginaries of the nation—portraying it as exclusionary and sick, especially toward subjects marked by Blackness, queerness, and poverty.

In later stanzas, Dávila writes:

> Dejen que llore cuan-do-me-dé-la-gana
> mientras friego o desconjelo el fríser, [. . .]
> probando las habichuelas
> [Let me cry when-I-feel-like-it
> while I scrub or defrost the freezer, [. . .]
> tasting the beans]

The poem then moves from domestic interiors to the streets, culminating in the powerful declaration "voy a cojer el monte" (I'm going to the mountain). This phrase references the historical figure of the *cimarrón*, the enslaved person who fled captivity to seek freedom in the mountains. She pictures herself among excrement, hallucinating, and full of wounds. This is the portrayal of a sick body. The cohabitation in the same verses of a sick body and nourishing actions, such as performing domestic tasks and cooking Puerto Rican food, can be read as a metaphor of a decaying national body. As a result, these verses become an attempt to poetically build a counternarrative to the hegemonic body of the nation and so portray it as a sick body that excludes and marginalizes the Black, the poor, the queer, and so on. At the end of the stanza, the poet is ready to "coger el monte." While the image of a woman wandering the streets might evoke homelessness or madness, the closing lines signal defiance and agency. Dávila invokes the memory of Black resistance as a mode of reappropriating erased histories and reclaiming space.

Yet the abjection[15] continues in the desire to disrupt beauty: the speaker wishes to destroy what is typically considered delicate or pure—flowers, butterflies, cocoons. Dávila offers an alternative aesthetic in which abjection and beauty coexist. Her gestures of spitting, snapping, vomiting, and frightening blur the boundaries of what is considered acceptable, proposing instead a poetics of refusal grounded in bodily excess and disruption.

The final verses intensify this rejection when the speaker's final plea is not only for solitude but for complete abandonment. This is a radical disavowal of the social, of community, and of the norms that define acceptable existence. In doing so, Dávila queers the very concept of existence by rejecting the value systems of a society that erases Blackness, poverty, and mental illness. Thus,

Dávila proposes another reality where the possibility of existence is committed to another value system that comes from the reality of those subjects that normally would be marginalized and labeled as abject in society, where her being lost, failing, and decaying is a praxis of antinormativity (Halberstam 2011) and disobedience (Halberstam and Nyong'o 2018). Her poetic voice enacts what Halberstam calls "the queer art of failure"—a refusal of normative success, visibility, and productivity (2011, 88). Dávila's urge to be left alone is a way to highlight her abject identity and is somehow a way of stressing her nonexistence within the context of her society. Consequently, Dávila's "failure" is an act of disobedience and a refusal of legibility within colonial and capitalist frameworks.

Moreover, by embracing abjection, Dávila queers both beauty and ontology, resonating with José Esteban Muñoz's concept of queerness as a mode of being "not-yet-here" (2009). Her final lines—"LET ME FALL APART—it will pass"—normalize the abject, suggesting that even collapse can be temporary, even necessary, in the reimagining of life. Through the lens of Halberstam and Muñoz, Dávila connects queer failure with utopian futurity, where disappointment and disobedience open paths toward imagining another world—antiracist, anticolonial, and anticapitalist.

The video performance *Soy la reencarnación de un alma esclavizada,* directed by Awilda Sterling-Duprey, visualizes this poetic vision. The cast includes local artists Paulina Pagán Picó, Aurelio Lima Dávila, Coqueta Daniel Sevilla Lebrón, and Awilda Rodríguez Lora. The performance opens with Sterling-Duprey, dressed in white, walking with a bamboo cane toward what appears to be an abandoned structure. There, she finds a book: *Incidents in the Life of a Slave Girl: An Authentic Historical Narrative Describing the Horrors of Slavery as Experienced by Black Women* by Linda Brent (the pseudonym of Harriet Jacobs), a formerly enslaved woman in the American South in the nineteenth century. Sterling-Duprey clutches the book to her chest and gazes out, her expression one of surprise and recognition.

This moment of embrace suggests a deep identification with the ancestral memory of Black womanhood and its historical erasures. In the next sequence, Sterling-Duprey looks directly at the camera as the image shifts to a fast-moving visual of trees, evoking speed and disorientation. This is followed by her arrival at a space populated by other performers. A disembodied masculine voice begins to recite Dávila's poem.

The visual interruptions—the silence, the jarring movement, and the interspersed imagery of historical texts—mirror the discontinuities in the histories of the enslaved, especially Black women. Additionally, these scenes may evoke Dávila's experience with Alzheimer's disease, metaphorically representing fragmented memory and the dissonance of cognitive decline. Her illness adds another layer of abjection and exclusion, reinforcing the urgency of finding a space for existence on one's own terms.

The artists' physical movements further embody the poem's themes. They move through liminal and uncomfortable spaces—lying in dust, caressing cracked walls, walking along narrow cornices—engaging in actions that resist utility or productivity. Like Dávila's poem, their gestures are deliberately nonnormative and unproductive within capitalist logics. Their embodied disobedience reiterates the text's queerness and the refusal to conform to colonial expectations of order and visibility.

The scenes set in the patio alternate between brief shots of Awilda Sterling-Duprey as she appeared in the opening sequence—gazing out at the landscape while holding a book—and images of rustling trees accompanied by a loud, ambient sound. These visuals are interspersed with rapid glimpses of an urban setting, such as a congested highway. Through this visual composition, Sterling-Duprey's capacity to bridge tradition, oral history, and the contemporary moment through her embodied performance is made strikingly evident. The transition from the mountain—a historically symbolic site of resistance for enslaved peoples—to a modern highway alludes to Puerto Rico's ongoing infrastructural crises, including insufficient urban planning, decaying transportation networks, and a lack of road maintenance. These systemic failures disproportionately impact the island's most marginalized communities, particularly those that are predominantly Black.

This performance visually translates the discomfort articulated in Ángela María Dávila's poem *Déjenme sola* [Leave me alone] by employing disjointed editing, fragmented imagery, and close-ups of body parts that resist a cohesive or comforting visual narrative. The sonic landscape alternates between abrupt, jarring noises and stark silences, further disrupting the viewer's sense of coherence. Sound and silence thus play a crucial role in shaping the affective experience of the piece. The performance closes with a question posed directly to the viewer: "¿Cuánta tensión cabe en un minuto de silencio?" [How much tension can be held in a minute of silence?] Here, silence operates as both an aesthetic and political strategy. It becomes a space of reflection that aligns with the poem's abject sensibility, inviting the viewer to enter into a place of tension and, within that space, to think, feel, and interpret from their own embodied position. As Rancière argues, this moment of engagement allows for a redistribution of the sensible, opening up a shared space where the viewer becomes a coparticipant in meaning-making (2011).

In this way, the performance *Soy la reencarnación de un alma esclavizada* and Dávila's poem *Déjenme sola* offer an alternative vision of reality—one that embraces abjection and reclaims marginality as a site of critical agency. The desire to wander aimlessly in the performance, or to be left alone in the poem, can be read as modes of resisting normative structures of recognition. These gestures foreground abject identities and simultaneously call attention to the historical, structural, and institutional erasure of Black people, especially Black women, in Puerto Rican society. The themes articulated by Dávila—a Black Puerto Rican woman—are translated visually and viscerally through Sterling-Duprey's own Black female body. In doing so, the artist not only recovers a suppressed history but does so from the doubly marginalized perspective of Black Puerto Rican women. This layered performative act engages what might be called metafeminine narratives, weaving together the voices and bodies of multiple Black women—Dávila, Harriet Jacobs (author of *Incidents in the Life of a Slave Girl*), and Sterling-Duprey herself—into a collective archive of resistance and remembrance.

The Centrality of the Black Puerto Rican Female Body in *Transparente desnudez, en-cierro, Lacks Criticality,* and . . . *blindfolded*

The centrality of the Black Puerto Rican female body—and its role in articulating and visually translating a Black anticolonial history from a distinctly feminine perspective—continues to evolve in the next group of performances under analysis: *Transparente desnudez* [What you see is what you get] (2015), *en-cierro* (2015–17), *Lacks Criticality* (2018–23), and . . . *blindfolded* (2019–23). While the performances discussed thus far already foreground themes such as Blackness, the visibility and agency of the Black female body, the community, and the historical legacies of Caribbean Blackness, these later works deepen and expand that exploration.

Together, these pieces form a conceptual and aesthetic continuum within Awilda Sterling-Duprey's broader body of work. They introduce new gestures, formal strategies, and symbolic elements, which are further developed across performances in a cumulative, iterative process. As is often the case in Sterling-Duprey's practice, these performances are shaped in real time by events unfolding in her personal life, in her community, and within the broader sociopolitical landscape of Puerto Rico. In all of these works, Sterling-Duprey's body functions as a conduit—a living archive—through which stories are told, refracted through the intersectional lenses of Blackness and womanhood. Her performances become embodied acts of testimony that insist on the presence, resilience, and complexity of Black Puerto Rican women, challenging both colonial erasures and dominant narratives of artistic production in the Caribbean.

TRANSPARENTE DESNUDEZ

Transparente desnudez [What you see is what you get] (2015) is a collaborative performance between Awilda Sterling-Duprey and Puerto Rican voice performance artist Ivette Román.[16] The work unfolds in three visually distinct moments over the course of a 19-minute video. In the first segment (approximately the first 10 minutes), Sterling-Duprey moves through the performance space with her body tightly wrapped in layers of plastic wrap, evoking themes of containment, vulnerability, and visibility. In the second segment (9:54–14:34), Román enters the space and assists in unwrapping Sterling-Duprey, revealing her nude body and introducing an intimate gesture of care, release, and transformation.

The final section of the performance reflects Sterling-Duprey's background as a visual artist. Here, she plays with stark contrasts of light and shadow, as well as with the interplay of predominantly black-and-white tones. Her movements generate dynamic patterns on the walls, where thick black lines intersect with white surfaces. She also interacts with her own shadow, which is projected onto a large white wall, emphasizing the visual and symbolic tension between presence and absence, materiality and trace. Sound and silence play a crucial role throughout the performance. Their alternation intensifies the affective and sensory experience of the piece, shaping the audience's perception of time, vulnerability, and embodiment.

Transparente desnudez begins with a striking image: the artist, nude but encased in plastic wrap, situates herself beneath a glass table filled with glass bottles. This evocative tableau sets the tone for the performance's broader exploration of fragility, opacity, exposure, and the politics of representation. The reflection of light through the glass bottles and the glass tabletop casts shimmering patterns across the surface of Awilda Sterling-Duprey's plastic-wrapped body. She begins by rolling side to side beneath the table, slowly lifting one arm, then the other, shifting into a doglike position, stretching her legs, and continuing to move in restrained, deliberate gestures. Although these movements are simple, the plastic wrap restricts her mobility, making each action visibly

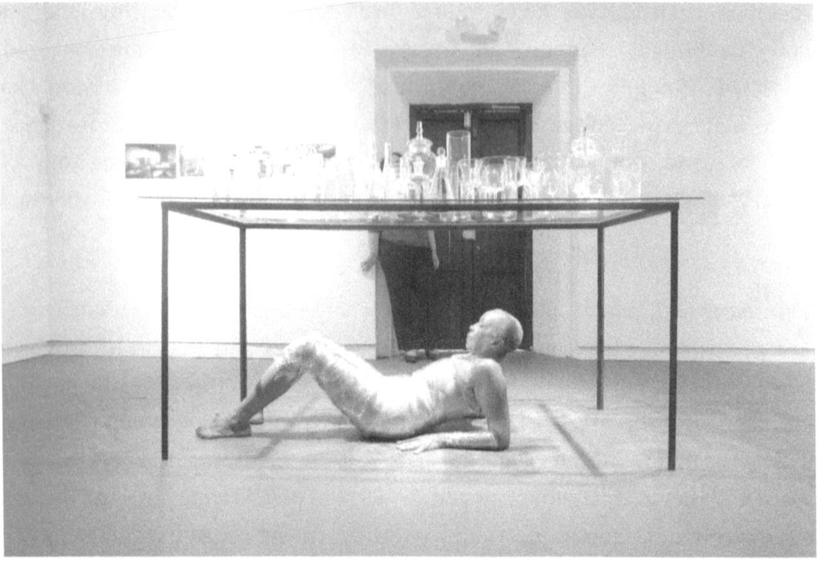

FIGURE 4.2. Awilda Sterling-Duprey, *Transparente desnudez*, 2014. Performance presented during the exhibition *Cosas: Notes on the Three-Dimensional Object in Contemporary Puerto Rican Art*, Arsenal de la Marina, Instituto de Cultura Puertorriqueña, San Juan, June 2014. In the image, the artist performs in front of works by Néstor Otero. Photograph: Abdiel D. Segarra Ríos. Courtesy of Abdiel D. Segarra Ríos.

more difficult and producing a persistent, rustling plastic sound that defines the first 10 minutes of the performance. During this time, Sterling-Duprey moves from one position to another—rolling, crawling, walking, and dragging herself across the floor—while Ivette Román, her collaborator, alternates between long silences and guttural, unintelligible vocalizations. These vocal emissions, paired with a prerecorded sound of dripping water, create an uncanny acoustic landscape. This initial sequence ends when Román uses a pair of scissors to cut away the wrap, slowly freeing Sterling-Duprey's body.

To better understand the conceptual and symbolic elements of this opening section, it is useful to return to the title of the performance: *Transparente desnudez*. The artist presents her body not merely as exposed but as *transparent*—a surface inscribed with untold histories, rendered visible through the very act of performance. The layering of translucent elements—the glass bottles, the glass tabletop, and the plastic wrap—produces a superimposition of reflective surfaces that evoke what Dolores Aponte-Ramos describes as "a kind of phantasmagoria charged with symbolic superpositions." For her, the work operates as an autobiographical gesture marked by "mystical accents fused with a naturalism of the everyday." According to Aponte-Ramos, *Transparente desnudez* creates a kind of verbal clarity that unfolds alongside the physical gestures leading Sterling-Duprey's body toward nudity. These parallel transparencies—the verbal and the corporeal—form an ambient condition through which the audience experiences the piece. In doing so, transparency challenges entrenched perceptions of gender, race, and embodiment. There is no evasion: the Black body emerges as an unavoidable and undeniable reality (2017, 54). The symbolic act of wrapping her body in plastic wrap, the refracted light through glass, and the eerie soundscape create a palimpsest of meanings: they reflect on the commodification and objectification of women's bodies, the hypersexualization of Black women, and the historical legacy of slavery, during which Black bodies were treated as property. Her nudity under the plastic references the specific and often sexualized violence inflicted upon enslaved Black women. Simultaneously, the constrained movements allude to the historical and contemporary limitations imposed on Black bodies, as well as the systemic constraints of heteronormative, patriarchal, and racialized social structures.

One particularly striking moment occurs when Sterling-Duprey sits beside a coffee table, positioning her legs beneath it while her chest remains behind it. Only her head is visible above the tabletop. This visual fragmentation creates the illusion that her body has been dismembered—plastic-wrapped limbs disjoined from her torso. She begins to breathe heavily, her open mouth fogging the glass surface. She pauses, then repeats the action several times. This gesture of sectioning the body while simultaneously clouding the glass metaphorically speaks to the historical fragmentation and commodification of the Black female body. Yet, her breath—life's most essential function—also serves as a reminder of her humanity. Through breath, she generates both transparency and opacity, illustrating the power of presence and the vulnerability of storytelling. This duality suggests that transparency is never absolute; the decision to reveal or conceal parts of one's history is an act of agency. It is precisely this tension between visibility and opacity that makes certain stories persist untold.

In the second part of the performance, Román carefully cuts away the plastic wrap with scissors, slowly liberating Sterling-Duprey's body, now fully nude before the audience. This act of unwrapping takes approximately 4 minutes and is accompanied by the artist's spoken narration of key moments from her personal and artistic life. Delivered without a microphone, her voice is barely audible, compelling the audience to lean in and listen with heightened attention. She recounts pivotal ages—twenty-five, thirty, thirty-five, and so on—

interweaving life experiences with milestones in her artistic career: becoming a mother, founding *Pisotón*—the first experimental dance collective in Puerto Rico, returning to the Escuela de Artes Plásticas at forty-five, and reengaging with experimental art in New York at sixty. She concludes with the declaration that, at sixty-seven, her age at the moment of the performance, she is bringing this chapter of her work to a close.

This act of sharing personal history while physically shedding the plastic carries profound symbolic weight. The difficulty of hearing her speech—arguably a deliberate choice—functions as a commentary on how women's voices are often overlooked or ignored, particularly when articulating the labor of motherhood. By recounting her life as a mother and artist simultaneously, Sterling-Duprey challenges romanticized notions of maternal instinct and the societal assumption that motherhood is "natural" and thus effortless. This cultural perception renders maternal labor socially invisible and devalues the emotional, physical, and intellectual toll it exacts—especially for Black women, and even more so for Black single mothers.

By requiring the audience to exert effort to hear her, Sterling-Duprey reclaims the attention that is so often denied to women's stories. The inclusion of her five-year-old son in the same breath as the founding of a national dance collective disrupts traditional narratives that frame motherhood and professional achievement as incompatible. Anyone who has had babies knows the physical, emotional, and psychological work that those and future years meant for Awilda Sterling. What might pass as unperceived, or what might be taken as a minor personal detail, carries the weight of centuries of abuse and neglect against women and mothers. This autobiographical gesture does not merely document her life; it rewrites cultural scripts that marginalize maternal labor. The sonic friction this moment generates—what Przybylski (2023) might describe as a "disturbed sonic movement"—becomes a political tool that demands the revaluation of Black maternal voices.

Additionally, the autobiographical timeline challenges normative expectations surrounding aging, productivity, and artistic relevance. Sterling-Duprey returns to art school at forty-five, restarts her experimental work in New York at sixty, and reflects on her life at sixty-seven. Within dominant capitalist and heteronormative frameworks, these life choices might be dismissed as belated or nonnormative. Yet, as Halberstam (2005) argues, queer and feminist temporalities offer alternatives to linear, teleological life trajectories. In this light, Sterling-Duprey's narrative becomes an assertion of nonnormative life paths that resist the pressures of productivity, youth, and conventional success.

This autobiographical narration unfolds as Awilda Sterling progressively disrobes, presenting her fully nude body before the audience. Her naked presence directly challenges capitalist and ageist ideologies that marginalize aging bodies, especially within the dance industry, where dancers are often deemed "too old" at a young age. By exposing her body, Sterling dismantles dominant discourses of youth, femininity, and productivity, particularly as they relate to Black women. Her nudity does not seek to shock or titillate; rather, it embodies what she describes as *transparente desnudez*—naked transparency, not nudity. Through her physical presence, she asserts a deeply personal yet collective truth about being a Black woman in a society that often renders such bodies invisible, hyper-visible, or inhuman.

She walks away from the audience, still nude, gently holding her breasts—organs often symbolically linked to motherhood and nourishment, yet also routinely eroticized through the lens of a heterosexual male gaze. As she moves through an installation of wooden sticks adorned with multicolored balloons resembling breasts, the gesture of holding her own breasts while walking among their inflated replicas underscores the performance's critique of how the female body, particularly the Black female body, is commodified and dismembered. This act also marks her transition into the final section of the performance.

A dramatic shift in lighting transforms the atmosphere of the performance. As Sterling enters this final space, the dim lighting renders her body a silhouette, and the projection of her shadow on the wall becomes exaggerated and dynamic. She slowly approaches a white wall marked with a curved black line and, with one finger, begins to trace it. Her movements generate a choreographic interplay between her body and its shadow, which morphs and transforms with each shift in posture and light.

This visual dimension of the performance foregrounds her background as a visual artist. In several interviews, Sterling has cited her admiration for abstract expressionism, particularly the work of Franz Kline (1910–1963), whose bold black strokes on white canvas and the physicality of his brushwork significantly inform her aesthetic. The stark contrast of black against white in this scene, and the gestural choreography of Sterling's movement, evoke this artistic lineage.

In this final space, her body appears unbound—liberated from the restrictive plastic wrap. Her gestures inscribe a narrative of emancipation, suggesting a trajectory from constraint to freedom. The performance closes with Sterling rubbing what appears to be charcoal across her skin, leaving black traces on

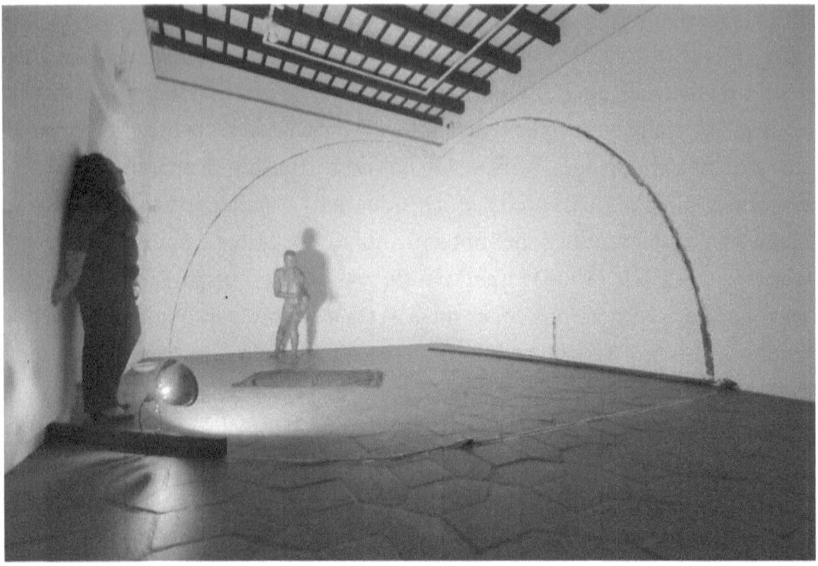

FIGURE 4.3. Awilda Sterling-Duprey, *Transparente desnudez*, 2014. Performance presented during the exhibition *Cosas: Notes on the Three-Dimensional Object in Contemporary Puerto Rican Art*, Arsenal de la Marina, Instituto de Cultura Puertorriqueña, San Juan, June 2014. In the image, the artist performs in front of a work by Jorge Rodríguez. Photograph: Abdiel D. Segarra Ríos. Courtesy of Abdiel D. Segarra Ríos.

her body and face. This act of marking—the visible residue of movement and memory—brings the performance to a somatic and symbolic conclusion.

Sterling's transition from a constrained, plastic-wrapped body to one that moves freely and leaves visible traces on itself enacts a powerful metaphor for historical memory, bodily resistance, and reclamation. The absence of verbal language throughout most of the performance—with the exception of the autobiographical interlude—returns the audience to a prelinguistic state where gesture, sound, and presence are primary forms of communication. As Aponte-Ramos writes, "Atrapar ese espacio trans-verbal implica la ambivalencia del tanteo, y la poesía de un estado de personificación/concreción de estados opuestos del sentimiento; el testimoniar la racialización en tanto proceso de jerarquización del poder como de toma de conciencia sociopolítica" [Capturing that trans-verbal space entails the ambivalence of speculation and the poetry of a state in which opposing emotional states are personified and materialized; it bears witness to racialization as both a process of hierarchical power and a mode of sociopolitical consciousness] (2017, 51).

Silence in the performance creates a space for introspection, compelling the audience to consider their own positionalities and epistemologies. The only moment of spoken language—when Sterling shares fragments of her personal and artistic trajectory—is deliberately difficult to hear. This sonic inaccessibility functions as a critical gesture, demanding intentional listening from an audience unaccustomed to attending to voices that have long been silenced. As Aponte-Ramos asserts, Sterling "nos exige como público escuchar la voz que no ha existido, la voz Negra" [demands that we, as an audience, listen to the voice that has not existed, the Black voice] (2017, 53).

The interplay of silence, sound, and voice in this performance contrasts with—and ultimately enhances—Sterling's corporeal presence onstage. Her moving body, producing subtle, inhuman sounds or barely audible narratives, becomes a vessel through which she foregrounds the historical erasure of Afro-diasporic subjects, particularly Black women. Through her *transparent nudity*, Sterling articulates stories that have long remained hidden: the stories of Black women, of Black mothers, and of Black women artists navigating oppressive structures of race, gender, age, and visibility.

EN-CIERRO

Awilda Sterling-Duprey's performance *en-cierro* [enclosed or in confinement] (2015–17; stylized in lowercase) marks a pivotal moment in her trajectory, bridging earlier works such as *Transparente desnudez* and later projects including *Lacks Criticality* (2018–23) and . . . *blindfolded* (2019–23). In *en-cierro*, Sterling revisits and expands key elements from her previous practice: the centrality of the Black female body, the evocative use of lighting and shadow (or the absence of light), abstraction in black and white, and the interplay of sound, silence, and gesture as metaphors for social, historical, and political constraints imposed on racialized bodies.

Simultaneously, *en-cierro* anticipates several techniques and themes that Sterling will explore more fully in her later performances. These include the incorporation of Caribbean elements—such as mimetic gestures of bushes swaying in the wind, natural soundscapes, and disorienting darkness—along with the recurring motif of movement while blindfolded. In *Lacks Criticality*, such features are revisited through the lens of Hurricane María (2017), which devastated Puerto Rico's infrastructure and exposed the island's colonial vulnerabilities. Likewise, the act of navigating space blindfolded, which begins in *en-cierro*, becomes central to the later work . . . *blindfolded*, where sensory deprivation acts as a metaphor for structural disenfranchisement and epistemic unknowing.

As its title suggests, *en-cierro* directly engages with notions of confinement, incarceration, and enclosure—conditions often experienced by marginalized communities. Sterling had already begun exploring this theme in her earlier performance *Maelo en el cuerpo* (2015), which drew on the life of singer Ismael "Maelo" Rivera, who was incarcerated for part of his life. Through Rivera—a revered yet controversial figure from Santurce—Sterling reflects on the criminalization of Blackness and poverty in Puerto Rico, the population that, in moments of crisis and natural disasters, pays the highest price. And in fact, retrospectively, *en-cierro* also acquires prophetic resonance (with the consequences that brought on the population): it prefigures the collective trauma of Hurricane María in 2017 and the global lockdowns of the COVID-19 pandemic (2020–22), which confined millions to domestic isolation.

Formally, *en-cierro* is an interdisciplinary work that integrates performance, experimental dance, installation, animation, video, and design. Its thematic core revolves around the politics of conduct, surveillance, and punishment—particularly the exclusion of behaviors deemed "antisocial" by hegemonic norms. Sterling's consistent aesthetic choices, such as dim lighting and stark black-and-white visual fields, recall the materiality of concrete and prison architecture. These elements invoke spaces of marginality and institutional control while also functioning as metaphors for classed, racialized, and gendered exclusion.

Moreover, *en-cierro* operates as a personal allegory. As a Black Puerto Rican woman artist practicing across disciplinary boundaries, Sterling challenges imposed racial expectations. Her embrace of abstract expressionism, her improvisational approach to *bomba* and *plena* folkloric dances, and her refusal to adhere strictly to cultural or academic conventions all speak to her pursuit of artistic freedom and self-definition. The metaphorical *en-cierro* is not only social and historical but also artistic—a reflection on the confinement of creative expression within identity-based constraints.

En-cierro has been performed in different countries and contexts, sometimes questioning, as a point of departure, the concept of identity,[17] and other times exploring the rhythmanalysis[18] of memory, times, and bodies in space.[19] However, the aesthetic is always very consistent where the lack of light and the exploration of the space with flashlights is predominant. One of these performances was staged in Berlin, Germany, in 2017 in collaboration with SAVVY Contemporary, Gintersdorfer/Klaßen, Q-Dance, Njelele Art Station, Hebbel am Ufer, FFT Düsseldorf, and Kampnagel, with support from the TURN Fund of the German Federal Cultural Foundation. My analysis of that presentation focuses on three aspects: (1) the predominance of darkness and its metaphorical functions, (2) movement through dark space with flashlights and branches, and (3) the sonic and visual strategies employed throughout the performance.

Darkness in *en-cierro* does more than set the scene—it engulfs the audience, implicating them physically and psychologically in the spatial dynamics of confinement. The lack of visibility disorients, while intermittent flashlight beams—controlled by both the artist and the audience—create shifting perceptual landscapes. At times, Sterling wears a headlamp, using it to illuminate elements like branches that she shakes in rhythmic response to the sound of heavy wind. These elements distort her silhouette, transforming her body and the performance space into a monstrous, ambiguous terrain. The audience, enveloped in shadow and sound, becomes both witness and participant in a space of sensory disarray.

The sound design reinforces this effect. Metallic noises, wind, and low-frequency vibrations collapse the distance between performer and audience, substituting sonic saturation for the absent senses of sight and speech. This rupture—this sonic violence—functions as a critique of capitalist and colonial order. As the German art collective GegenSichKollektiv explains, "Noise, with its epistemic violence, counters the division between activity and passivity. By making us aware of our inability to decipher it, noise alienates us. [. . .] We cannot find reaffirmation of our accepted positions (either audience or performer)" (2012, 194). In *en-cierro,* noise serves not only to destabilize roles but also to generate new affective and epistemological conditions. The chaos and density of the sonic field become anticapitalist, anticolonial strategies for disrupting linear narratives, hierarchies, and systems of control. The built system of signs and sounds in *en-cierro* creates a universe of monstrosities and chaos as the only way to raise awareness and interconnect bodies and histories of oppression, gender, age, and race. Unveiling, facing, and embracing erased histories becomes the way to exorcise any dystopic outcome.

Within this dark and noisy atmosphere, Sterling introduces ritualistic gestures reminiscent of Afro-Caribbean religious practices. The use of branches, drumming, and embodied movements evoke the spiritual aesthetics of Santería, forging a cultural bridge between the performer and Afro-Caribbean ancestral traditions. These moments are often juxtaposed with restricted, minimal movements—sitting, reclining, slowly shifting across the floor—which seem to resist spectacle in favor of introspection. I interpret them as a way to slow down the present to create space for memory of erased stories. But also, these moments speak to the limitations of the body, both as a social citizen that is also Black and a woman, and as a reference to the physical restrictions in dance due to aging. This last reference, then, could be a critique to the dance academy that can be very discriminatory based on race and age of the dancers. Thus, these choreographies not only recall erased histories but also speak to the limitations imposed on bodies by race, gender, and age. Sterling thus critiques both social norms and institutional dance frameworks that exclude older and nonwhite bodies from dominant paradigms of beauty, discipline, and virtuosity.

In *en-cierro,* Awilda Sterling-Duprey offers a powerful counternarrative to dominant representations of aging dancers. Projecting black-and-white abstract imagery onto the walls while performing live, she stages a transition from two-dimensional visual media—such as painting, drawing, and video—to a dynamic, three-dimensional space activated by her moving body. This performative gesture challenges traditional notions of what the dancing body can signify or achieve. By embodying abstraction, Sterling reimagines the body itself as a living canvas—one capable of transforming reality and envisioning alternative futures for those historically marginalized, particularly Black communities, even from within the confines of *en-cierro.*

The abstract visual language that unfolds onstage serves not only as an aesthetic strategy but also as a declaration of artistic and personal freedom. As a Black Puerto Rican artist, Sterling resists the racialized expectations imposed upon her—expectations that seek to dictate how Black bodies should move, paint, or perform. Emerging from darkness, she moves deliberately and silently toward an abstract, three-dimensional freedom—an embodied rejection of normative scripts. Moreover, *en-cierro* becomes a metaphorical and political reference to Puerto Rico's colonial status—an island both geographically and politically enclosed. In the shared silence and darkness of the performance space, Sterling's body and those of the audience inhabit a collective *en-cierro.* Yet within this confinement, they find grounding—a reconnection to the self and to each other. This intimate experience, both physical and affective, creates the conditions for imagining futures beyond their current state of enclosure. The *en-cierro* performance is a dense, multidimensional meditation on confinement, resistance, and the haunting persistence of colonial and patriarchal systems. It invites audiences to sit with discomfort—to feel disoriented, alienated, and immersed in a universe of monstrosity and memory. The performance insists that unveiling and embracing repressed histories is the only path toward healing and transformation.

LACKS CRITICALITY

In 2018, Awilda Sterling-Duprey developed the performance *Lacks Criticality* (2018–23), a piece that expands her long-standing investigation into the expressive potential of the moving body. As noted in *The Dance Journal,* the work conceptually continues Sterling-Duprey's engagement with Henri Lefebvre's theories on movement in diverse spatial and architectural contexts, especially his *Rhythmanalysis,* which posits rhythm as a central organizing principle of life and the universe.[20] Sterling-Duprey explains that her goal is "to make the audience active participants, not just passive observers," seeking to speak her personal and cultural history through bodily encounters with audience members.[21]

Indeed, *Lacks Criticality* explores the body's rhythms beyond music and sound, offering movement as a visual and affective testimony of survival and resistance. As is common in Sterling-Duprey's work, the performance blends installation, dance, live music, visual art, and video. This chapter draws on two recorded iterations of the piece: a 1-minute, 11-second version performed at the fifteenth Puerto Rico Festival in 2020, and a 59-minute version presented as part of the exhibition *No existe un mundo posthuracán* [There is no post-hurricane world] at the Whitney Museum of American Art in March 2023. While each iteration contains unique elements, both share a core choreographic and conceptual vocabulary: the use of projected video, the presence of other performers (dancers or musicians), the invocation of African diasporic rhythms and Puerto Rican bomba, and scenes performed in near-complete darkness with the aid of flashlights. *Lacks Criticality* resonates with Sterling-Duprey's earlier works—*Toque de tambores para las diosas, Transparente desnudez,* and *en-cierro*—through its exploration of Afro-Caribbean spirituality, shadow play, and embodied resistance in the dark. It also anticipates her subsequent performance . . . *blindfolded* (2019–23), suggesting a conceptual and aesthetic continuity across her oeuvre.

Conceived as a response to the catastrophic impact of Hurricane María in 2017, *Lacks Criticality* addresses both the environmental devastation of the storm and the structural violence of colonial neglect. The performance critiques the inadequate and delayed response of both the US federal government and the Puerto Rican authorities, which resulted in thousands of deaths and left much of the island without electricity, potable water, or essential services for nearly a year. The title itself is a searing indictment of the governmental claim that the situation in Puerto Rico "lacked criticality"—a phrase that Sterling-Duprey repurposes to highlight the erasure of urgency in a context of evident crisis. *Lacks Criticality* responds to the damage inflicted on both the bodies and the environment of Puerto Rican citizens because of the devastation left behind by Hurricane María. But also, it addresses the devastation caused by the colonial state of the island. The title creates a paradoxical reference to the lack of criticality established by the government in a situation that was obviously urgent and critical. Thus, the artist, through her work, with her body, finds a cathartic way to stay alive and freely express the emotional pain and traumatic experience that belongs to her and to the Puerto Rican community.

Through movement, Sterling-Duprey crafts a space for collective mourning, embodied memory, and imaginative resistance. Both recorded versions of *Lacks Criticality* foreground community by involving other performers and alternating between solo and ensemble sequences. In both iterations, the artist transitions between dynamic movement, stillness, seated gestures, and dragging herself across the floor. These choreographic shifts suggest a metaphorical engagement with the improvisational tactics Puerto Ricans had to adopt to navigate the literal and bureaucratic wreckage left in María's wake.

In the 2023 version, Sterling-Duprey introduces movements that evoke the body's resistance to hurricane winds or the difficulty of wading through flooded streets—gestures also present in the 2020 version but more fully developed here. At one moment, a projected video shows Sterling-Duprey dancing in a skirt made from a black trash bag, superimposed over meteorological footage of Hurricane María. Her blindfolded head aligns with the hurricane's eye, creating a powerful visual conflation of artist and storm. She then vanishes behind a curtain, leaving only the hurricane's image behind, while her live counterpart reemerges onstage carrying a trash bag, which she manipulates in ways that echo bomba's flowing skirt movements.

This choreographic moment, in which the artist symbolically becomes the hurricane and reclaims its destructive force, enacts a kind of embodied catharsis. Sterling-Duprey restages a traumatic emergency in a safe, aesthetic space, where the physical memory of crisis can be transformed into a tool of consciousness and resistance (13:00–19:00, 2023 version). As she dances with the trash bag, its crinkling evokes the sound of storm winds and water, while its swirling motion visually references bomba, the Afro–Puerto Rican music and dance tradition developed by enslaved Africans in the seventeenth century. The substitution of the traditional skirt with a trash bag—a mundane object associated with waste—becomes a metaphor for how Puerto Ricans, particularly Black Puerto Ricans, were treated in the aftermath of the storm: disposable, neglected, abject. Rather than reject this abjection, Sterling-Duprey embraces it as a site of ancestral power. Like the Santería deity Oyá—who governs storms, winds, and transformation—she becomes the hurricane, wielding destruction not as an end but as a precondition for renewal. Her performance channels an Afro-diasporic spiritual epistemology that reclaims trauma as a catalyst for liberation.

The interplay of silence, sound, and live music—particularly drums and jazz—functions throughout the performance as a strategy for breaking colonial structures and imagining alternative futures (Przybylski 2023). Reshaping the traumatic experience of Hurricane María allows new structures that go beyond and against the colonial order that neglected Puerto Ricans. In a climactic moment (23:00), Sterling-Duprey places the trash bag over her head as if suffocating, a gesture that powerfully encapsulates the suffocating conditions of colonial subjugation and post-María neglect. Yet, from this act of constraint emerges a warrior figure, drawing on ancestral strength to confront destruction with fearless vitality. As projected images of Hurricane María and scenes of survival flash across the screen, live drums underscore her bodily resilience and spiritual defiance, summoning a collective Afro–Puerto Rican call to perseverance.

Later, images of people navigating ruined landscapes are accompanied by jazz music, suggesting that even amid devastation, Puerto Ricans continue to dream, create, and reimagine their sociopolitical reality. Visual abstraction, particularly in the form of black, white, and gray lines produced through lighting effects and movement, recalls Sterling-Duprey's interest in abstract expressionism. Therefore, black, gray, and white lines are drawn in the space through the presence or absence of light. The artist's silhouette moves through this visual field with flashlights worn or held, evoking the literal and symbolic darkness endured after the hurricane, as well as the lack of institutional "illumination" or care.

Her movements deform her shadow into monstrous shapes, expanding and contracting its scale, sometimes isolating specific body parts like a foot. These distortions communicate a sense of presence even in a dystopic reality and challenge dominant visual tropes of the dancer's body—especially the Black female dancer's body—as graceful, predictable, or ornamental. In defying these norms, Sterling-Duprey refutes the colonial image of Puerto Ricans as obedient and docile.[22]

This aesthetic disobedience is also enacted through her use of abstract expressionism, a genre from which Black artists have often been excluded or pigeonholed. Through that aesthetic disobedience and by appropriating abstraction and merging it with Afro-Caribbean performance, Sterling-Duprey asserts a decolonial visual language rooted in nonconformity and political critique. Her disobedient gestures address a decolonial power that comes to life onstage through her ancestral bodily movements.

The two performance endings reinforce this project of historical unveiling and speculative resistance. In the 2020 version, Sterling-Duprey removes her blindfold while pointing a flashlight at her face—struggling to open her eyes under the harsh light, a gesture that suggests both revelation and discomfort. In the 2023 version, she dances with two machetes in hand to the sound of live drums, embodying a fierce, combative energy. Both conclusions insist on the necessity of seeing clearly, reconnecting with ancestral memory, and confronting oppression with embodied courage. Sterling-Duprey invites her audience to join her in imagining a future rooted not in fear or abandonment, but in visionary resistance.

In *Lacks Criticality,* Awilda Sterling-Duprey transforms the stage into a space of embodied memory, political reckoning, and spiritual resurgence. Through her choreography, she bears witness to the layered violences of colonialism, ecological catastrophe, and systemic neglect, while simultaneously reactivating Afro-diasporic rhythms and ancestral knowledges as forms of resistance. Her use of darkness, silence, abstraction, and the symbolic trash bag skirt become a radical aesthetic strategy—one that refuses legibility within dominant frameworks and instead insists on an affective, embodied critique of the structures that deem Puerto Rican suffering as noncritical. Sterling-Duprey's performance does not merely represent the aftermath of Hurricane María; it enacts the storm's lingering psychic and political force through the body, resignifying vulnerability as power, and dispossession as a call to collective action. In doing so, *Lacks Criticality* emerges not only as a memorial to loss, but as a choreographic manifesto for survival, sovereignty, and decolonial futurity.

. . . *BLINDFOLDED*

In both *en-cierro* (2015–17) and *Lacks Criticality* (2018–23), Awilda Sterling-Duprey introduces a gesture that would become central to her later performance . . . *blindfolded* (2019–23): the act of performing while blindfolded. This embodied experiment, which lends its name to the work itself, represents a synthesis of Sterling-Duprey's multiple artistic lineages—as a painter, dancer, and performance artist. In . . . *blindfolded,* she enacts a dance-drawing while blindfolded, marking large-scale paper surfaces affixed to the walls in response to music—primarily jazz, but also genres such as salsa, bossa nova, bomba, and others. Her movements produce abstract, jittery, and expressive lines that trace a corporeal response to rhythm and sound.

In an interview with Jenny Gill for the Joan Mitchell Foundation, Sterling-Duprey describes . . . *blindfolded* as the series that "brings everything together," referring to the centrality of improvisation throughout her practice, which reaches new dimensions in this work through the sensorial constraint of blindness. Recounting her first blindfolded experiment, she notes that it happened unexpectedly during a 2020 performance at El Cuadrado Gris (The Gray Square), an alternative art space in San Juan. Faced with a moment of uncertainty, she improvised by blindfolding herself: "I didn't know how to deal with the situation. . . . So I said, 'Well, I'm going to blindfold myself.'" What began as a spontaneous gesture quickly became a methodology. Sterling-Duprey explains that being blindfolded heightens her tactile sensitivity: she navigates the space through her hands, identifying boundaries and obstacles, and selects colors—usually oil sticks—arranged on the floor according to a predetermined palette. Guided by instrumental jazz, each sonic element provokes a corresponding mark: "If the music goes, 'bap, bap, bap,' then I do the same on the surface." The artist describes the experience as a synesthetic one—transcending the five senses and activating a heightened form of awareness through sound, touch, and movement.[23]

In her conversations about the work, Sterling-Duprey frequently underscores how improvisation liberates her from the obligation to "know" in advance what she is doing or intends to do. As she states in an interview with Miguel Trelles, "While making those images . . . I am enjoying grasping the concept" (24:12).[24] This process of *grasping* becomes a metaphorical articulation of resistance—where disobedience takes the form of navigating without a clear map, rejecting fixed outcomes or expectations. The blindfolded body defies the presumed visual and choreographic constraints of both painting and dance. Sterling-Duprey thus challenges conventional understandings of rhythm, sonic embodiment, gesture, and visuality. In the space of rupture she creates, there emerges a zone of possibility—a suspended moment where alternative modes of existence and perception are enacted. In this way, she performs what Przybylski calls "the choice to name the uncomfortable reality of violence against women and girls" (2023, 211). Drawing from Przybylski's theory of sonic disruption as a refusal of normative order, Sterling-Duprey's work asserts the presence of an undisciplined Black female body that claims space freely—an act often met with social resistance or repression.

In . . . *blindfolded*, this act of bodily disruption becomes a critique of colonial systems of control, Eurocentric standards of discipline, and heteropatriarchal surveillance. Through abstraction, improvisation, and the audacity of not-seeing, Sterling-Duprey invokes incoherence and wildness as deliberate queer and decolonial strategies—what Tavia Nyong'o and Jack Halberstam (2018) theorize as necessary modes of being that unsettle the civilizational logics of whiteness and empire.

Silence, another recurring motif in Sterling-Duprey's practice, also plays a key role in . . . *blindfolded*. Both interior and exterior silences—particularly those amplified when sight is suspended—create a heightened perception of energy, bodily memory, and ancestral connection. The silence becomes a site of deep listening and presence, where the artist's movements—especially those of her feet and shoulders—echo the embodied memory of African diasporic lineages in the present. This sensorial practice allows her to bypass the rigid frameworks that seek to regulate and contain Black female bodies. Her choreographic experimentation breaks through stereotypes, opening space for alternative affective and spatial imaginaries.

Indeed, . . . *blindfolded* encapsulates the core of Sterling-Duprey's abstract aesthetic sensibility: a willingness to take risks, to follow intuition, and to build art in the moment. The improvisational structure, closely tied to jazz, allows her to navigate between two-dimensional and three-dimensional spaces—the painted surface and the dancing body. In this fusion, dance becomes painting, and painting becomes movement, gesture, and trace. The resulting images are not premeditated compositions but records of motion, expressions of embodied rhythm, and visual articulations of lived experience. The viewer, in turn, is drawn into a state of uncertainty, mirroring the precarious sociopolitical conditions of Puerto Rico. Improvisation—like music, dance, and rhythm—is thus central not only to the performance but also to understanding coloniality and its discontents. As Sterling-Duprey traverses genres such as bomba and *danzón*, she activates the cultural memories and musical landscapes that shaped her, transforming them into tools for decolonial rupture. . . . *blindfolded* presents an experimentalism that creates new aesthetics to imagine new ways of Puerto Ricanness beyond colonization. At the same time, improvisation is central to Afro-Caribbean traditions. The culture informs the movement, and the culture is informed and defined by Africa. Thus, in making improvisation the protagonist of . . . *blindfolded* the artist is making a statement of sociopolitical and cultural awareness as a Black person.

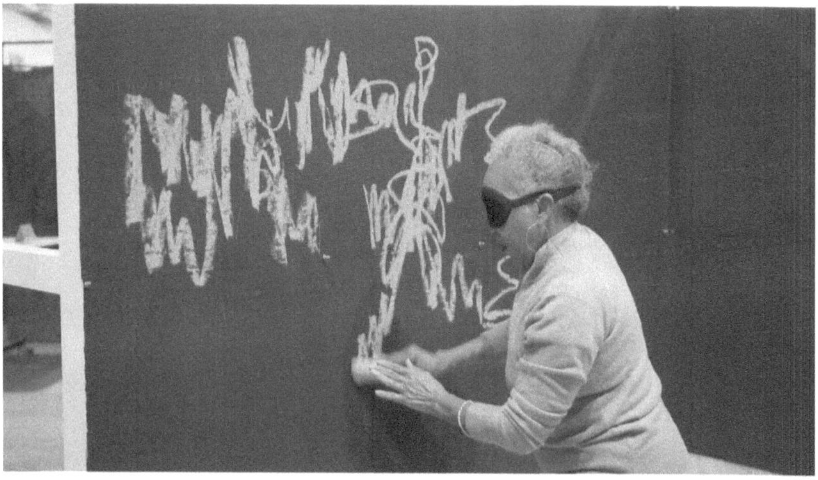

FIGURE 4.4. Awilda Sterling-Duprey, . . . *blindfolded* (2020–). Performance, *Whitney Biennial 2022. Quiet as It's Kept,* Whitney Museum of American Art, 2022. Courtesy of the Whitney Museum of American Art, New York.

Moreover, the ephemeral traces of rhythm upon the body are translated into a visual language through the paintings produced during the performance. These works function like an open book of unwritten histories—stories captured in vibrant oil-stick marks, a medium whose pasty texture and semitransparency reflect the paradox of oral histories: dense and vital yet persistently marginalized by official narratives. Sterling-Duprey's use of this medium symbolically inscribes the erased stories of the enslaved, the disenfranchised, and the minoritized. Through this process, . . . *blindfolded* becomes not only a performance but a radical act of transcription—one that translates embodied Afro-Caribbean memory into visual form, breaking the silence imposed by colonial historiography and reclaiming Black feminist presence as both archive and future.

The graphic expression in . . . *blindfolded* remains visibly inscribed on paper despite the transparency of the pigment and the absence of direct visual control over the surface, given that the artist is blindfolded. The visual component of the performance, therefore, captures the otherwise invisible sonic improvisations of the musical genres Sterling-Duprey selects as a means of breaking both visual and performative conventions. She predominantly chooses straight-ahead jazz—a genre that privileges improvisation and spontaneity. In several

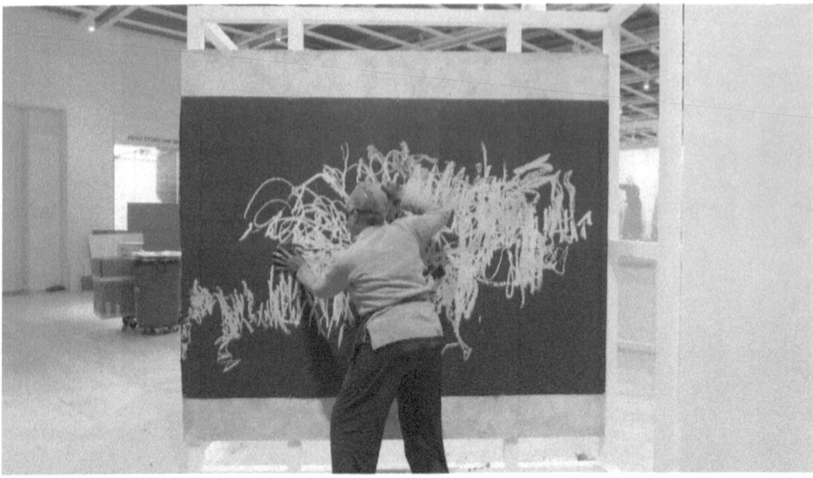

FIGURE 4.5. Awilda Sterling-Duprey, . . . *blindfolded* (2020–). Performance, *Whitney Biennial 2022. Quiet as It's Kept,* Whitney Museum of American Art, 2022. Courtesy of the Whitney Museum of American Art, New York.

interviews about . . . *blindfolded,* Sterling-Duprey explains that this particular style of jazz was also the music favored by Franz Kline (1910–1962) during his creations, her favorite painter.[25] In this way, her musical selection becomes a bridge that links her visual, performative, and choreographic training. Much like the improvisational gestures of abstract expressionist painting, the improvisations of straight-ahead jazz serve to bring her visual mark-making (inspired by Kline and abstract expressionism more broadly) into close alignment with her embodied, performative movements.

The result is . . . *blindfolded,* a performance that returns to the theme of transparency—through both color choice and concept, which Sterling-Duprey began exploring in *Transparente desnudez*—and to the motif of moving in darkness, a concern also central to *en-cierro* and *Lacks Criticality.* These movements are guided by a commitment to process, to the spontaneity of the moment, and to following where intuition and the body might lead. As metaphor, . . . *blindfolded* becomes a reflection on life itself: the embrace of unplanned processes and the pleasure found in that which resists control but emerges instead from internal and ancestral truths.

At the close of the performance, the artist wipes her hands clean of the oil paint crayons used during the piece and, rather than discarding the towels, she—still blindfolded—hangs them on a surface. In her interview with the Joan

Mitchell Foundation, Sterling-Duprey describes this gesture as "building her own continent" for those whose stories have been erased. Her movement across the canvas, approached as a three-dimensional space, becomes an introspective and spiritual act. Informed by her Afro-Caribbean experience, each color's vibration and each gesture recall the way ancestral memory is expressed through rhythm and embodied practice. When painting blindfolded, Sterling-Duprey allows her body to surrender to a feeling of abandonment—a surrender that mirrors the neglected architectural spaces of Puerto Rico. These abandoned spaces, in turn, become metaphors for the island's emotional, physical, political, and social neglect. Through this framework, . . . *blindfolded* becomes a means of un-drawing and reimagining a continent—of dismantling and rebuilding—and of marveling at where this process of imagination leads. Sterling-Duprey's body, in this performance, becomes a legible text, one that speaks through movement to a community of forgotten and marginalized people. Her aim is to recover a collective memory that has been systemically erased—one that survives only through embodied rituals and performative gestures that resist historical amnesia (Connerton 1989).

The preceding analysis highlights how improvisation functions as a central and sustained methodology in Sterling-Duprey's artistic practice. In a kind of circular return, the study of her work brings us back to its origins: the graphic mark, the exploration of form, light, and shadow, the expressive use of color, and a deep engagement with the tonal range of grays, blacks, and whites. These visual elements are not only formal concerns but also carriers of meaning and memory. From this foundation, Sterling-Duprey has developed a transdisciplinary practice rooted in movement, abstraction, and improvisation as strategies for reclaiming erased histories, recovering cultural memory, and imagining new artistic and political possibilities. Her work speaks on behalf of her Black Puerto Rican community, her colonized homeland, and her own embodied experience as a Black Caribbean woman navigating—and resisting—systems of marginalization.

Improvising Presence: Toward a Black Puerto Rican Aesthetic

In tracing the multifaceted trajectory of Awilda Sterling-Duprey's work—from her gestural drawings and improvised dance performances to her explorations of silence, rhythm, and ancestral memory—it becomes clear that her artistic practice is one of profound resistance and reclamation. Whether painting blindfolded to the unpredictable cadences of jazz or inscribing her body into the political landscapes of the Puerto Rican archipelago, Sterling-Duprey embraces abstraction and improvisation as decolonial tools. Her performances do not simply represent but enact the tensions between visibility and invisibility, control and surrender, memory and erasure. Through improvised movements, mark-making, and sonic attunement, she constructs ephemeral yet enduring archives and aesthetics to recuperate Afro-Caribbean identities and Black feminist embodiments.

Sterling-Duprey's commitment to improvisation offers a radical alternative to colonial narratives that demand order, linearity, and legibility. Instead, she invites us into a space of disorientation—a choreographic and visual terrain where the body feels its way through darkness, where memory is tactile, and where silence resonates with ancestral echoes. Her work gestures toward a future rooted in refusal, experimentation, and collective memory, offering an embodied politics that refuses to be contained. In this way, Sterling-Duprey's art becomes not only a mode of expression but a queer practice of imagining freedom beyond imposed borders—geographic, aesthetic, and epistemological.

Awilda Sterling-Duprey's work embodies a powerful constellation of *artistic articulations*—each gesture, mark, and silence becoming a mode of visual and corporeal speech. Her *visual movements* traverse and transgress aesthetic, cultural, and historical boundaries, forging a language rooted in improvisation, opacity, and embodied memory. Through these movements, she—as an Afro-Caribbean woman and through queer practices of disobedience and disruptions—reclaims presence for Black Puerto Rican subjectivities as they have been historically rendered invisible or illegible. Sterling-Duprey's practice does not merely respond to colonial frameworks—it reimagines the very terms of artistic engagement, challenging the visual and choreographic norms that constrain Black and feminine expression. Her work *has always been here,* at once intimate and insurgent, leaving behind a living archive of resistance and an ever-evolving grammar for Afro-Caribbean futures.

FIVE

Conclusion

"Estoy Jayá"

> [P]ersonal happiness [. . .] seems so easy, but it is not . . .
> my work has to do with that [. . .]
> [. . .] the truth is that I wanted to try to do a job that would contribute
> to something,
> that would make the world a little better, or a little easier for others.
> [. . .] *jayá* was about that . . .
> to do something that is even more,
> more emotional, a hymn!
>
> Gisela Rosario Ramos / Podcast recorded on March 7, 2024, with the author

The term *jayá* that titles this last section "can be used as a noun (jayaera, jayación), as a verb (jáyate, jayo, jayaré), as an adjective (jayá, jayau, jayadite), as an adverb (jayadamente), or as a noun with adjective modifier (jayaera combativa). [. . .] Fast forward to 2019 and there is an observable tendency to further label *jayaera* as combative" (Rivera-Velázquez 2024, 155). This book opened in the streets of San Juan, where the *perreo combativo* protests and *jayaera combativa* of July 2019, and particularly of the night of July 24, 2019, transformed the plaza and the cathedral in old San Juan into a site of Afro-queer feminist resistance.

The perreo and jayaera combativa reflected "the integration of cuir and trans-feminists politics within more traditional feminist spaces" (Rivera-Velázquez 2024, 155). That night, dancing bodies defied the intertwined forces of colonialism, patriarchy, homophobia, and religious conservatism through what Rivera-Velázquez defines as *cuir bliss*—the author's interpretation of the initial meaning of *jayá*, a deeply internal and odd feeling of joy that arises from freely expressing oneself, rooted in self-acceptance and the flourishing of one's singular identity. That feeling, shifted into a collective experience catalyzed by the perreo combativo, fueled "cuir irreverence" in social justice movements (Rivera-Velázquez 2024). The *jayaos'* disobedient movements—twerking, chanting, voguing—reclaimed public spaces through irreverent joy and embodied dissent. This protest did not emerge in isolation. It was the culmination of decades of creative, corporeal, and political labor by Afro-queer Puerto Rican women artists who had long been mapping other ways of existing, resisting, and imagining. It is from that genealogy that this book draws its purpose and momentum.

Across four chapters, this study has traced an intergenerational and intersectional choreography of disobedience—from Gisela Rosario Ramos's multimedia artwork of joy, jayaera, multiplicity, and refusal; to Awilda Rodríguez Lora's embodied politics of self-love, queer motherhood, and Black existence; to the radical sensuality and border-crossing vulnerability of Helen Ceballos; and to the foundational work of Awilda Sterling-Duprey and her abstraction of Black Puerto Rican femininity. Disobedience is a shared denominator for unbuilding the world they inhabit, reformulating social expectations, and reorganizing existence. Their artistic practices blur normative boundaries between ability and disability, youth and age, femininity and masculinity, queerness and Blackness. While differing in form and medium, each artist mobilizes movement—both literal and conceptual—as a method to unsettle coloniality, resist normativity, and make space for Afro-queer life.

This is how Gisela Rosario Ramos (chapter 1) performs through radical joy. Joy, in her work, is not a retreat from politics but a form of feminist counterviolence. Macha Colón's irreverent characters and carnivalesque aesthetics explode normative codes of gender, beauty, and romantic love. Her work celebrates bodies deemed too fat, too loud, too improper—proposing instead a queer, decolonial model of feminine excess that disrupts colonial aesthetics of whiteness, thinness, and passivity. The recuperation of the word *jayá*—once denigrated as rural and improper—becomes a symbolic gesture of empowerment and reterritorialization. In the music video "Jayá," the queer wedding staged by Macha as reverend is both satire and utopia: it stages a queer disorder as the only viable structure for sustaining Black and queer community.

Similarly, Awilda Rodríguez Lora (chapter 2) deploys disobedient movement in her choreographic and performance work to explore and embody *sustento*—support—for queer mothers, Afro-descendant women, and the broader community. Her performances, such as *La tortillera, Mamá Awilda,* and *La Mujer Maravilla,* challenge heteropatriarchal norms around motherhood, domestic labor, and beauty through acts of nudity, vulnerability, and care. In works like

La Rosario and *Bailar todos los días,* dance becomes both aesthetic language and social practice, positioning Rodríguez Lora as a community leader and caretaker within the Afro-queer artistic movement in Puerto Rico. Her female body—Black, queer, and positioned in sites of abjection and invisibility—emerges as a site of aesthetic agency and embodied resistance.

Helen Ceballos (chapter 3) proposes a cartography of queer Caribbean movement. Her disobedience lies in a fragmented poetics of gesture, often marked by repetition, refusal, and failure. Her work resists the linearity of nationalist narratives and capitalist temporality, insisting instead on incomplete, nonlinear, and affectively saturated modes of performance. Her stories—of migration, undocumented life, Blackness, queerness, and diaspora—are stitched together through performative gestures that become political inscriptions of memory and resistance. Through anticapitalist and anticolonial movements, she carves out a space for being an Afro-Caribbean woman on her own terms.

Joy, resilience, queerness, and racialized embodiment are also central to the work of Awilda Sterling-Duprey (chapter 4). Her visual and corporeal movements—whether painted on canvas or enacted in performance—destabilize racialized and gendered logics of legibility. Sterling-Duprey's gestural abstract expressionism translates bodily pain, silence, and joy into a visual language that foregrounds the experience of being a Black Puerto Rican woman artist. In performances such as . . . *blindfolded,* her movements offer a visual grammar of what lives beyond the visible, producing a space of queer Afro-Caribbean futurity in which the failure of sight opens the door to other forms of knowing and being.

This circular movement between generations is not incidental; it is central to the political and aesthetic argument of this book. By beginning and ending with the most experienced artists—Rosario Ramos and Sterling-Duprey—I have sought to emphasize the importance of memory, continuity, and inherited forms of rebellion. In doing so, the chapters do not present a linear narrative of progress, but rather a constellation of embodied responses to shared histories of erasure, violence, and marginalization. These artists, each in her own way, inhabit the fissures of colonial temporality and state-sanctioned order, reclaiming disobedience as both method and meaning. Their movements become *wild* and undisciplined, to borrow from Halberstam and Nyong'o—not because they lack form, but because they reject containment.

Movement, as explored in this book, is not merely choreography or gesture. It is a politics: a refusal to be still, to be silenced, to be legible on colonial and heteronormative terms. Movement becomes the language through which these artists narrate Afro-queer life in the Puerto Rican archipelago—a life that is often precarious, but never without power (pun intended). Whether dancing in protest, embodying ancestral memory, or occupying public space with unapologetic presence, these women remind us that the body is a critical site of history and futurity. Their performances disarticulate the supposed order of things and generate a politics of disorder—rooted in joy, irreverence, vulnerability, and collective imagination.

Methodologically, the book outlines the careful development of artistic conceptualizations of race, gender, and sexuality that together build a contemporary Afro-queer canon of artivism—highlighting the links between the body and decolonial action in the Puerto Rican archipelago. The project weaves together close reading, performance analysis, visual culture studies, decolonial and queer theory, and feminist ethnography. It emerges from sustained engagement with the artists and their communities—through interviews, participant observation, digital archives, art exhibits, shared drafts, and live performances.

This approach foregrounds relational and situated knowledge, rejecting distanced objectivity in favor of embodied, affective, and politically accountable scholarship. I lived in Puerto Rico for four months as a single mother of a breastfed newborn and a toddler. I navigated impossible urban planning, daycare selection, and the economic consequences of colonialism—from food and formula prices to gas and electricity. Being in Puerto Rico intellectually sustained this book, and in turn, I received *sustento* that made this book possible. *Sustento,* then, becomes not only a theme but a methodology—alongside listening, watching, and feeling with the artists.

I also write as a woman who is an immigrant in the United States, whose first language is not English, and who comes from a complex geopolitical space: the Mediterranean. It is a geography often overlooked in this part of the world, yet one that I carry under my skin and that shares much with the Caribbean, including African heritage, the intersection with other assets of power such as colonialism and patriarchy, and the historical and cultural whitening of our cultures. For these reasons—and certainly offering a responsible reflection on the shared foundations of colonial oppression, while preserving the complexities and differences that belong to the "pluriversality" of each geography—I think that this is a very specific contribution, limited and personal (Fauzia and Amenta 2024, 25). And it could not be otherwise, because I can only share what my physical, intellectual, and political body has experienced. Yet, this is a perspective from a geographical wide angle, with a different baggage, but still from the United States. This perspective is part of the book's unique contribution: a geographically broad but politically grounded viewpoint from within the United States but not entirely of it.

This research and lived experience have shaped my interpretive lens and affirmed the epistemic value of the body in academic inquiry—especially when engaging with artistic practices that resist textual, disciplinary, and institutional norms. They have also given me permission to claim the right to make mistakes and to change my mind—or, as Rachele Borghi calls it, quoted by Claudia Fauzia and Valentina Amenta, the right to "sbaglieranza" [the right to get things wrong]—that is, "una presa di responsabilità collettiva che consideri lo sbaglio intrinseco a qualsiasi tentativo di decostruire lo status quo per immaginare nuovi mondi" [a collective assumption of responsibility that considers error as intrinsic to any attempt to deconstruct the status quo in order to imagine new worlds] (2024, 13). Embracing *this* right has allowed me to approach knowledge-making as a dynamic, embodied, and relational practice, always open to revision and collective transformation.

Thus, this book can be used as a tool grounded in a methodology that privileges embodied listening, affective witnessing, and collaborative knowledge production. Rather than imposing a fixed critical framework on the artists' works, I approached each piece with openness to the movements it provoked—intellectually, emotionally, and politically. The methodology, informed by queer, Black, and decolonial feminisms, treats the lived experiences of the artists as theoretical and political archives in their own right, and as a collective way of resistance, deconstruction, and opposition to the different established categories of power outside the colonial prism of modernity. Through slow engagement, direct dialogue, and participation in the spaces where these works are created and shared, I have come to understand disobedience as not only aesthetic but also as a relational and epistemological practice.

My time in Puerto Rico, my participation in artistic spaces like La Goyco, and the generosity of the artists were vital to this process. For example, on March 7, 2024, during a UNCF/Mellon research fellowship that allowed me to spend a semester in Puerto Rico, I met the artists individually first, and then all together to record the podcast. My intention was to break with the academic pedestal and engage in dialogue with the artists I had been writing about for years. This act was, for me, a performative academic gesture—appropriate to an academic book on queer performance. I wanted to discuss together their practices, their approaches, and their existence as artists, as Afro–Puerto Ricans, as queer women, but especially as human beings in this complex equation called life. We gathered at La Calle Loíza Recording Studio, managed by Joanne Gil

Rivera in the Community Center La Goyco (Taller Comunidad La Goyco), in the neighborhood of Santurce in San Juan, Puerto Rico. By then, I had completed the first version of two chapters, was finalizing the third chapter, and had followed these artists' work for over a decade.

After the recording of the podcast—of which several quotes are included throughout this book—we transformed our conversation into a roundtable at *La Cumbre Afro* [The African Summit] held in Puerto Rico on March 18–23, 2024, organized by Afro–Puerto Rican writer Mayra Santos-Febres, with Helen Ceballos as producer through her *Plataforma Eje*. The roundtable took place at the University of Puerto Rico, Río Piedras (UPR), on March 21, and was titled "Feminidad, cuirness y raza en el performance Afro Boricua" [Femininity, queerness, and race in the Afro–Puerto Rican performance]. The auditorium quickly filled with students, faculty, academic colleagues, and artists. The roundtable also featured Edrimael Delgado Reyes, not included in this book but fully deserving of attention, and whose text from that event now appears in the *CENTRO Journal* (Summer 2024).[1] After these two main events that brought author and artists into dialogue, the book was completed in August 2024. A few final steps in the editing process followed, bringing this project into the form you now hold in your hands.

This methodological stance rejects extractivism and centers reciprocity, community, and situatedness. As Helen Ceballos described it during our podcast conversation, this is "a manual, a map for the reader who approaches the text to see how these Caribbean women did it in their context, under what conditions." I recognize that analyzing disobedient bodies requires a parallel commitment to rigor when employing disobedient strategies within academic practices—embracing emotion, partiality, and the messiness of research as valid forms of knowledge-making. The women featured in this book, through their disobedience, move past institutional and social barriers, dismantle racialized and sexist boundaries, and continue to forge paths in irreverent and unruly ways. They are shaping an Afro-Caribbean *herstory*—one I am honored to bring into an academic space, committed to be written, read, and remembered.

Yet, this study is only a beginning. The scope of this book—necessarily limited—only scratches the surface of the vibrant queer, Black, and feminist performance scenes in Puerto Rico and across the Caribbean. Many artists and collectives—Edrimael Delgado Reyes, Pó Rodil, Pepe Álvarez Colón, Javier Cardona Otero, Las Nietas de Nonó, Antonio Ramos, Lionel Villahermosa, Perra Mística, Lale Namerrow Pastor, Mima, Eduardo Alegría, nibia pastrana santiago, Viveca Vázquez, Pati Cruz, María José, Kairiana Núñez Santaliz, and

La Sombrilla Cuir, among many others—are creating transformative work that demands further scholarly attention. Future research should explore how these and other artists theorize through performance, curate community, and embody resistance within and beyond the archipelago.

Additionally, comparative studies across the Caribbean and its diasporas could further enrich our understanding of how disobedience takes shape through diverse languages of movement, gender, race, and geography. How does queer disobedience manifest in contexts such as the Dominican Republic, Haiti, Cuba, or diasporic spaces like New York and Miami? How do Afro-Caribbean performance practices intersect with trans-Caribbean and global movements for racial, gender, and migrant justice? And what methodologies best honor the ephemeral, affective, and relational nature of these performances?

The implications of this work extend beyond the Puerto Rican context. The frameworks of Afro-queer movement, disobedience, and indisciplinarity proposed here offer analytical tools for understanding other performances of minoritized embodiment across the Caribbean and its diasporas. Future research might extend this intergenerational lens to take up the challenge of tracing how Afro-queer aesthetics are transmitted, transformed, or resisted across generations, media, and borders. It might also examine the infrastructural and institutional conditions that enable—or constrain—the emergence of such performances.

In the face of escalating state violence, climate catastrophe, and neoliberal precarity, the artistic interventions analyzed here remind us that performance is not simply a reflection of crisis—it is also a method of survival, a speculative tool, and a blueprint for otherwise futures. This work calls for expanded academic engagement with art as a legitimate mode of theorizing and worldmaking. It also urges institutions to recognize the intellectual labor of artists and to take seriously the political force of joy, failure, irreverence, and desire.

Returning to the spirit of perreo combativo, we witness how this ethos resonates across generations: a shared impulse to move against erasure, to dance toward liberation. The Afro-queer Puerto Rican women artists at the center of this study offer more than aesthetic interventions—they gift us with new vocabularies of resistance and relation. Their bodies—unruly, luminous—carry the weight of history and the promise of what might still be born through movement. As Awilda Sterling-Duprey expressed in our podcast conversation: "This book also challenges certain mindsets [about race, what/who is Black, and the use of words such as *negrito/a*] [. . .]. It will provoke a lot of curiosity regarding concepts that academia has already established . . . [. . .]

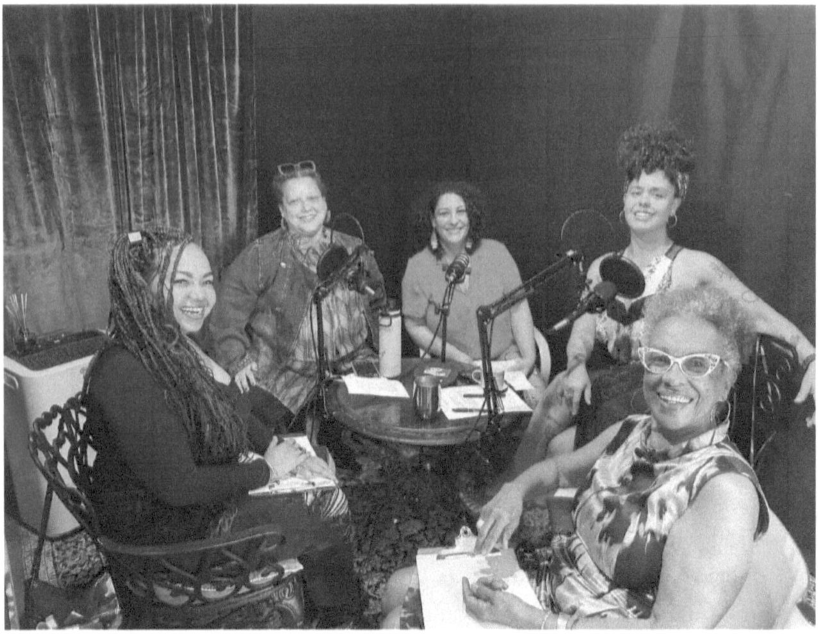

FIGURE 5.1. Recording session of the podcast conversation on March 7, 2024, in the studio of La Calle Loíza Inc. in La Goyco, Cangrejos, Puerto Rico. *From the bottom right*: Awilda Sterling-Duprey, Awilda Rodríguez Lora, Anastasia Valecce, Gisela Rosario Ramos, and Helen Ceballos. Photo credit: Joanne Gil Rivera. Courtesy of the author and Joanne Gil Rivera.

breaking paradigms [. . .] that [are] different from what they know in the United States [. . .]." Indeed, in a territory where coloniality continues to dictate daily precarity—through lack of food sovereignty, crumbling infrastructure, and systemic violence against women, Blacks, and trans people—disobedience, as well as the challenging of fixed mindsets, as artistic and academic practice, becomes more than resistance: it is a mode of survival. Caribbean Afro-queer disobedience destabilizes dominant scripts of respectability, gender normativity, and aesthetic discipline. To be wild, to be irreverent, to refuse the codes of proper behavior—especially in public space, onstage, or in media—is to enact decolonial gestures that make room for other ways of being and knowing.

Disobedient Women allowed me to begin a conversation about the rich tapestry of disobedience, resilience, decolonial self-care techniques, creativity, and cultural and artistic defiance in a colonized territory navigating postcolonial conditions. This is a study that speaks to the sociopolitical dimensions of the Puerto Rican archipelago through the lens of art, showing how, through performance, these women challenge social norms simply by moving their bodies as they wish. At the same time, they carve out spaces of empowerment and visibility for the marginalized, working from an intersectional perspective.

This book is a beginning—an effort to amplify these voices, advocate for their recognition, and understand the transformative power of art in reimagining identity and societies. The artists featured in *Disobedient Women,* and those mentioned above, among others, are irreverent and unruly in how their bodies move and exist in a patriarchal, heteronormative, capitalistic, and colonized society—one that often reduces femininity as a monolith and women to commodities for the masculine gaze. This book is an invitation to embrace disobedience as a praxis—to reclaim a space of weirdness, unconformity, and queerness.

Ultimately, *Disobedient Women* can be read as a performative invitation to look beyond limits, norms, and social standards—an invitation to abandon one-size-fits-all notions of success and to embrace the weird, the wild, and the yet-unknown territories of queerness and possibility. These pages became more than analysis; they became a practice in listening to disobedient bodies and learning from them. This book is a promise that anecdotes—such as the one shared by Sterling-Duprey during the recording of the podcast on March 7, 2024, and included in the opening of chapter 1—where a fat woman (Macha) can eat *carne frita* while performing a song on feminine sexual desire onstage, and a sixty-year-old woman (Sterling-Duprey) can shout *¡Agárrame las tetas!* to the audience—represent a world that is not just possible, but desirable, and politically urgent.

Disobedient Women is not only a chronicle of performance—it is itself a performance of refusal, of tenderness, of scholarly insubordination. It gestures toward futures where queer, Black, Caribbean women are not merely included but centered as theorists of movement, desire, resistance, and joy. These performances remind us that disobedience is not just an act of defiance—it is a method of survival and a way of dreaming. May this book—like the bodies it celebrates—keep moving, dancing, and disrupting, carving space for what is yet to be. Finally, may these movements create places where saying *estoy jayá* is not merely disobedience, but a bold declaration of personal, cultural, social, and political freedom.

NOTES

INTRODUCTION Undisciplined Measures

1 Perra Mística is the professional stage name of a DJ and artist based in Puerto Rico. She is known for her work as a DJ, with a focus on creating an engaging and experimental musical experience for her audience. Her DJ sets often include a blend of tropical, electronic, Caribbean, and world music genres.

2 All translations in the book are mine.

3 Edrimael Delgado Reyes (he/him) is an interdisciplinary Puerto Rican artist, cultural worker, and dancer who explores forms of reconciliation between Queer and Afro-Caribbean identities through performance and community practices. Delgado develops performance convergence spaces for the LGBTQ+ community in Puerto Rico through LaBoriVogue, the first vogue laboratory in the island using Ballroom as an agent of liberation, individual transformation, and collective justice. To watch the described perreo combativo performance, see https://www.youtube.com/watch?v=aX2VCrB2Rno.

4 Many scholars have narrated and analyzed the events of perreo combativo and the historical circumstances that led to that moment, such as Arnaldo Cruz-Malavé, Rocío Zambrana, and Consuelo Martínez Reyes, among others.

5 I establish a critical distinction between the terms *feminine* and *femme* within contemporary queer theoretical frameworks. *Feminine* denotes the socially constructed expectations and performances of femininity conventionally assigned to cisgender women operating within heteronormative structures. This concept also encompasses the mechanisms through which femininity becomes subject to surveillance and regulation when expressed beyond these prescribed boundaries. Conversely, *femme* emerges from queer community discourse, signifying queer individuals who deliberately embody and articulate femininity as an integral component of their nonheteronormative identity. Femme subjects fundamentally challenge heteronormative assumptions regarding the legitimate expression of femininity and its appropriate manifestations. Simultaneously, they disrupt conventional expectations within LGBTQ+ communities by asserting diverse and fluid performances of femininity across a spectrum of identities—including trans-

gender men and women, lesbians, gay men, and other queer positionalities. While this study focuses on four cisgender queer women, their artistic production serves as a lens through which to reconceptualize the broader meanings and political possibilities of femininity, moving beyond essentialist biological frameworks and normative gender prescriptions to explore more expansive articulations of gender expression and agency.

6 Edrimael Delgado Reyes, "Perreo combativo frente a la Catedral: Una perspectiva cuir," Todas periodismo feminista, July 28, 2019, https://www.todaspr.com/perreo-combativo-frente-a-la-catedral-una-perspectiva-cuir/.

7 I write the word *wild* in italics because I am referring to the way in which scholars Halberstam and Nyong'o use the term in their edited volume (2018) and the way Halberstam later goes back to it and articulates it in his book *Wild Things* (2020). They reframe the term *wild* within queer theory to refer to disrupting norms and conventions related to gender, sexuality, and identity, emphasizing the fluidity and multiplicity of identities and desires that defy traditional boundaries. I often rely on the term *wild* throughout the book to define the artists' artistic movements because that is how they defy social norms.

8 Within this study, I define performance art as creative work generated through actions executed by the artist or other participants, encompassing both live presentations and recorded documentation, whether spontaneous or carefully scripted. This definition extends to film, video, photography, and installation-based works that document or transmit these performative actions. Beyond its formal characteristics, I approach performance as a mode of direct engagement with social realities, spatial configurations, and the complex politics of identity formation and expression.

9 https://www.bbc.com/news/world-latin-america-41340392

10 https://observatoriopr.org/feminicidios

11 Throughout the book I refer to Gisela Rosario Ramos with her legal name, or with her artistic name in all of its forms and without distinction: Macha Colón, or just Macha.

12 As I specify in the conclusion of this book, "[T]his study is only a beginning. The scope of this book—necessarily limited—only scratches the surface of the vibrant queer, Black, and feminist performance scenes in Puerto Rico and across the Caribbean. Many artists and collectives—Edrimael Delgado Reyes, Pó Rodil, Pepe Álvarez Colón, Javier Cardona Otero, Las Nietas de Nonó, Antonio Ramos, Lionel Villahermosa, Perra Mística, Lale Namerrow Pastor, Mima, Eduardo Alegría, nibia pastrana santiago, Viveca Vázquez, Pati Cruz, María José, Kairiana Núñez Santaliz, and La Sombrilla Cuir, among many others—are creating transformative work that demands further scholarly attention. Future research should explore how these and other artists theorize through performance, curate community, and embody resistance within and beyond the archipelago."

13 Grosfoguel argues that the capitalist accumulation processes in history "are related to a racial/ethnic hierarchy and its derivative classifications of superior/inferior, developed/underdeveloped, and civilized/barbarian people." He also notes that "the notion of 'coloniality' conceptualizes the process of colonization of the Americas and the constitution of a capitalist world-economy as part of the same entangled process" (2003, 17).

14 More information on the exhibit *Puerto Rico Negrx* can be found on the web page and social media pages of the MAC museum.

15 I use the term "Spanish Caribbean" to refer to a geographic place that is located in the Caribbean and in which the predominant contemporary spoken language is Spanish. However, I am aware of the complexity of terms such as "Spanish Caribbean" or "Hispanic Caribbean" as they can also refer to the colonized past of this geographic area under Spain. I do not intend to neglect such meaning, but to shift the attention to the more contemporary colonial state of Puerto Rico in its relation with the United States, since it is in tune with the topics covered in this book. At the same time, I note that Puerto Rico is Spanish Caribbean to highlight that it is a Caribbean island (and not—or not simply—a US territory) and that despite the linguistic impositions of English, Spanish is the primary language in Puerto Rico.

16 https://static1.squarespace.com/static/5af199815cfd796ad4930e20/t/5dca948508f69e3b5b6c85c9/1573557399490/La+persistencia+de+la+indolencia+2019.11.12-vf.pdf. This data is from the Observatorio de Equidad de Género de Puerto Rico [Observatory of Puerto Rican Gender Equity] and refers to femicides between 2014 and 2018. That time frame coincides with the beginning period of this book and with the moment during which I was first drafting this introduction. On their website, https://observatoriopr.org/, data on other years until the present are available (also included in the conclusion of this book).

17 While the artists featured in this book have engaged in mentorships and collaborations (among themselves and with other artists) that have nourished their practices over time, establishing a clear artistic lineage remains elusive. Although many acknowledge inspiration from Caribbean and non-Caribbean artists, their work resists being reduced to direct lines of influence. Their aesthetic and political trajectories emerge through complex, nonlinear processes shaped by personal experience, local conditions, and communal exchange. These relationships, while meaningful, often unfold through embodied, affective, and ephemeral interactions—rehearsals, improvisations, gestures, or conversations—that leave little archival trace. Unlike literature or visual art, where influence can be traced through intertextuality or citation, performance is transmitted in situational, often undocumented ways. In the Caribbean, where archives are fragmented and performance frequently intersects with daily life and resistance, genealogies

are further complicated by the medium's fluid and fugitive nature. For instance, while Awilda Sterling-Duprey evokes Sylvia del Villard in her engagement with Afro-Caribbean ancestry, or Franz Kline in her visual language, these connections do not manifest as direct artistic influence. Similarly, Helen Ceballos's work may invite comparison to Ana Mendieta's, yet such affinities suggest resonances rather than traceable inheritances.

CHAPTER ONE Filming, Performing, and Singing Disobedient Femininities

1 This is an anecdote shared by Awilda Sterling-Duprey during the recording of the podcast on March 7, 2024.

2 The artistic name Macha Colón was born gradually as the artist came to perform as a singer around 2007. It is a name connected to her musical production when she wrote a song titled "Las tetas" [Tits] with artist and her friend Gloria Soto. They presented the song before a small audience and introduced themselves with the names of Mary and Macha, Las hermanas Colón [The Colón's sisters]. Later Rosario Ramos put together the two names Mary + Macha, alluding to the insult "marimacha" to refer to masculine and/or homosexual women. That is also the moment in which the artist decided to embrace the label of being a queer artist. Consequently, adopting the insult "marimacha" became a strategy to own an insult to transform it into something positive: if a man can be macho, she could be Macha. Macha is Macha Colón, referring to the historical conqueror Cristobal Colón, putting together and grouping in her artistic name both the queer aspect and the colonial condition of Puerto Rico.

3 I propose Gisela Rosario Ramos's work as a tool of "radical joy" that brings a message of celebration of life in all of its aspects. The most explicit examples of it are in the song "Jayá," which, in the lyrics, performance, and aesthetic of the video (as I will explore in this chapter), is the quintessential of the practice of radical joy as a tool of survival to create community. Celiany Rivera Velázquez, in an article published in 2024, extensively studies the concept of *jayaera* in the work of Macha Colón. The article discusses the evolution of the neologism *jayaera* from 2008 to 2024. However, the author addresses an unfortunate forgetfulness from 2020 that often misplaces the intrinsic connection between Macha Colón and jayaera, with many newer generations using the neologism without awareness of its origin story, despite Macha's seminal work on rescuing the word and expanding its meaning. However, Rivera Vásquez talks about how Gisela (Macha Colón) continues to build on the concept's spiritual component. I agree with Rivera Velázquez's argument of the expansion of the *jayá* concept in Gisela's work. In her films and songs analyzed in this chapter, I found a constant practice of

radical joy that is connected to the idea of jayaera. The characters of her movies, as well as the lyrics of her songs and the aesthetic of her videos, are a way to show the importance of being fulfilled as a human being by doing what makes you feel at peace and what makes you feel an integral part of your community. I find that these themes come back often in the works analyzed. Thus, I do not refer to radical joy as a tool that enforces joy in a "toxic positivity" kind of way. Instead, I see the practice of what I define as "radical joy" in her works, as a way to be "radical" because "joy" is not what society thinks the queer subject is entitled to or deserving of. Consequently, Rosario Ramos proposes the practice of radical joy as a strategy of survival that offers a way to shape paths into the deconstruction and reimagination of femininity, spirituality, beauty standards, and how the queer body can move in the physical space.

4 This idea of "disobedient/irreverent" femininities follows what I describe in the introduction chapter of this book as my way to identify people who decide to live outside of the heteronormative productive standards as theorized by Jack Halberstam in his book *In a Queer Time and Place*. Thus, I address them as "disobedient/irreverent," or as it would be said in colloquial Spanish "malcriadas" women, and I put those terms in quotes, since this is how they are often perceived by those who adhere to a heteronormative and patriarchal society. In the context of this study, it is more of a provocative way to deconstruct what is perceived as a "disobedient/irreverent" behavior based on gender standards. Also, as specified in the introduction, I detach the term *woman* from *womanhood* by treating any expression of femininity as valid regardless of the subject who embodies it. Therefore, these "disobedient/irreverent" femininities are expressed by women who are queering the ways in which we look at beauty standards and gender expression. They are queer beyond their sexual preferences and orientation. Instead, they are embodying, through their art, the complex multilayered reality of being queer.

5 All translations from Spanish into English of titles, song lyrics, and quotes throughout the book are mine.

6 I was able to work with the material included in this chapter thanks to the generosity of Gisela Rosario Ramos. Although her films have been screened at festivals and in movie theaters and her album is available for purchase and online streaming, Gisela graciously granted me access to the films so that I could revisit them as many times as necessary during the writing process. She also gifted me a copy of her album *Tanquecito de amor*.

7 https://www.nalac.org/es/members/2708-gisela-rosario-ramos/

8 Eva Aladro-Vico (2018) defines artivism as the use of art to foster social change and transformation. The term *art*ivist is composed of the words artist + activist and can be traced to the late 1990s among Chicano artists from Los Angeles. The artivist uses their artistic talents to fight and struggle against injustice and

oppression. The artivist merges commitment to freedom and justice. The artists included in this book, including Rosario Ramos, are artivists since their productions open discussions on social, cultural, and political topics, such as patriarchy, sexism, colonialism, and the like. Also, they often intersect their artistic production to community service. This is also the case of Gisela Rosario Ramos, who has worked, for example, for El hogar del buen pastor (2023–24), a place for homeless people. Rosario Ramos was offering workshops for them, or she was organizing movie nights and other activities. I am not expanding on this specific service for two reasons: (1) it falls outside of the time period studied in this book (2013–23), and (2) I focus on how their artistic productions (aesthetics, lyrics, movement, etc.) open space for discussions around sociopolitical and cultural concepts.

9 *Bomba* is both a traditional dance and a musical style of Puerto Rico. Its origins are rooted in the island's history of African slavery, and today it has evolved into a community expression of Puerto Rican culture. While bomba can be used as the generic name for a number of rhythms, it is truly about a creative, interactive relationship between dancers, percussionists and singers. According to anthropologist Bárbara Abadía-Rexach, the original goal of bomba is "visibilizar lo que históricamente ha sido marginado: la Negritud" [to make visible what historically has been marginalized: Negritude] (2015, 11). Also, the author points out that nowadays there is "el nuevo movimiento de la bomba" (NMB; the new movement of bomba). NMB is a new initiative practiced "a favor de la educación sobre la cultura Negra y nacional puertorriqueña [que] va[n] a la par con otras que manifiestan las desigualdades que existen" [in favor of the education of Black national Afro Puerto Rican culture and at the same time it covers other manifestations of inequalities]—for example "los derechos de la comunidad LGBTT" [the rights of the LGBTT community]. As a result, these initiatives "han logrado crear un ambiente general de resistencia y lucha en Puerto Rico" [managed to create a climate of general resistance and fight in Puerto Rico] (2015, 13). However, Abadía-Rexach problematizes the role of NMB because—in her opinion—it nuances "las tensiones raciales existentes, donde la discriminación y el prejuicio hacia los Negros continúa" [the racial tensions that exist, where discrimination and prejudice toward the blacks continue] (2015, 13–14). Thus, the scholar proposes a study of the understanding of Puerto Rican Blackness through the musical discourse, especially focusing on the genre of bomba (Abadía-Rexach 2012, 17–18). However, as Jade Power-Sotomayor argues in her article "Corporeal Sounding: Listening to Bomba Dance, Listening to Puertorriqueñxs," Afro–Puerto Rican bomba is a sonic-centered practice that challenges the Western emphasis on dance as a primarily visual spectacle, redirecting attention to what Ashon Crawley terms the "choreosonic"—the inseparable relationship between movement and sound.

The author highlights how bomba dance generates rhythmic diversity through deliberate movement choices that both emerge from and shape the sonic landscape of drumming and dance. This practice demands a form of listening that creates relational dynamics capable of disrupting colonial, white supremacist, and heteropatriarchal structures that seek to discipline Puerto Rican bodies. By closely analyzing various expressions of bomba, the article explores how dancers assert not just spatial occupation but a relational presence—drawing bodies into collective social experience and challenging linear temporal constraints. It contends that bomba's resurgence on the island and in the diaspora reveals its power to enact a mode of "listening to flesh," particularly attuned to subaltern, racialized, and femme-marked embodiments. In a similar way, throughout this book I argue that movement in relation to physical, domestic, public, metaphorical, and digital spaces addresses how the relation to cultural, political, and social issues can be rethought, dismantled, questioned, and reformulated through a queer lens. It is in this perspective that I study the case of the bomba dances of Lío Villahermosa and their representations on screen. In this section, I do not dive into the racial discourse in relation to bomba, but I focus on the queer aspect that artist Lío Villahermosa conjugates with the genre of bomba, within the context that Abadía-Rexach recognizes as NMB. I also focus on how he—by "listening to flesh" (Power-Sotomayor 2020)—queers the movements in the last scene of his bomba dance and so transforms his relation to space, memory, family history, and identity.

10 The topic of the hegemony in the queer production (especially in film production) is a wider topic that I do not include in this section. However, I briefly mention it to make visible the innovation that *El hijo de Ruby* constitutes when representing the queer topic on screen. Several critics mention the lack of variety within the queer topic in cinema. The majority of queer films favor topics on male homosexuality. Often the characters respond to a heteronormative aesthetic; they are white, young, and respond to specific beauty canons. Even those films that try to show the complexity of the LGBTQ+ community often fall in the same patterns. Among scholars that study this topic, Lawrence La Fountain-Stokes, in his analysis of documentary film *Mala Mala,* about the transsexual community in Puerto Rico, highlights that "en la película se nota un discurso de blanqueamiento" [in the movie there is a whitening tendency] (2016, 193). Jonathan Montalvo speaks of a hypermasculine and heteronormative simulation in his analysis of Dominican film *Sanky Panky* in a context of global capitalism and sexual consumerism (2016, 221–26). Jack Halberstam explores the resistance in associating queerness with Blackness, and he speaks about the tendency in literature and cinema to focus on white gay men when people write about queerness (12, 2005). Finally, José Esteban Muñoz talks about queerness as a phenomenon often considered "'a white

thing' fantasy [. . .] strangely reflected in reverse by the normativity of whiteness in mainstream North American gay culture" (1999, 9) and as a "normative rubric that has policed the sex/gender system" (1999, 58) in the critical proposal to resist the term "masculinity." As I explain in this chapter, *El hijo de Ruby* breaks with binarisms of an expectation of what a queer aesthetic should look like through the narrative structure of the documentary. Refer to the bibliography for more details on the works mentioned.

11 I use the concept of memory as British social anthropologist Paul Connerton defines it in his book *How Societies Remember* (1989). According to Connerton, social memory, rituals, and traditions are essential to understanding the construction of individual memory and collective memory through tools such as dancing, among other tools. Thus, I use this theoretical framework to talk about memory, dance, and tradition in the context of the documentary *El hijo de Ruby.* I also take into consideration the definition of utopia, memory, and future that José Esteban Muñoz develops in *Cruising Utopia,* as I explain in detail in the article.

12 I am thinking here of temporality as it is explained by Jack Halberstam in his book *In a Queer Time and Place,* where what is expected by the members of any society is always based on a heteronormative logic that establishes how the present should be lived according to one's age, sex, etc. Halberstam proposes a queer living as an alternative to escape the rigid parameters of adulthood. I connect Halberstam's reading of time to Muñoz's utopia because when you can shape your own present (by escaping the rigidity of it), the future can hold the potential that Muñoz talks about—a future that can offer endless possibilities of living outside of a heteronormative logic.

13 I go back to Abadía-Rexach when she defines the New Bomba Movement (NMB) as "syncopated identities [that] are interwoven on Puerto Rican race, nationality, culture, gender, and class" (2019, 40). Abadía-Rexach emphasizes how NMB showcases a cultural manifestation that reconfigures Blackness in a complex way to reflect how race is treated and perceived in the Archipelago. According to Abadía-Rexach, these new spaces still allow racist practices and the folklorization of Blackness. In the context of this analysis, as previously specified, I do not focus on the racial role within the history of Lío Villahermosa and his father, who are not dark-skinned Afro–Puerto Ricans. I focus instead on something that has more to do with the queering of bomba performed by Lío in a traditionally patriarchal and sexist space such as bomba music, and the effects and meanings of that message visually represented on screen through the work of Gisela Rosario Ramos. For more information on the racial history of bomba, its contemporary evolution, and its patriarchal structure read Abadía-Rexach, Cartagena, Quintero Rivera, and Rodríguez Juliá, among others.

14 Jerry Ferrao, the singer of the group, is known to be a controversial figure in his circles. He is known for writing songs that bring to light uncomfortable stories about other bomba singers. For example, he had historic conflicts with other authority figures of bomba, such as the late Héctor René "Tito" Matos Otero (June 15, 1968–January 18, 2022), a Puerto Rican percussionist who played the requinto drum, a key instrument in plena music, and one of the founders of the bomba and plena band Viento de Agua. Consequently, it is accurate to say that there is a possibility that Jerry Ferrao was not interested in taking sides, and that he was more interested in being polemical.

15 https://www.youtube.com/watch?v=yqiCevRVA4k

16 It is essential to consider that Abadía-Rexach (2015, 2019) examines how bomba has gained popularity across racial lines over the past twenty years, and how this shift has been facilitated by emphasizing its cultural value while sidelining its racial dimensions. The claim in Ferrao's song that bomba belongs to "el pueblo" [the people] reflects this turn toward the cultural framing of bomba—a move that, as Abadía-Rexach notes, often renders its racial significance invisible. Nevertheless, and while acknowledging Abadía-Rexach's valuable insights, I would argue that the expansion of bomba dancing to include individuals whose identities intersect race with other axes, such as queerness, also opens up space for new forms of belonging. These individuals claim their place in the community through a socially recognized body language—bomba dancing—that affirms their presence and agency.

17 In order to understand the structure of bomba and how it is played and danced, Juan Cartagena explains that the term bomba refers to both the music and the dance. The common element includes percussions of two or more bomba drums. These are the *buleador* (as it is called in the north of the main island), or *tambor segundo* (as it is called in the south of the main island), "a drum which keeps the rhythmic base through a deeper, bass timbre; and a second drum, called *primo* or *subidor* in the north, and *tambor primero* in the south, with a higher pitch timbre used to mark the dancer's steps. [. . .] The interplay between the lead dancer and lead drummer has been characterized as a 'dialogue' or a 'challenge' that produces competition, at times joyful and feigned, and at times serious, that is at the heart of *bomba*" (17).

18 The concept of the "virility of the nation" is in conversation with Puerto Rican scholar Rubén Ríos Ávila. In his essay "Queer Nation" the scholar states, "[L]as figuraciones de la nación puertorriqueña suelen ser, de hecho, como en tantos otros lugares, bastante previsiblemente heteronormativas: o se trata de la nación viril, macha, [. . .], fundada en un heroismo de la hombría, o se trata de la nación femenina [. . .], una isla doncella" [The representations of the Puerto Rican nation are usually one, in fact, as in many other places, fairly and predictably heteronor-

mative: it either is of the virile and masculine nation [. . .] founded on the heroism of masculinity, or it is the feminine nation [. . .], a damsel island] (2009, 1130–31). Ríos Ávila sees the Puerto Rican nation far from recognizing its queer artists, writers, and people. I retake this concept published in an essay in 2009 to propose the work of Macha Colón in 2014 with *El hijo de Ruby* as a concrete proposal to question the binary nation that Ríos Ávila talks about. Gisela Rosario Ramos's work at large is a concrete step forward to queer a nation.

19 Isabel understands contemporary events, such as the earthquakes that afflicted Puerto Rico during the first months of 2020 with disastrous architectural, social, and political consequences. In the scene, although the two women do not discuss anything specific, Isabel says that she is scared, almost as a subliminal message to indicate a concern that does not have to do with the natural event only, but that can be extended to the ways in which natural disasters are politically handled in Puerto Rico, politics that also keep women at the bottom. In the second above-mentioned scene, the protesters on TV want "justice for Keishla." The killing of Keishla—as published by NBC News—was "the latest in a string of at least 21 femicides on the island since January." See the news at https://www.nbcnews.com/news/latino/puerto-rico-mourns-keishla-rodriguez-s-death-boxer-f-lix-n1266598.

20 As previously explained, the term *jayar* is Puerto Rican slang common among people who live in the mountains in Puerto Rico. It refers to when someone feels great and at peace inside. Gisela Rosario Ramos is the first one who rescues the term and makes it widely known in all Puerto Rico through her song "Jayá." I will analyze this song in the next section of this chapter. Mima, who debuted this song on the set of *Perfume de gardenias* by Rosario Ramos, includes in the lyrics a term that recalls and connects with the film director's work.

21 This song is interpreted by Eduardo Alegría and Macha Colón. The video that Tata's son is watching on TV is from Eduardo Alegría's concert Se nos fue la mano [We lost control] by the music group Alegría Rampante. The concert was held in Tapia theater in San Juan, Puerto Rico, on November 18, 2016.

22 The symbolic references at Julia's funeral include the red shoes, a reminder of the feminist fights for all those lives lost because of feminicides, but it is also a reminder of, again, all the lives lost in hurricane María. The rainbow flag is, of course, the symbol of the LGBTQ+ community, and Isabel's souvenirs are small Puerto Rican flags in color and in black and white to represent the country and its grief. The black-and-white version of the flag made its first appearance in 2016 after the establishment of "La Junta de Control Fiscal" (the Fiscal Control Board) and the PROMESA act (the Puerto Rico Oversight, Management, and Economic Stability Act). So, the flag in black and white is a sign of national sorrow for the economic state that the country had been put in, with those extreme measures of austerity that are still affecting the country nowadays.

23 See Christina Sharpe's book *In the Wake: On Blackness and Being* (Duke University Press, 2016). In this book Sharpe interrogates literary, visual, cinematic, and quotidian representations of Black life that compose what she calls the "orthography of the wake." Sharpe illustrates how Black lives are swept up and animated by the afterlives of slavery, and she delineates how the sign of the slave ship marks and haunts contemporary Black life in the diaspora and how the specter of the hold produces conditions of containment, regulation, and punishment, but also something in excess of them. As I explain in the chapter, Sharpe's theory speaks to the ways in which Puerto Rico, especially after María, deals with grief between resilience and trauma in the "hold" of neoliberalism.

24 Yoani María Sánchez Cordero (b. 1975) is a Cuban blogger and journalist internationally recognized for her critical portrayal of life under Cuba's current regime. Her widely translated blog *Generación Y* defies government censorship through creative digital dissemination. Sánchez's video interview with Puerto Rican artist Gisela Rosario Ramos highlights the long-standing historical and political connections between Cuba and Puerto Rico—two "sister islands" united by shared struggles for independence, resistance, and audacity. By engaging in this cross-Caribbean dialogue, Sánchez invokes a legacy of rebellious solidarity and feminist defiance. The interview's title, *Sin pelos en la lengua,* reflects their mutual commitment to outspoken, uncensored expression in times of crisis.

25 Although the album has 2016 as its release date, I understand that some of the songs have probably been released as singles between 2011 and 2016. For example, the song "Jayá" celebrated ten years since its release in 2022.

26 Fernando Picó, for example, explores how fugitive slaves in Puerto Rico used the rugged terrain to establish settlements, engaging in subsistence farming, clandestine trade, and even negotiations with colonial authorities. Lebrón Ortiz investigates how these maroon spaces functioned not just as sites of escape, but as models for alternative political and economic organization that challenged plantation economies. Marronage created alternative ways of living outside colonial control. These maroon communities, such as those found in the mountainous regions of Puerto Rico, transformed the physical landscape into a political space—one where survival, cultural preservation, and resistance were enacted collectively, and it is essential to understand this past to engage with twenty-first-century Caribbean history. Finally, Chuco Quintero examines how contemporary Afro-Caribbean and Indigenous movements navigate between autonomy and institutional recognition, showing how countermarronage operates through policies that claim to include marginalized groups while ultimately maintaining control over them by absorbing or pacifying radical resistance. Quintero explores how this process can be seen, for example, in the co-optation of Afro-Caribbean cultural traditions into nationalist discourses that erase their subversive potential. I use this theoretical

framework to reflect on the sense of community of the neighborhood that Rosario Ramos sings about. The neighborhood becomes a physical space that acquires political meanings as communities come together to resist contemporary displacements (such as gentrification), respond to political abandonment, and create alternative ways of living and being part of society.

27 https://www.youtube.com/watch?v=uNpPQvupacM

28 The strong reaction against a Black female body from men is not new or exclusively experienced by Macha Colón. In fact, there are other examples of this form of manifested misogyny. One of them is the case of the mural *Paz para la mujer* by the collective Moriviví. The mural was completed in January 2015, and in the same year it was vandalized by a few men who painted underwear and a brassiere with white paint to cover the portrayed Black women's breasts and genitals. In reaction to what many understood as an act of censorship, feminists protested in front of the mural. Taking off their tops and posing like the figures in the mural, the women formed a human chain. These events brought forth a much-needed conversation around the control exerted over women's bodies and the different forms violence takes. The story got coverage in all the local news outlets and some online coverage directed to the Latinx community in the US. After that, Colectivo Moriviví did not restore the mural to its original appearance. Instead, the artists intervened. The second figure was restored. Nevertheless, a photomontage of the protests in front of the mural, arranged to look like censorship pixels, was installed over the chest of the first figure. Over time the mural has needed periodic restoration, and each restoration brings some changes. For more info, see https://www.colectivomorivivi.com/2021-paz-mujer.

29 In this section on the visual aesthetic of Rosario Ramos I speak in general of her aesthetic without focusing on all or specific interviews, and I omit many performances that could have a place in this section. This is partially due to space constraints within the chapter, and because I aim to revisit the visual dimensions of Macha Colón, album covers, and songs previously analyzed from different perspectives. Yet, it is worth noting that Gisela Rosario Ramos's appearance—even outside of performance—consistently offers a statement about her position regarding alternative understandings of beauty standards.

30 Macha Colón is periodically invited to recreate *templos de la jayaera*. For example, she created one during the Cumbre Afro [African Summit] organized in March 2024 at the Universidad de Puerto Rico–Río Piedras. I mention the one from December 2022 for two reasons: it marked the anniversary of the song, and it falls within the time frame of this study. This is part of the expansion of the concept of *jayaera* instilled with a spiritual aspect that Celiany Rivera Velázquez analyzes in her article on Macha Colón and the term *jayá* (2024).

31 In Puerto Rican Spanish, *jevota* is a colloquial and gendered term that comes from the word *jeva*, which is slang for a woman—often meaning a girlfriend, a hot woman, or a desirable woman. The -ota suffix is an augmentative that adds emphasis, so *jevota* roughly translates to a super-hot woman, a badass woman, or a confident, sexy, powerful woman. It often implies that the woman in question carries herself with a lot of presence—she's not just attractive, but also unapologetically bold, stylish, and commanding attention, giving an empowering meaning to the term from a feminist or queer perspective. In feminist or queer circles, in fact, it can be reclaimed as a term of pride, signaling an empowered, self-possessed, sensual woman who challenges norms. Thus, addressing a woman as a jevota becomes an act of resistance and self-celebration.

CHAPTER TWO Wonder Woman Dances Every Day

1 Note that even if the artist's pronouns are she/her/hers, when she speaks in Spanish, she uses an inclusive and nonbinary language. So, for instance, she calls the body "la cuerpa" but in Spanish it would be "el cuerpo"; she speaks of "les artistes" instead of "los artistas," and she says "nosotres" instead of the "nosotros" pronoun as it is in standard Spanish. These specific words are not possible to reproduce in English, where words like "body," "us," and "artists" have no gender, grammatically speaking. However, it is important to keep in mind that Awilda uses a gender-inclusive and nonbinary language in her Spanish.

2 The concept of abjection has been widely theorized. I understand abjection as a social tendency of marginalizing otherness because it is considered threatening for society. Julia Kristeva is the first theorist who provides a theory of abjection in *Powers of Horror* (1982). According to her, the abject represents the contamination of the self by otherness. The self—according to Kristeva—can no longer distinguish itself from the other and so threatens the subject with the possibility of its own annihilation. As mentioned in the chapter, Judith Butler looks at abjection from a queer standpoint in her book *Bodies That Matter* (1993). David Sibley, in *Geographies of Exclusion* (1995), demonstrates how the dynamics that establish social exclusion follow the oppressive logic of abjection. He refers especially to queer groups along with other intersecting social groups that deviate from social norms based on race, class, sexuality, immigration status, religion, gender, etc. These groups are abject because they threaten social homogeneity and therefore can destabilize existing social structures. Finally, Arnaldo Cruz-Malavé thinks of present colonialism in Puerto Rico as a form of abjection.

3 Some dates of the performances are approximate since the digital material is partially organized and videos sometimes do not date the year of the work. However, I was able to chronologically reconstruct the work of this artist

through her website, her curriculum vitae, videos on Vimeo and on YouTube, and the artist's collaboration.

4 The misspelling of the word "country," written "cuntry," is intentional by the artist, and I will explain the reasons behind this misspelling later in the chapter.

5 Among the four artists studied in this book, Awilda Rodríguez Lora is perhaps the one with the most organized digital archive of her work. Most of her performances and video performances are accessible through her personal website, Vimeo, and YouTube. Nevertheless, the assistance and generosity of the artist were fundamental in granting access to additional videos, photographs, and contextual information about several of her projects.

6 Lynda Carter was a Mexican American actress who, in the 1970s, embodied the superheroine Wonder Woman, becoming a cultural icon and a symbol of female empowerment during a pivotal moment in US popular culture. Notably, her Mexican heritage—on her mother's side—was rendered invisible, as she was presented (and could pass) according to North American standards of whiteness. It is especially significant that Awilda Rodríguez Lora reclaims this American (whitened) icon, re-Browning and re-Latinizing the figure of Wonder Woman, challenging dominant racialized narratives of representation and power.

7 Las Nietas de Nonó are two Black siblings who, in their creative process, evoke ancestral memory through personal archives. Their practice incorporates performance, found objects, organic materials, ecology, fiction, video, and installation. They are based in Carolina, Puerto Rico. https://www.lasnietasdenono.com/bio-1.

8 As I mentioned, this list is the result of a long archival search. However, it still is an incomplete list of the explorations of *La Mujer Maravilla.* I also indicated the first date in which the explorations have been performed. However, in many cases there have been multiple performances of chapters of *La Mujer Maravilla,* as in the case of *Cuerpa,* or INDIA$, for example.

9 This is an important exploration, as the framing of breastfeeding as "naked exposure" or as being indecent has deep roots in US and Puerto Rican histories, tied to broader social anxieties around gender, sexuality, race, and public space. For example, in the United States it was not until 2018 that breastfeeding in public became legal in all fifty states. However, enforcement and social attitudes still vary. The Puerto Rican archipelago has mirrored many of the US's cultural tensions, though with its own colonial and racial dynamics. However, a law that guarantees a woman's right to breastfeed in any public or private place was passed much earlier than in the US (Law 95, 2004). Nevertheless, despite legal protections, critiques of public breastfeeding—especially in working-class or Afro-Boricua communities—persist, often framed through moral or religious lenses. The idea of breastfeeding as "naked exposure" ties into longer histories of policing the visibility of femme, racialized, and reproductive bodies. Awilda Rodríguez Lora and

many others artivists, especially in feminist and Afro-Caribbean contexts, have pushed back on these norms by reclaiming breastfeeding as a public, political, and communal act. This exploration of *La Mujer Maravilla* is an example of it. For more information on maternity and motherhood in Puerto Rico and in the Caribbean, read works by Ivette Guzmán Zavala, Consuelo Martínez Reyes, Elena Valdez, and Adli Mariann Cordero Espada, among others.

10 https://vimeo.com/laperformera.

11 https://vimeo.com/laperformera.

12 The artist titles the piece *Cuerpa,* which translates as "Body" but with a feminine declination, while in standard Spanish grammar the word "body" has a masculine declination, "cuerpo." This is part of the artist's way of applying the gender-inclusive language that is used increasingly more often in Spanish by LGBTQ+ people, allies, and anyone who prefers a gender-inclusive language.

13 The concept of "cuntry"—a queer, racialized, and often vulgar performance of femininity and nation—can be read as a powerful deconstruction of white Latinidad, particularly as it is critiqued by Jossianna Arroyo in *Caribes 2.0: New Media, Globalization, and the Afterlives of Disaster.* In this work, Arroyo analyzes how Latinidad—especially in postcolonial and digital contexts—often operates as a white, neoliberal script that flattens difference and erases Blackness, Indigeneity, and queerness. Latinidad, in her critique, is a transnational, marketable identity that emerges through circuits of new media and globalization, promoting sanitized narratives of resilience, multiculturalism, and recovery—especially in the wake of disaster. These narratives tend to exclude those bodies and voices that do not fit neatly into the frame of the upwardly mobile, mestiza/o, and respectable Latinx subject. In relation to *Caribes 2.0,* "cuntry" represents the afterlives of disaster not through narratives of resilience or recovery, but through a noisy, excessive, queer Black and Brown presence that defies containment. It resists the erasures embedded in state discourses, media representations, and cultural policies that often rely on whitewashed aesthetics of Latinx identity. Instead, it sounds out survival in the rhythms of *perreo,* in the vernaculars of barrio life, and in the disobedient bodies that dance, curse, lactate, and scream their way into visibility. "Cuntry," as performed by Awilda Rodríguez Lora, works as a queer, anti-respectable, and deeply embodied refusal of that scripted Latinidad. The term itself—blending "country" with the sexualized insult "cunt"—serves to queer both national belonging and gendered decorum. It reclaims the abject, the hypervisible, the "inappropriate," and the racialized feminine as sites of power and survivance. This aesthetic and political mode interrupts neoliberal logics of visibility and consumption by centering the flesh, the local, and the grotesque, refusing the idea that Latinidad must be legible to dominant US-centered frameworks.

14 "¡El pueblo unido jamás será vencido!" is a Chilean protest song first released in 1975 whose music was composed by Sergio Ortega Alvarado and the text written in conjunction with the Quilapayún band. This is one of the most successful songs of the Nueva canción chilena [New Chilean song] movement. The motto has been used in various protests around the world against either left- or right-wing dictatorships and has been translated into many languages around the world.

15 This is a salsa song from 1982 by Bobby Valentín and Cano Estremera.

16 Ignacio Jacinto Villa Fernández (Guanabacoa, Cuba, September 11, 1911–Mexico City, October 2, 1971), better known by his stage name Bola de Nieve, was a Cuban pianist, composer, and singer.

17 The reference to violence as a legacy of patriarchy and colonialism converses with Saidiya Hartman's theory of the afterlives of slavery and colonialism. In her book *Lose Your Mother: A Journey Along the Atlantic Slave Route,* Hartman develops the concept of the afterlives of slavery and colonialism to describe the enduring effects of racial slavery long after its formal abolition. This concept highlights how the legacies of violence, displacement, and dehumanization continue to shape Black life in the present—not as mere historical residue, but as persistent structures of inequality and social death. The continuity of violence, strategies of dispossession and rootlessness, and the erasure in official history and archives all contribute to the continuation of a culture of slavery. The afterlives of slavery exist in these historical absences and the epistemic violence of colonial recordkeeping. The work of Awilda Rodríguez Lora addresses these topics and, through her artistic practice, proposes a way to reimagine the past and reexamine cultural ways of treating Black and Brown female queer bodies. Hartman suggests an ethical responsibility to show how the global racial order—especially the treatment of Black people—is rooted in the plantation, the slave ship, and the colonial encounter. In doing so, she connects historical atrocity to contemporary anti-Blackness.

18 *El puertorriqueño dócil* is a 1967 essay by René Marqués that defines the Puerto Rican personality in different literary and political scenarios. It uses as a starting point the definition of the Puerto Rican as docile, obedient, and easy to subjugate.

19 https://laperformera.org/La-Rosario-1

20 After losing the original *La Rosario* apartment in Santurce due to gentrification and rising rental costs, Awilda Rodríguez Lora relocated the project to the community space of La Goyco, also located in Santurce. While *La Rosario* at La Goyco is no longer a residential space, it now functions as a multipurpose room equipped with a wooden stage, table, and chairs—available for artists to rent for performances, rehearsals, seminars, and other gatherings. This iteration maintains *La Rosario*'s dual model: both a sustainable capitalist framework and a community-based ethos. Since 2021, Rodríguez Lora has been developing *La futura Rosario,* an initiative aimed at recovering the original lodging component of the project.

21 The *coquí* is a common frog in Puerto Rico. It is named after the onomatopoeic sound that the males of two species make at night.

22 Interview with Sarah G. Sharp titled *A Call for Sustento—Interview with Awilda Rodríguez Lora by Sarah G. Sharp,* Performance Is Alive, July 11, 2018, https://www.performanceisalive.com/news/a-call-for-sustento-interview-with-awilda-rodriguez-lora-by-sarah-g-sharp.

23 Since *Sustento* encompasses live performance, community-based projects, and video performance, the title has occasionally appeared in different forms. In some instances, the live performance has been presented as *Sustento capital,* while in others it is referred to simply as *Sustento.* The image chosen in this book comes from the performance *Sustento capital.*

24 I am writing the words "aesthetics" and "aesthesis" as they appear in Mignolo's and Vazquez's article "Decolonial AestheSis: Colonial Wounds/Decolonial Healings—Social Text." The capitalization of the "T" and the "S" in the article serves to exaggerate the different spellings of the two words to avoid any confusion in the reader. According to the authors, while aestheTic became a colonized term, the use of the term aestheSis represents a decolonial alternative to senses and perception of the arts beyond the "Modern aestheTics [that] have played a key role in configuring a canon, a normativity that enabled the disdain and the rejection of other forms of aesthetic practices, or, more precisely, other forms of aesthesis, of sensing and perceiving." See https://socialtextjournal.org/periscope_article/decolonial-aesthesis-colonial-woundsdecolonial-healings/, section 2, second paragraph.

25 https://sites.lsa.umich.edu/cwps-blog/asynch-awilda-rodriguez-lora/

26 https://vimeo.com/841980895. The video performance of *Sustento* was in the making as I was writing this chapter and was screened for the first time while I was finishing the first version of the chapter. I then watched the video at the Museum of Contemporary Art in January 2024 during my stay in Puerto Rico as a fellow of the UNCF/Mellon Residency Program to finish the writing of this book. The artist kindly shared a copy of it with me, so I was able to incorporate this section after the trip to Puerto Rico, when I edited all the chapters.

27 The apparent contradictions between the external funding of artistic projects—particularly from US-based organizations—and Awilda Rodríguez Lora's community-centered practice warrant critical attention. Rather than undermining her decolonial commitments, these tensions are precisely what her work brings into focus. Rodríguez Lora's performances are fundamentally rooted in conviviality and collective care, centering queer, feminist, and Afro-Caribbean communities often erased from dominant cultural narratives. When I refer to her work as a decolonial practice, I highlight how it challenges the foundational logics of coloniality: namely, the heteronormative, patriarchal, and capitalist

structures that define success, value, and belonging. Through queer embodiment, Rodríguez Lora contests normative ideals of family, productivity, and visibility—resonating with critiques articulated by Jack Halberstam—and cultivates a space for alternative modes of living and relating. Importantly, her receipt of financial support through US fellowships or residencies does not negate these politics; rather, it constitutes a strategic reversal of colonial power dynamics. By using such resources to amplify historically silenced voices and to build platforms for marginalized communities, Rodríguez Lora asserts a form of agency that subverts the traditional hierarchies of patronage and voice. In this reclamation, I read not contradiction, but an embodied decolonial act of resistance and reparation.

28 This is how the artist creates a pun on her name in the video performance *Mamá Awilda,* phonetically emphasizing "Awilda" as "A-WILD-a" to highlight the wildness and disobedience with which she lives her queer life.

29 Awilda Rodríguez Lora is not alone in using rest as an epistemological and artistic tool with decolonial and anticapitalist implications. Her work forms part of a rich global tapestry of creative and intellectual practices that challenge dominant ideologies of productivity. For instance, the New York–based organization The Nap Ministry, founded by Tricia Hersey, frames rest as a form of resistance against systemic pressures that valorize overwork and exhaustion. Similarly, *Black Power Naps,* a project founded by Dominican American artists Navild Acosta and Fannie Sosa, proposes "reparations through rest" by creating sleep sanctuaries for BIPOC communities. Their work explicitly challenges the racialized denial of rest and recuperation historically imposed on Black and Brown bodies, offering an overtly anticapitalist and decolonial intervention. Other artists address related themes through distinct lenses: Rafa Esparza (US/Mexico) explores Brown labor and its connections to colonial and labor histories; Autumn Knight (US) investigates Black womanhood, emotional labor, and psychic rest; and Puerto Rican performer and academic nibia pastrana santiago—who occasionally also collaborates with Rodríguez Lora—foregrounds laziness, stillness, and rest as part of a slow, anticapitalistic movement. These practices collectively underscore the increasing relevance of rest as a critical and embodied response to productivity regimes and neoliberal ideologies.

CHAPTER THREE Entre Islas

1 The term *macota* in Dominican Spanish refers to a notebook.

2 *Yola* is a Dominican term that refers to a raft, an improvised and rudimental boat that moves undocumented immigrants. All the translations from Spanish into English are mine. Translated words and titles will only be translated into English the first time that I mention them.

3 The immigration of Dominicans to Puerto Rico has been studied by several scholars, including Jorge Duany, Yolanda Martínez-San Miguel, Jossianna Arroyo, and Marisel Moreno, among others. Duany, for example, in *Los dominicanos en Puerto Rico: Migración en la semi-periferia* (1990), offers a comprehensive examination of Dominican migration to Puerto Rico, situating it within the broader context of global migration patterns and the dynamics of semi-peripheral regions. Duany conceptualizes Puerto Rico as occupying a semiperipheral position in the global economic system, a positioning that influences the nature of Dominican migration. He also explores the labor market experiences of Dominican migrants and the impact of their presence in Puerto Rico on the formation of a transnational identity that reshapes concepts of citizenship and belonging. Martínez-San Miguel, in her article "De ilegales e indocumentados: Representaciones culturales de la migración dominicana en Puerto Rico" (1998), addresses the theme of *dominicanidad* in Puerto Rico, examining how Dominican migration has been represented in Puerto Rican culture. She focuses on constructions of identity, the dynamics of racialization, and the tensions between legality and illegality. Martínez-San Miguel analyzes how these cultural representations reflect and reinforce social perceptions of Dominican immigrants, exploring the complexities of their integration into Puerto Rican society. Arroyo, in her chapter "Caribbean Mediascapes: Ruins and Debt in Puerto Rico," featured in the edited volume *Caribbean Migrations* (2020), examines the intersections of media, migration, and the socioeconomic challenges faced by Caribbean societies, including Puerto Rico. While the chapter broadly addresses Caribbean mediascapes, it provides context for understanding how media representations influence perceptions of migrant communities, such as Dominicans in Puerto Rico. Finally, Marisel Moreno, in *Crossing Waters: Undocumented Migration in Hispanophone Caribbean and Latinx Literature & Art* (2022), delves into the complexities of Dominican migration to Puerto Rico. She offers a nuanced examination of how literature and visual art portray undocumented migration within the Spanish-speaking Caribbean, particularly focusing on Dominicans navigating the perilous Mona Passage to reach Puerto Rico. Moreno also specifically addresses the gendered dimension of migration, highlighting the unique challenges faced by Dominican women. She examines how these women confront both the physical dangers of sea crossings and the societal prejudices encountered upon arrival in Puerto Rico. All of these works reflect histories that resonate with Helen Ceballos's personal story as an undocumented Dominican immigrant in Puerto Rico and with some of the central themes in her artistic work.

4 Most of Helen Ceballos's performances, video performances, photographs, and images do not circulate publicly and have been made accessible to me through the generosity of the artist herself. Some materials—such as video excerpts, inter-

views, and the photo-essay *Cerezas por papeles*—are available on digital platforms like YouTube and Facebook. However, Ceballos does not maintain a personal archive or website, and much of her digital, performative, and visual work exists only through personal recordings or photographs, which has posed a significant challenge in reconstructing the trajectory of her artistic practice.

5 The performances have been selected following four criteria: (1) The time period I cover in this book (2013–23); (2) The topics explored that related to migration, the Caribbean, mourning and loss, and queerness and the female body; (3) Talking to the artist and making her part of the selection; (4) The ways in which these performances are connected with other works, projects, or cultural initiatives.

6 Once more, I would like to go back to the work of Marisel Moreno—particularly her book *Crossing Waters: Undocumented Migration in Hispanophone Caribbean and Latinx Literature & Art* (2022)—which addresses a variety of topics that helped me conceptualize the work of Ceballos. For example, Moreno discusses how the Caribbean Sea, often romanticized as a site of leisure or cultural hybridity, is in fact a space of death, displacement, and racialized state violence. She conceptualizes the sea as a borderland without fixed lines on land—a fluid, unstable, and deadly space. In this framework, the Caribbean Sea becomes a racialized, militarized, and gendered border where undocumented migrants are surveilled, detained, or left to perish. Moreno argues that while water may suggest openness or freedom, for migrants it often represents containment, risk, and invisibility. The "sea as borderland" is where legal status, humanity, and even life itself are negotiated—and often denied. This understanding of the sea is visually represented in Ceballos's work. The artist connects her personal experiences and migration traumas to her art, where themes of displacement and migration are central. In this way, Moreno and Ceballos enter into a dialogue in which the Caribbean Sea ceases to be a paradise and instead becomes a dangerous borderland. Dominican migrant women are also central to both Moreno's and Ceballos's work, as they explore how women experience the border through their bodies—from the constant risk of sexual violence to social exclusion, exploitation, and sex work.

7 https://sitiadadehelenceballos.blogspot.com/

8 https://www.youtube.com/watch?v=eWNYeaXOxxE

9 https://www.youtube.com/watch?v=k2v4OvtXmiI

10 https://ishbelcora.wordpress.com/2018/11/11/helen-ceballos-mi-cuerpo-es-mi-unica-patria/

11 https://vimeo.com/369036373. At the 34:42–36:34 mark.

12 https://www.youtube.com/watch?v=Fn_VDa2heQA

13 https://www.youtube.com/watch?v=5HAShiC3bjU

14 Oshun (or Ochún) is a recurring spiritual presence in Afro-Caribbean aesthetics, especially within Santería/Lukumí and other Yoruba-derived traditions. Ceballos

invokes Oshun not only as a symbol of sensuality, fertility, and beauty, but also as a protector of the vulnerable, particularly migrant women and queer bodies who traverse hostile environments.

15 Rebeca Hey-Colón theorizes water as a carrier of memory, spirituality, and epistemology within Afro-Caribbean and Latinx cultural production. Water is a way to channel its power, both salty and sweet, in sustaining connections between past, present, and not-yet-imagined futures. She explores how water deities—especially Yoruba orishas like Ochún, Yemayá, and Olokun—are not just mythic figures but active presences in diasporic identity, resistance, and healing practices. Ceballos's performance can be read as part of these aquatic epistemologies—knowledges that flow through the body, through trauma, and through diasporic memory. Other authors that touch on the topic of Afro-Caribbean spirituality in connection to the ocean as sites of resistance and self-making are Jossianna Arroyo, who touches broadly on Afro-Caribbean spiritual-political dimensions and resistance through spirituality in works such as *Travestismos culturales* (2003) and *Writing Secrecy in Caribbean Freemasonry* (2013). Also, Omise'eke Natasha Tinsley in her book *Ezili's Mirrors: Reflections of Feminist Black Atlantic* shows how Caribbean water spirits like Ezili—and by extension, Ochún—are not just nurturing but also erotic, dangerous, and powerful. This complexity is echoed in Ceballos's work, which mixes softness with rage, and sensuality with trauma.

16 https://www.youtube.com/watch?v=fUcH4VoOqug

17 The "body without organs" is a concept that Deleuze and Guattari mobilize in opposition to the organism and its organization, in opposition to the functional specificity of organs, so as to release the decoded and deterritorialized flows of desire. The BwO is the "anorganism of the body" a bundle of virtual affects in a nonorganic and nonorganized multiplicity.

18 https://drive.google.com/file/d/1g3EnefSZZGmq7JpADqoROILbllO7Adom/view

19 https://www.youtube.com/watch?v=Rv1AmJ1DSLs

20 https://www.youtube.com/watch?v=aS1-RuSVuOs

21 As mentioned, Oshun is a goddess in the Yoruba religion of West Africa. Oshun is a river deity and is associated with water, purity, fertility, love, and sensuality. She also represents the combination of death and rebirth.

22 Some of the gestures and images that Helen Ceballos creates in her performances recall the work of Cuban artist Ana Mendieta (1948–1985). Earth and water are sacred, maternal elements in the work of both artists. They are drawn to Indigenous, Yoruba, and Afro-Cuban spiritual traditions, often invoking female deities and elemental forces such as earth, fire, blood, and water. In both cases, nature is gendered and spiritualized, offering alternative cosmologies to Western, patriarchal frameworks. Though separated by generations and geopolitical contexts, Ceballos and Mendieta share profound aesthetic, thematic, and spiritual affinities in their

performance-based work. Both artists use the body as a site of political, spiritual, and decolonial intervention, turning to nature, ritual, and Afro/Indigenous epistemologies to articulate complex experiences of displacement, gendered violence, and belonging. This parallel is worth highlighting since—as previously noted—Ceballos's identity and artistic practice reflect the interconnectedness of the Hispanic Caribbean. This transtemporal comparison underscores how certain forms of expression and media reemerge to address enduring realities rooted in the history, politics, and coloniality of these geographies, revealing their continued urgency and relevance.

23 *Santería* is a syncretic religion that combines traditional Yoruba beliefs from West Africa with Catholicism and Spiritism. It was originally developed in Cuba and then spread through Latin America.

24 https://www.afrolatinoforum.org/pensamientos-blog/cerezas-por-papeles-cherries-for-documents, translation from Spanish into English by Rojo Robles. However, in my opinion, "el premio no iba a llegar" would have been more accurately translated as "the prize was not going to arrive." In this statement, the artist captures the profound disillusionment that many migrants face: while the act of migration is often driven by the hope of achieving something better—framed as "arriving" or "winning"—the reality upon arrival is frequently one of continued struggle, marginalization, and precarity.

25 In Spanish and in Caribbean slang the *cherrie* also indicates the woman's vulva or virginity—the phrase "pop your cherry" refers to losing your virginity. This scene, then, could also refer to tourist economies in the Dominican Republic, sex work, sex violence, abuse, and the exploitation of women's bodies.

26 https://www.afrolatinoforum.org/pensamientos-blog/cerezas-por-papeles-cherries-for-documents. Translation from Spanish into English by Rojo Robles.

27 https://drive.google.com/file/d/1UMqcVCPuVM1UH9tHSmzL62wt6BTKVmoq/view

28 The artist uses the word *cuerpa,* which in Spanish changes the grammatical genre of the word *cuerpo* [body] into *cuerpa.* The meaning is not altered, but the intent is to propose a decolonial language that deconstructs patriarchal structures through language. I left it in Spanish in the English translation because there is not a corresponding term in English.

29 https://drive.google.com/file/d/1MHSyYLmLna_cX_wOnWJPn7vI6-kleyZe/view

30 https://open.spotify.com/episode/3x3EqhdpJ2xINKEIZ5CbOy

31 This is the text sent by the curators to Miami Art Week and shared with me by Helen Ceballos.

32 https://web.archive.org/web/20230726212850/https://plataformaeje.pr/

33 Manuel Ramos Otero (1948–1990) was a pioneering Puerto Rican writer, poet, and openly gay intellectual whose work broke ground in articulating queer desire, exile, and marginality from a Caribbean and diasporic perspective. Born in

Manatí, Puerto Rico, and later based in New York City, Ramos Otero's writing traverses themes of sexuality, colonial displacement, and the aesthetics of resistance, often blending autobiographical elements with experimental forms. His influential collection *Invitación al polvo* (1991), published posthumously, reflects a poetics of fragmentation and survival in the face of AIDS (the cause of his death), homophobia, and cultural alienation. Through his literary and political interventions, Ramos Otero forged a critical space for queer Caribbean expression that continues to resonate across contemporary artistic and academic landscapes.

CHAPTER FOUR Artistic Articulations

1 *Cimarrona* is in Spanish the feminine declination of the word *cimarrón*, which means runaway slave.

2 https://www.youtube.com/watch?v=_FiJ8tuTvIU

3 https://www.youtube.com/watch?v=rxfEzk_m4cY

4 https://www.youtube.com/watch?v=_FiJ8tuTvIU

5 https://www.youtube.com/watch?v=VcoOygyOx-M

6 I am referring here to the reactions of the audience recorded in the video that is available online. However, I am certain that every audience exposed to this piece would have a similar reaction. Hence, this is an analysis that is true beyond the single performance taken in consideration here.

7 Tego Calderón is using in this song two culturally specific words to refer to Black people. They are *negrito* and *niche*. The word "negrito" technically means "little Black person" and it was coined by sixteenth-century Spanish missionaries operating mainly in the Philippines, but then it was borrowed by other Spaniard colonialists. In contemporary Spanish it still translates to "little Black man." However, it is generally not considered a racial slur in Latin America and often has a positive meaning, such as a term of endearment. The word comes from the Spanish word negro, which means "Black." The word "niche," instead, has an offensive potential for Black people. It is more of a local word that in the past was used to also refer to a Black person. However, it is not much used in the present anymore and, when used, it is because it culturally remembers the famous Black Puerto Rican singer Ismael Rivera and his song "El niche." Here, I decided to translate both terms in English with the word "Black," which ultimately is what they both mean. The word "niche" might resemble the N word as used in US English. However, I think that the N word in the United States has different negative connotations. For that, I translated both times with the word "Black."

8 The question was: "¿Cómo fue, para una mujer afroantillana, representar y desmantelar, tanto internamente en movimiento como en consciencia social, lo que es el patriarcado usando una figura tan amada como Maelo, y terminar desha-

ciendo algo que ni siquiera estaba materializado? ¿Cómo eso se reflejó, luego de terminar esa pieza, en Awilda como profesional del movimiento y del arte?" [How was it, for an Afro-Caribbean woman, to represent and dismantle, both internally in movement and in social consciousness, what the patriarchy is using a figure as beloved as Maelo, and end up undoing something that wasn't even materialized? How did that reflect, after finishing that piece, on Awilda as a professional of movement and of art?]

9 The resurgence of interest in Cangrejos, Cortijo, and Maelo within Puerto Rican academic and cultural discourse reflects a broader movement to reclaim Afro-Caribbean heritage and challenge historical erasures. This revival is evident in recent scholarly works and artistic performances that center Afro–Puerto Rican contributions to the island's cultural identity. One significant contribution to this discourse is the dissertation by César Colón Montijo, which delves into the life and legacy of Ismael Rivera. Colón Montijo's research offers an in-depth analysis of Rivera's musical career, his role in Afro–Puerto Rican identity formation, and the sociopolitical contexts that shaped his artistry. This work not only highlights Rivera's influence on Puerto Rican music but also situates him within the broader narratives of resistance and cultural affirmation. Similarly, Marisel Hernández's publication on Rafael Cortijo provides a comprehensive examination of Cortijo's impact on Puerto Rican music and culture. Her work explores how Cortijo's fusion of Afro-Caribbean rhythms with traditional Puerto Rican music challenged prevailing racial and cultural norms, paving the way for greater acceptance and celebration of Afro–Puerto Rican heritage. These scholarly endeavors, alongside performances like Awilda Sterling-Duprey's *Maelo en el cuerpo,* signify a deliberate effort to recenter Afro–Puerto Rican figures in the island's cultural narrative. By revisiting and reinterpreting the contributions of artists like Rivera and Cortijo, contemporary scholars and artists are actively engaging in a process of cultural reclamation and redefinition. This academic and cultural resurgence not only honors the legacies of these influential figures but also fosters a more inclusive understanding of Puerto Rican identity—one that acknowledges and celebrates its Afro-Caribbean roots.

10 Casa de América is a public consortium whose purpose is to strengthen bonds between Spain and Latin America through seminars, roundtables, exhibitions, master classes, conferences, film screenings, discussions, presentations, workshops, and other activities. The consortium was founded in 1990 by the Ministry of Foreign Affairs and Cooperation in Madrid, Spain.

11 https://www.youtube.com/watch?v=ox6a6yGrHOc

12 *Regla de Ocha* considers that all things have a spirit—people, rivers, plants, and stones. This belief is connected to the idea that *Orishas* gods manifest themselves

in the human world through nature. *Santería* is another name for *Regla de Ocha,* also known as *Regla Lucumí* or *Lucumí.* It originated in Cuba in the late nineteenth century amid a process of syncretism between the Yoruba religion of West Africa, the Catholic religion brought by Spaniard colonizers, and Spiritism. There is no central authority in control of the practices of *Regla de Ocha/Santería*; thus, much diversity exists among practitioners.

13 https://www.youtube.com/watch?v=sFhpBEI1ODg

14 This poem can be analyzed in multiple ways, and the racial aspect of it is not the only aspect that it is worth analysis. Precarity, social class, and the condition of the poet are all aspects that are present in this poem. However, in this context I am analyzing the poem in relation to the video performance by Sterling-Duprey. In that optic, I pay particular attention to the racial aspect of it.

15 See note 50 for a better understanding of the term "abject" from a theoretical standpoint.

16 https://www.youtube.com/watch?v=fxwTfwEe9tg

17 https://www.youtube.com/watch?v=dWkAwZFAoBo

18 This is a term explored in the work of French Marxist philosopher and sociologist Henri Lefebvre (1901–1991). He posits that the human body is composed of several rhythms; in order to observe rhythms outside of the body, the rhythmanalyst must use her or his own rhythms as a reference to unify the rhythms under analysis. Consequently, the rhythm is the conjunction of the rhythmanalyst and the object of the analysis. This is a method for analyzing the rhythms of urban spaces and the effects of those rhythms on the inhabitants of those spaces. This is a concept that Awilda Sterling-Duprey takes into consideration to develop her performative work, especially *en-cierro* and *Lacks Criticality.*

19 https://vimeo.com/320755905

20 Henri Lefebvre, as mentioned, authored a collection of essays titled *Rhythmanalysis: Space, Time and Everyday Life.* In this book he outlined a method for analyzing the rhythms of urban spaces and the effects of those rhythms on the inhabitants of those spaces.

21 See the fourth paragraph of "2018 Reflection: Response Commission presents Awilda Sterling Duprey's Lacks Criticality, Sept 21 & 22," Philadelphia Dance.org, September 15, 2018, archived August 11, 2020, at https://web.archive.org/web/20200811134549/https://philadelphiadance.org/dancejournal/2018/09/15/2018-reflectionresponse-commission-presents-awilda-sterling-dupreys-lacks-criticality-sept-21-22/.

22 I am thinking here of works such as *El puertorriqueño dócil* [The docile Puerto Rican] by René Marqués (1919–1979). Published in 1967, the essay focuses on the problem of national identity in relation to the language, literature, and social

conditions in Puerto Rico. Specifically, Marqués in this essay defines the personality of a Puerto Rican as docile and obedient to whoever is in power as a form of critique regarding colonialism and the subordinate state of the island, and he determines the docility as a deterrent to achieving independence.

23 Jenny Gill. "In the Studio: Awilda Sterling." Joan Mitchell Foundation. June 9, 2023. https://www.joanmitchellfoundation.org/journal/in-the-studio-awilda-sterling. See especially last six paragraphs.

24 LATEA Tertulia/REMOTO conversation in Spanish with Awilda Sterling-Duprey on the occasion of her participation in the Whitney Biennial that closed on September 5, 2022. https://www.youtube.com/watch?v=rxfEzk_m4cY.

25 Franz Kline was an American painter. He is associated with the Abstract Expressionist movement of the 1940s and 1950s.

CHAPTER FIVE Conclusion

1 Edrimael Delgado Reyes, "Cuando bailo soy mujer," *CENTRO Journal* 36, no. 2 (Summer 2024): 237–39.

BIBLIOGRAPHY

Abadía-Rexach, Bárbara. "Centro y periferia: Las identidades en el nuevo movimiento de la bomba puertorriqueña." *CENTRO Journal* 31, no. 2 (Summer 2019).

———. *Musicalizando la raza: La racialización en Puerto Rico a través de la música.* Ediciones Puerto, 2012.

———. "¡Saludando al tambor! El nuevo movimiento de la bomba puertorriqueña." Doctoral thesis, University of Texas at Austin, 2015.

Alvarado, Leticia. *Abject Performances.* Duke University Press, 2018.

Aponte-Ramos, Dolores. "Awilda Sterling, autobiografía menipea de la danzante, del ojo que la mira, del oído que la escucha." *Revista del ICP (Instituto de Cultura Puertorriqueña),* 3rd series, no. 6 (2017).

Arroyo, Jossianna. "Caribbean Mediascapes: Ruins and Debt in Puerto Rico." In *Caribbean Migrations: The Legacies of Colonialism,* edited by Anke Birkenmaier. Rutgers University Press, 2020.

———. *Caribes 2.0: New Media, Globalization, and the Afterlives of Disaster.* Rutgers University Press, 2023.

Austin, J. L. *How to Do Things with Words.* Edited by J. O. Urmson, and Marina Sbisà. 2nd ed. Harvard University Press, 1975.

Bach, Kent. "Speech Acts." In *Routledge Encyclopedia of Philosophy,* edited by Edward Craig, 2014.

Barthes, Roland. *Camera Lucida: Reflections on Photography.* Hill and Wang, 2010.

Bonilla, Yarimar. "The Coloniality of Disaster: Race, Empire, and the Temporal Logics of Emergency in Puerto Rico, USA." *Political Geography* 78 (2020).

Bonilla, Yarimar, and Marisol LeBrón, eds. *Aftershocks of Disaster: Puerto Rico Before and After the Storm.* Haymarket Books, 2019.

Brent, Linda. *Incidents in the Life of a Slave Girl: An Authentic Historical Narrative Describing the Horrors of Slavery as Experienced by Black Women.* Harvest/Harcourt, 1983. Originally published 1861.

Briggs, Laura. *Reproducing Empire: Race, Sex, Science, and U.S. Imperialism in Puerto Rico.* University of California Press, 2003.

Brusi, Rima, Yarimar Bonilla, and Isar Godreau. "When Disaster Capitalism Comes for the University of Puerto Rico." *The Nation*, September 20, 2018, https://www.thenation.com/article/archive/when-disaster-capitalism-comes-for-the-university-of-puerto-rico/.

Burt, Ramsay. "Genealogy and Dance History: Foucault, Rainer, Bausch, and de Deersmaeker." In *Of the Presence of the Body: Essays on Dance and Performance Theory*, edited by André Lepecki, 29–46. Wesleyan University Press, 2004.

Butler, Judith. *Bodies That Matter.* Routledge, 1993.

———. *Gender Trouble: Feminism and the Subversion of Identity.* Routledge, 1990.

———. *Notes Toward a Performative Theory of Assembly.* Harvard University Press, 2018.

Byrd, Jodi A. "Beast of America: Sovereignty and the Wildness of Objects." *South Atlantic Quarterly* 117, no. 3 (2018): 599–615. Publication edited by Jack Halberstam and Tavia Nyong'o.

Cartagena, Juan. "When Bomba Becomes the National Music of the Puerto Rico Nation . . ." *CENTRO Journal*, 16, no. 1 (Spring 2004).

Chambers-Letson, Joshua. *After the Party: A Manifesto for Queer of Color Life.* New York University Press, 2018.

Claudio, Karla. "Ni Una Más: Boricua Women Fight Misogyny with Art." *ArtsEverywhere.* October 7, 2019. https://www.artseverywhere.ca/boricua-women/.

Connerton, Paul. *How Societies Remember.* Cambridge University Press, 1989.

Contreras Capó, Vanesa, and Nicole Delgado. "Debt and Structural Gender Violence." *Critical Times* 4, no. 1 (April 1, 2021): 167–69.

Cooper, Carolyn. *Sound Clash: Jamaican Dancehall Culture at Large.* Palgrave Macmillan, 2004.

Cruz-Malavé, Arnaldo. *Bailando en un encierro: Duelo, danza y activismo en las manifestaciones del verano boricua de 2019.* Editora Educación Emergente, 2023.

———. "'What a Tangled Web!': Masculinidad, abyección y la fundación de la literatura puertorriqueña en los Estados Unidos." *Revista de crítica literaria latinoamericana* 23, no. 45 (1997): 327–40.

Dávila, Arlene, and Yasmin Ramirez, eds. *Nuyorican and Diasporican Visual Art: A Critical Anthology.* Duke University Press, 2025.

Decenas, Carlos Ulises. *Circuits of the Sacred: A Faggotology in the Black Latinx Caribbean (Writing Matters!).* Duke University Press, 2023.

Deleuze, Gilles, and Félix Guattari. *A Thousand Plateaus: Capitalism and Schizophrenia.* 1st ed. University of Minnesota Press, 1987.

Delgado Reyes, Edrimael. "Cuando bailo soy mujer." *CENTRO Journal* 36, no. 2 (Summer 2024): 237–39. Special issue on *Caudal: Rasanblaj of Contemporary Feminist and Queer/Cuir Perspectives on Puerto Rico and the Dominican Republic*, edited by Celiany Rivera Velázquez and Carlos Ulises Decena.

———. "Perreo combativo frente a la Catedral: Una perspectiva cuir." *El Nuevo Día*, July 28, 2019. https://www.todaspr.com/perreo-combativo-frente-a-la-catedral-una-perspectiva-cuir/.

Dolan, Jill. *The Feminist Spectator as Critic*. University of Michigan Press, 2012.

———. *Geographies of Learning: Theory and Practice, Activism and Performance*. Wesleyan University Press, 2001.

———. *Utopia in Performance: Finding Hope at the Theater*. University of Michigan Press, 2005.

Duany, Jorge. *Los dominicanos en Puerto Rico: Migración en la semi-periferia*. Ediciones Huracán, 1990.

Ellis, Nadia. *Territories of the Soul: Queered Belonging in the Black Diaspora*. Duke University Press, 2015.

Fauzia, Claudia, and Valentina Amenta. *Femminismo terrone: Per un'alleanza dei margini*. Tlon Edizioni, 2024.

Franko, Mark. "Given Movement: Dance and the Event." In *Of the Presence of the Body: Essays on Dance and Performance Theory*, edited by André Lepecki, 113–23. Wesleyan University Press, 2004.

Freeman, Elizabeth. *Time Binds: Queer Temporalities, Queer Histories*. Duke University Press, 2010.

García Peña, Lorgia. *The Borders of Dominicanidad: Race, Nation, and Archives of Contradiction*. Duke University Press, 2016.

———. *Translating Blackness: Latinx Colonialities in Global Perspective*. Duke University Press, 2022.

Gardiner, Judith Kegan, ed. *Provoking Agents: Gender and Agency in Theory and Practice*. University of Illinois Press, 1995.

GegenSichKollektiv. "Anti-Self: Experience-less Noise." In *Reverberations: The Aesthetics, Affect and Politics of Noise*, edited by Michael Goddard, Benjamin Halligan, and Paul Hegarty, 193–206. Continuum International, 2012.

Glissant, Édouard. *Poetics of Relation*. Translated by Betsy Wing. University of Michigan Press, 2006. Originally published in French by Gallimard, 1990.

Goddard, Michael, Benjamin Halligan, and Paul Hegarty, eds. *Reverberations: The Philosophy Aesthetics and Politics of Noise*. Continuum International, 2012.

Godreau, Isar, and Yarimar Bonilla. "Nonsovereign Racecraft: How Colonialism, Debt, and Disaster are Transforming Puerto Rican Racial Subjectivities." *American Anthropologist* 123, no. 3 (2021): 452–66.

Grosfoguel, Ramón. *Colonial Subjects: Puerto Ricans in a Global Perspective*. University of California Press, 2003.

Halberstam, Jack/Judith. *Female Masculinity*. Duke University Press, 2018.

———. *In a Queer Time and Place: Transgender Bodies, Subcultural Lives*. New York University Press, 2005.

———. *The Queer Art of Failure.* Duke University Press, 2011.

———. *Wild Things: The Disorder of Desire.* Duke University Press, 2020.

Halberstam, Jack, and Tavia Nyong'o, eds. *Wildness.* Special issue of *South Atlantic Quarterly* 117, no. 3. Duke University Press, 2018.

Hey-Colón, Rebeca. *Channeling Knowledges: Water and Afro-Diasporic Spirits in Latinx and Caribbean Worlds.* University of Texas Press, 2023.

Homar, Susan, and nibia pastrana santiago, eds. *Habitar lo imposible: Danza y experimentación en Puerto Rico.* Beta Local, 2022.

hooks, bell. *Art on My Mind.* New Press, 1995.

Irigaray, Luce. *This Sex Which Is Not One.* Cornell University Press, 1985. Originally published in French in 1977.

Irobi, Esiaba. "The Philosophy of the Sea: History, Economics and Reason in the Caribbean Basin." *Worlds and Knowledges Otherwise* 1, dossier 3 (2006). Post Continental Phylosophy.

Jackson, Zakiyyah Iman. "*Theorizing in a Void:* Sublimity, Matter, and Physical in Black Feminist Poetics." *South Atlantic Quarterly* 117, no. 3 (2018): 617–48. Publication edited by Jack Halberstam and Tavia Nyong'o.

Kalyva, Eve. "The Rhetoric of Disobedience: Art and Power in Latin America." *Latin American Research Review* 51, no. 2 (2016): 46–66.

Kincaid, Jamaica. *A Small Place.* Farrar, Straus and Giroux, 1988.

King, Rosamond. *Island Bodies: Transgressive Sexualities in the Caribbean Imagination.* University Press of Florida, 2016.

Kontopoulos, Kyriakos. *The Logics of Social Structures.* Cambridge University Press, 1993.

LaBelle, Brandon. *Background Noise: Perspectives on Sound Art.* 2nd ed. Bloomsbury, 2015.

La Fountain-Stokes, Lawrence. "Mala Mala y la representación transgénero y transformista en el cine puertorriqueño." In *Nuestro Caribe: Poder, raza y poscolonialismo desde los límites del mapa LGBTQ,* edited by Mabel Cuesta, 185–200. Isla Negra Editores, 2016.

———. *Queer Ricans: Cultures and Sexualities in the Diaspora.* University of Minnesota Press, 2011.

———. *Translocas: The Politics of Puerto Rican Drag and Trans Performance.* University of Michigan Press, 2021.

Lara, Ana-Maurine. *Queer Freedom: Black Sovereignty.* Afro-Latinx Futures Series. State University of New York Press, 2021.

———. *Streetwalking: LGBTQ Lives and Protest in the Dominican Republic.* Critical Caribbean Studies Series. Rutgers University Press, 2020.

Lazzara, Michael J., and Vicky Unruh, eds. *Telling Ruins in Latin America.* Palgrave Macmillan, 2009.

Lebrón Ortiz, Pedro. *Filosofía del cimarronaje*. Editora Educación Emergente, 2020.

———. "Maroon Logics as Flight from the Euromodern." *Transmodernity: Journal of Peripheral Cultural Production of the Luso-Hispanic World* 9, no. 2 (2019).

Lefebvre, Henri. *Rhythmanalysis: Space, Time and Everyday Life*. Bloomsbury Academic, 2013.

Lepecki, André. *Of the Presence of the Body: Essays on Dance and Performance Theory*. Wesleyan Dance Series. Wesleyan University Press, 2004.

Lugones, María. "Toward a Decolonial Feminism." *Hypatia* 25, no. 4 (2010): 742–59.

Maldonado-Torres, Nelson. "Towards a Combative Decolonial Aesthetics." In *The Routledge Companion to Decolonizing Art History*, edited by Tatiana Flores, Florencia San Martín, and Charlene Villaseñor Black, 583–90. Routledge, 2023.

Manalansan, Martin F. "Messy Mismeasures: Exploring the Wilderness of Queer Migrant Lives." *South Atlantic Quarterly* 117, no. 3 (2018): 491–506. Publication edited by Jack Halberstam and Tavia Nyong'o.

Marqués, René. *El puertorriqueño dócil y otros ensayos, 1953–1971*. Editorial Antillana, 1977.

Martínez Reyes, Consuelo. "La fluidez del género como estrategia en el cine y la literatura lésbicos del Caribe hispano." In *Nuestro Caribe: Poder, raza y poscolonialismo desde los límites del mapa LGBTQ*, edited by Mabel Cuesta, 136–50. Isla Negra Editores, 2016.

———. "From Alienation to Revolution: Female Characters as Decolonial Tools in J. L. Torres's *The Accidental Native*." *Revista Canadiense de Estudios Hispánicos* 46, no. 1 (2021): 169–89.

Martínez-San Miguel, Yolanda. "De ilegales e indocumentados: Representaciones culturales de la migración dominicana en Puerto Rico." *Revista De Ciencias Sociales* 4 (1998): 113–73.

Masiello, Francine. "Scribbling on the Wreck." In *Telling Ruins in Latin America*, edited by Michael J. Lazzara and Vicky Unruh. Palgrave Macmillan, 2009.

Massumi, Brian. "Floating the Social: An Electronic Art of Noise." In *Reverberations: The Philosophy Aesthetics and Politics of Noise*, edited by Michael Goddard, Benjamin Halligan, and Paul Hegarty, 40–57. Continuum International, 2012.

Mignolo, Walter. *The Darker Side of Renaissance: Literacy, Territoriality and Colonization*. University of Michigan Press, 1995.

———. *Local Histories/Global Designs: Essays on the Coloniality of Power, Subaltern Knowledges and Border Thinking*. Princeton University Press, 2000.

Montalvo, Jonathan. "¿Dónde está el bugarrón? Exclusión e inclusión de un modelo de masculinidad y sexualidad alterno en la película Sanky Panky y la novela Sirena Selena vestida de pena." In *Nuestro Caribe: Poder, raza y poscolonialismo desde los límites del mapa LGBTQ*, edited by Mabel Cuesta, 221–36. Isla Negra Editores, 2016.

Moreno, Marisel. *Crossing Waters: Undocumented Migration in Hispanophone Caribbean and Latinx Literature & Art.* University of Texas Press, 2022.

Muñoz, José Esteban. *Cruising Utopia: The Then and There of Queer Futurity.* New York University Press, 2009.

———. *Disidentifications: Queer of Color and the Performance of Politics.* University of Minnesota Press, 1999.

Nixon, Angelique. *Resisting Paradise: Tourism, Diaspora, and Sexuality in Caribbean Culture.* University Press of Mississippi. 2015.

Pérez Royo, Victoria. *¡A bailar a la calle! Danza contemporánea, espacio público y arquitectura.* Universidad de Salamanca, 2009.

Picó, Fernando. *Libertad y servidumbre en el Puerto Rico del siglo XIX.* Edición Uracán, 1983.

Pitts, Andrea, Mariana Ortega, and José Medina, eds. *Theories of the Flesh: Latinx and Latin American Feminisms, Transformation, and Resistance.* Oxford University Press, 2020.

Power-Sotomayor, Jade. "Corporeal Sounding: Listening to Bomba Dance, Listening to puertorriqueñxs." *Performance Matters* 6, no. 2 (2020): 43–59.

Przybylski, Liz. *Sonic Sovereignty: Hip Hop, Indigeneity, and Shifting Popular Music Mainstreams.* New York University Press, 2023.

Quijano, Aníbal. "Coloniality of Power, Ethnocentrism, and Latin America." *NEPANTLA* 1, no. 3 (2000): 533–80.

———. "'Raza,' 'etnia' y 'nación' en Mariátegui: Cuestiones abiertas." In *José Carlos Mariátegui y Europa: El otro aspect del descubrimiento,* edited by Roland Forgues, 104–20. Empresa Editorial Amauta, 1993.

Quijano, Aníbal, and Immanuel Wallerstein. "Americanity as a Concept, or the Americas in the Modern World-System." *International Journal of Social Sciences* 134 (1992): 583–91.

Quiles Rodríguez, Edwin R. *San Juan tras la fachada: Una Mirada desde sus espacios ocultos (1508–1900).* Editorial Instituto de Cultura Puertorriqueña, 2003.

Quintero Rivera, Ángel G. "La cimarronería como herencia y utopía." In *Antología del Pensamiento Crítico Puertorriqueño Contemporáneo,* edited by Anayra Santory and Mareia Quintero. CLACSO, 2018.

———. *Cuerpo y cultura: Las músicas "mulatas" y la subversión del baile.* Iberoamericana-Vervuert, 2009.

Quintero Rivera, Ángel G., and Mariana Ortega Breña. "Migration, Ethnicity, and Interactions Between the United States and Hispanic Caribbean Popular Culture." *Latin American Perspectives* 34, no. 1 (2007): 83–93. https://www.jstor.org/stable/27647997.

Quiroga, José. *Tropics of Desire.* New York University Press, 2000.

Rancière, Jacques. *The Emancipated Spectator.* Verso, 2011.

Ríos Ávila, Rubén. "Queer Nation." In *Los otros cuerpos: Antología de temática gay, lésbica y queer desde Puerto Rico y su diáspora*, edited by Luis Negrón, Moisés Agosto Rosario, and David Caleb Acevedo, 293–307. Editorial Tiempo Nuevo, 2007.

———. "Queer Nation." *Revista Iberoamericana* 75, no. 229 (2009): 1129–38.

Rivera Montes, Zorimar. "It's About Time We Fail: A Puerto Rican Poetics of Exhaustion." *Public Books*, May 25, 2023. https://www.publicbooks.org/its-about-time-we-fail-a-puerto-rican-poetics-of-exhaustion/.

———. "¿Quién le debe a quién? A Poetics of Feminist Debt Refusals in Puerto Rico." *CENTRO Journal* 36, no. 2 (Summer 2024): 101–29. Special issue on *Caudal: Rasanblaj of Contemporary Feminist and Queer/Cuir Perspectives on Puerto Rico and the Dominican Republic*, edited by Celiany Rivera Velázquez and Carlos Ulises Decena.

Rivera-Servera, Ramón H. *Performing Queer Latinidad: Dance, Sexuality, Politics*. University of Michigan Press, 2012.

Rivera-Velázquez, Celiany. "Jayaera: The Multimedia Joy of Afro-Caribbean 'Cuir Bliss' (2008–2024)." *Feminist Media Histories* 10, no. 4 (October 2024): 149–66.

Rivera Velázquez, Celiany, and Carlos Ulises Decena, eds. *Caudal: Rasanblaj of Contemporary Feminist and Queer/Cuir Perspectives on Puerto Rico and the Dominican Republic*. Special issue of *CENTRO Journal* 36, no. 2 (Summer 2024).

Rodríguez, Juana María. *Queer Latinidad*. New York University Press, 2003.

———. *Sexual Futures, Queer Gestures, and Other Latina Longings*. New York University Press, 2014.

Ruiz, Sandra. *Ricanness: Enduring Time in Anticolonial Performance*. New York University Press, 2019.

Saketopoulou, Avgi, and Ann Pellegrini. *Gender Without Identity*. Unconscious in Translation Press, 2023.

Santana, Analola. *Freak Performances*. Ediciones Callejón. 2018.

Santiago-Ortiz, Aurora. "Testimonio as Stitch Work: Undoing Coloniality Through Autoethnography in Puerto Rico." *Chicana/Latina Studies: The Journal of Mujeres Activas en Letras y Cambio Social* 20, no. 2 (2021): 122–48.

Saunders, Patricia Joan. *Buyers Beware: Insurgency and Consumption in Caribbean Popular Culture*. Rutgers University Press, 2022.

Saunders, Rebecca. *Bodies of Work: The Labour of Sex in the Digital Age*. Palgrave Macmillan, 2020.

Sharpe, Christina. *In the Wake: On Blackness and Being*. Duke University Press, 2016.

Spillers, Hortense J. "Mama's Baby, Papa's Maybe: An American Grammar Book." *Diacritics* 17, no. 2 (1987): 65–81.

Spivak, Gayatri. "Can the Subaltern Speak?" In *Colonial Discourse and Post-Colonial Theory, A Reader*, edited by Patrick Williams and Laura Chrisman, 66–111. Columbia University Press, 1996. Essay originally published 1988.

Suárez Findlay, Eileen J. *Imposing Decency: The Politics of Sexuality and Race in Puerto Rico, 1870–1920.* University of North Carolina Press, 2000.

Taylor, Diana. *The Archive and The Repertoire: Performing Cultural Memory in The Americas.* Duke University Press, 2003.

———. *Performance.* Duke University Press, 2016.

———. *¡Presente! The Politics of Presence.* Duke University Press, 2020.

Tinsley, Omise'eke Natasha. *Ezili's Mirrors: Imagining Black Queer Genders.* Duke University Press, 2018.

Valecce, Anastasia. "El hijo de Ruby: Memorias de un futuro queer." In "Revisiting Queer Puerto Rican Sexualities: Queer Futures, Reinventions, and Un-Disciplined Archives," edited by Lawrence La Fountain-Stokes and Yolanda Martínez-San Miguel. *CENTRO: Journal of the Center for Puerto Rican Studies* 30, no. 2 (2018).

Venkatesh, Vinodh. *New Maricón Cinema: Outing Latin American Film.* University of Texas Press, 2016.

Villanueva, Joaquín, Micol Seigel, Jordan T. Camp, Stuart Schrader, Beverley Mullings, Jenna M. Loyd, and Marisol LeBrón. Review of *Policing Life and Death: Race, Violence, and Resistance in Puerto Rico,* by Marisol LeBrón. *The AAG Review of Books* 8, no. 3 (2020): 170–82. https://doi.org/10.1080/2325548X.2020.1760653.

Warren, Calvin L. *Ontological Terror: Blackness, Nihilism, and Emancipation.* Duke University Press, 2018.

Watlington, Emily. "Yvonne Rainer's Radical Return." *Art in America,* July/August 2023.

Weinbaum, Alys Eve. "Hortense Spillers and the Ungendering of (Re)productive Racial Capitalism." *History of the Present* 14, no. 1 (2024): 20–49.

Zambrana, Rocío. *Colonial Debts: The Case of Puerto Rico.* Duke University Press, 2021.

Videos and Online Material

INTRODUCTION

BBC. "Hurricane Maria: Puerto Rico May Be Months Without Power." September 21, 2017. https://www.bbc.com/news/world-latin-america-41340392.

Delgado Reyes, Edrimael. "Perreo combativo frente a la Catedral: Una perspectiva queer." *Todas,* July 28, 2019. https://www.todaspr.com/perreo-combativo-frente-a-la-catedral-una-perspectiva-cuir/.

Observatorio de Equidad de Género Puerto Rico. July 8, 2024. https://observatoriopr.org/download/2024-trimestre-ii-feminicidios-desapariciones-y-violencia-de-genero-2024-4-de-julio-de-2024-2/.

"Puerto Rico Negrx." Museo de Arte Contemporáneo de Puerto Rico, October 20, 2023. https://www.museomac.org/arte/exhibiciones/puerto-rico-negrx.

"Residente se une al perreo de Fortaleza." Video uploaded January 20, 2020. https://www.youtube.com/watch?v=aX2VCrB2Rno.

Romero, Ivette. "Exhibition: Puerto Rico Negrx" (review). October 28, 2023. Page archived January 28, 2024, at https://web.archive.org/web/20240128062158/https://repeatingislands.com/2023/10/28/exhibition-puerto-rico-negrx-review/.

CHAPTER ONE / GISELA ROSARIO RAMOS

Acevedo, Nicole. "As Puerto Rico Mourns Keishla Rodríguez's Death, Boxer Félix Verdejo Is Indicted in Her Killing." NBC News, May 6, 2021. https://www.nbcnews.com/news/latino/puerto-rico-mourns-keishla-rodriguez-s-death-boxer-f-lix-n1266598.

Chipaumire, Nora. "The Black, African, Female, Body: Nora Chipaumire at TEDx-CalArts." Video uploaded June 18, 2014. https://www.youtube.com/watch?v=uNpPQvupacM.

Colectivo Moriviví. "Restoration paz para la mujer." 2021. https://www.colectivomorivivi.com/2021-paz-mujer.

"El arca de mima." Single. Mima. Premiered June 13, 2021. https://www.youtube.com/watch?v=2_p2HoO6eZ4.

"El Gay." From the album *Tiempo al tiempo*. Los Rebuleadores de San Juan. Video uploaded September 8, 2012. https://www.youtube.com/watch?v=yqiCevRVA4k.

El hijo de Ruby. Directed by Gisela Rosario Ramos. Corporación de Cine de PuertoRico. 2014. https://vimeo.com/90163383/.

Everitt Howe, David. "Niv Acosta and Fannie Sosa." *Art in America*. March 1, 2019. https://www.artnews.com/art-in-america/aia-reviews/niv-acosta-and-fannie-sosa-62635/.

Irizarry, Yoryie. 2014. "¿Puerto Rico odia a las mujeres?" 80 grados. April 25, 2014. https://www.80grados.net/puerto-rico-odia-a-las-mujeres/.

Macha Colón (Gisela Rosario Ramos). NALAC. 2018. https://www.nalac.org/es/members/2708-gisela-rosario-ramos/.

Martínez, Kiko. "Trailer for 'Perfume de Gardenias' Features Elderly Boricua Who Lands Job Customizing Funerals." June 3, 2021. https://remezcla.com/film/trailer-perfume-de-gardenias-tribeca-film-festival/.

Miel. Single. Gisela Rosario Ramos. Video uploaded November 21, 2019. https://www.youtube.com/watch?v=1F8AIYKi8VQ.

Paz para la mujer. Mural by Colectivo Moriviví. 2014. At "Restoration: Paz para la mujer," https://www.colectivomorivivi.com/2021-paz-mujer.

"Perfume de Gardenias: About the Film." https://www.perfumedegardenias.com/en/aboutthefilm. Last accessed July 2024.

Rosario Ramos, Gisela. 2014. *El hijo de Ruby*. Corporación de Cine de Puerto Rico. https://vimeo.com/90163383.

Sánchez, Yoani. "Macha Colón: sin pelos en la lengua." Video uploaded September 3, 2019. https://www.youtube.com/watch?v=sJ_EOLNnrSs.

"Tanquecito de amor." Gisela Rosario Ramos. 2016. https://soundcloud.com/macha-colon/sets/tanquecito-de-amor.

"Todo en su sitio." From the album *Poblado.* 2022. https://alegriarampante.bandcamp.com/track/todo-en-su-sitio.

CHAPTER TWO / AWILDA RODRÍGUEZ LORA

"Bailar todos los días." La Performera. January 2015. https://laperformera.org/bailartodoslosdias-1.

"Catapult LVS 32: Awilda Rodríguez Lora (La Performera) & Raquel Paiewonsky." Streamed live on November 20, 2020. https://www.youtube.com/watch?v=ckVvqBsQ-pk.

La Fountain-Stokes, Lawrence. "ASYNCH \\ Performing the Moment, Performing the Movement." Larry La Fountain-Stokes in conversation with Awilda Rodríguez Lora. April 16, 2021. Page archived October 7, 2025, at https://web.archive.org/web/20251007221339/https://sites.lsa.umich.edu/cwps-blog/asynch-awilda-rodriguez-lora/. Video uploaded April 13, 2021, at https://www.youtube.com/watch?v=mwtOGkbUrn4.

———. "*Sustento* and the Queer Feminist Politics of Awilda Rodríguez Lora's *La Mujer Maravilla.*" Lecture at the University of Toronto. May 19, 2023. https://www.cinema.utoronto.ca/events/sustento-and-queer-feminist-politics-awilda-rodr%C3%ADguez-loras-la-mujer-maravilla.

La Performera. Videos. https://vimeo.com/laperformera, and https://laperformera.org/. Last accessed August 2023.

"La Rosario." La Performera. November 2014. https://laperformera.org/La-Rosario-1.

"La Rosario Proyectos." Copráctica: Live Art Must Live. https://fundraising.fracturedatlas.org/sustento. Last accessed August 2023.

Las Nietas de Nonó. https://www.lasnietasdenono.com/bio-1. Last accessed August 2024.

La Tortillera. *I Wanted to Be a Cheerleader but My Cuntry Didn't Have It.* https://laperformera.org/DUOS/i-wanted-to-be-a-cheerleader-but-my-cuntry-didn-t-have-it.

Livable Futures. "Awilda Rodriguez Lora." https://livablefuturesnow.org/awilda-rodriguez-lora. Last accessed August 2023.

Mignolo, Walter, and Rolando Vazquez. "Decolonial AestheSis: Colonial Wounds/Decolonial Healings." July 15, 2013. https://socialtextjournal.org/periscope_article/decolonial-aesthesis-colonial-woundsdecolonial-healings/.

"Mujer Maravilla: Cuerpa." Video uploaded September 16, 2019. https://vimeo.com/360351074.

Rodríguez Lora, Awilda. Instagram account. https://www.instagram.com/laperformera. Last accessed August 2023.

Sharp, Sarah G. "A Call for Sustento—Interview with Awilda Rodríguez Lora." July 11, 2018. https://www.performanceisalive.com/news/a-call-for-sustento-interview-with-awilda-rodriguez-lora-by-sarah-g-sharp.

"Sustento Teaser." Uploaded July 3, 2023. https://vimeo.com/841980895.

"Wex Artist Talk: Awilda Rodríguez Lora." Video uploaded July 3, 2023. https://wexarts.org/talks-more/awilda-rodriguez-lora.

CHAPTER THREE / HELEN CEBALLOS

Ceballos, Helen. 2021. "Cerezas por papeles" [Cherries for papers]. Translation from Spanish into English by Rojo Robles. Article published June 28, 2023. https://www.afrolatinoforum.org/pensamientos-blog/cerezas-por-papeles-cherries-for-documents.

———. "Hasta las luces de Helen Ceballos." Peakd.com. November 10, 2023. https://peakd.com/hive-10053/@limaescritora/hasta-las-luces-de-helen.

———. "Helen Ceballos." Materic.org. https://www.materic.org/helen-ceballos/. Last accessed April 2024.

"Circuito de Helen Ceballos." Vide uploaded September 24, 2019. https://www.youtube.com/watch?v=9KoxMKV-ByA.

"Coito bucal." Video uploaded November 27, 2019. https://www.youtube.com/watch?v=Fn_VDa2heQA.

Collazo, Maria. "Invitadxs a esta cena: MEZCOLANZA." *Claridad*, February 1, 2024. https://claridadpuertorico.com/invitadxs-a-esta-cena-mezcolanza/.

"Comen de mi." Video. Created December 21, 2023. https://drive.google.com/file/d/1MHSyYLmLna_cX_wOnWJPn7vI6-kleyZe/view.

"Cuerpos fronterizos Helen Ceballos." Video. Created February 22, 2024. https://drive.google.com/file/d/1UMqcVCPuVM1UH9tHSmzL62wt6BTKVmoq/view.

"Cuerpxs Queers en el Caribe: Fronteras e Identidades Artist Talks by Helen Ceballos and Lío Villahermosa." Hemispheric Institute. October 17, 2019. https://hemisphericinstitute.org/en/events/cuerpxs-queers-en-el-caribe-fronteras-e-identidades.html.

"El cuadrado gris." https://www.facebook.com/elcuadradogris/videos/hoy-viernes-7-mayo-en-vivo-3pm-por-veobo-la-artista-helen-ceballos/375991897036009/. Last accessed February 2024.

"El cuerpo y la ruina: The 19th Annual Stonewall Performance and Artist Conversation." Dartmouth College. March 28, 2019. https://theater.dartmouth.edu/news/2019/03/artist-helen-ceballos-perform-bentley-theater.

"El destrence de Helen Ceballos." Video uploaded November 27, 2019. https://www.youtube.com/watch?v=eWNYeaXOxxE.

Fermaint, Renia. "Mezcolanza: Una invitación a experimentar lo híbrido." *90 grados*. January 21, 2018. https://90grados.com/arte/mezcolanza-una-invitacion-a-experimentar-lo-hibrido.

"Fue esa la vía." Video uploaded June 23, 2023. https://vimeo.com/839067789.

"Golpe de agua." https://www.youtube.com/watch?v=5HAShiC3bjU. Last accessed February 2024.

"Hablar de la prole." Canales abiertos//Open Channels. Video uploaded July 8, 2020. https://www.youtube.com/watch?v=Rv1AmJ1DSLs.

"Helen Ceballos: Acacia Network Orgullo Nuestro Award." Acacia Network. Video uploaded October 24, 2018. https://www.youtube.com/watch?v=OKKkc2k-XxE.

"La Mirada Boricua/The Boricua Gaze: Helen Ceballos." Dartmouth University. https://journeys.dartmouth.edu/boricuagaze/helen-ceballos/. Last accessed April 2024.

Lowell-Fiet. "El camino a Santiago de Cuba: Rumbos del teatro caribeño (2)." *Claridad,* August 2, 2022. https://claridadpuertorico.com/el-camino-a-santiago-de-cuba-rumbos-del-teatro-caribeno-2/.

———. "El camino a Santiago de Cuba y el Festival del Caribe, parte I." *Claridad,* July 26, 2022. https://claridadpuertorico.com/el-camino-a-santiago-de-cuba-y-el-festival-del-caribe-parte-i/.

"*Memoria.*" Combo Chimbita. Video uploaded September 7, 2021. https://www.youtube.com/watch?v=aS1-RuSVuOs.

"No voy a pedirle a nadie que me crea." Canales abiertos//Open Channels. Video uploaded June 23, 2021. https://www.youtube.com/watch?v=fUcH4VoOqug.

Plataforma Eje. Page archived July 26, 2023, at https://web.archive.org/web/20230726212850/https://plataformaeje.pr/.

"Rito de paso." https://vimeo.com/776721808. Last accessed February 2024.

Robles, Rojo, and Rebeca L. Salois. "Bonus: Entrevista con Helen Ceballos." *Latinx Visions.* Podcast. May 2023. Spotify. https://open.spotify.com/episode/3x3EqhdpJ2xINKEIZ5CbOy.

Rodríguez, Ishbel Cora. "Helen Ceballos: 'Mi cuerpo es mi única patria.'" November 11, 2018. https://ishbelcora.wordpress.com/2018/11/11/helen-ceballos-mi-cuerpo-es-mi-unica-patria/.

Segarra-Ríos, Abdiel D. "Unspoken Identities." February 15–March 31, 2023. https://www.anamasprojects.com/exhibitions/unspoken-identities/.

"Sitiada de Helen Ceballos." September 8, 2020. https://sitiadadehelenceballos.blogspot.com/.

"Tener tus piernas." Video created February 22, 2024. Modified May 6, 2024. https://drive.google.com/file/d/1g3EnefSZZGmq7JpADqoROILblIO7Adom/view.

UPR Diálogo. "Helen Ceballos: 'Mi cuerpo es mi única patria.'" March 19, 2018. https://dialogo.upr.edu/helen-ceballos-mi-cuerpo-es-mi-unica-patria/.

Velez Burr, Amber Lee. "Sitiada con raíces al aire." 80 Grados. August 26, 2011. https://www.80grados.net/sitiada-y-con-raices-al-aire/.

CHAPTER FOUR / AWILDA STERLING-DUPREY

Alvarez, José. "Awilda Sterling-Duprey: (Un)Drawing the Continent Blindfolded." *Contemporary And.* July 27, 2022. https://www.contemporaryand.com/en/america-latina-magazine/texts/awilda-sterling-duprey-undrawing-the-continent-blindfolded.

"Artista Awilda Sterling presenta nueva pieza sobre Maelo." *El Nuevo Día.* April 10, 2015. https://www.elnuevodia.com/entretenimiento/cultura/videos/artista-awilda-sterling-presenta-nueva-pieza-sobre-maelo-165128/.

"Awilda Sterling: 'Con ton y son . . .' en la Liga de Arte." 80 Grados. July 12, 2019. https://www.80grados.net/awilda-sterling-con-ton-y-son-en-la-liga-de-arte/.

"Awilda Sterling: En-Cierro (Enclosed) | SAVVY Contemporary 2017." Video uploaded March 1, 2019. https://vimeo.com/320755905.

Calderón, Tego. "Loíza." From the album *El Abayarde.* 2002.

Casa Afro. "Awilda Sterling Duprey." https://casaafro.org/portfolio/parentesis-awilda-sterling-duprey/. Last accessed June 2024.

———. "Paréntesis: 25 años después." https://casaafro.org/parentesis-galeria/. Last accessed August 2024.

———. "Sobre Paréntesis." https://casaafro.org/sobre-parentesis/. Last accessed August 2024.

"Con ton y son: Apropriaciones y exploraciones de un proceso personal." Autogiro. Published July 2, 2019. Last updated February 8, 2023. https://autogiro.cronicaurbana.com/es/awilda-sterling-duprey-con-son-y-ton/.

"Danza contemporánea y performance 'Maelo en el Cuerpo' a cargo de Awilda Sterling." Puerto Rico Art News. April 2015. https://www.puertoricoartnews.com/2015/04/danza-contemporanea-y-performance-maelo.html.

Dávila, Ángela María. "Déjenme sola." March 30, 2018. https://projectzudotcom.wordpress.com/2018/03/30/un-poema-de-anjelamaria-davila/.

"De Maelo al hip-hop." La Calle Loíza Facebook account. April 21, 2015. https://www.facebook.com/lacalleloiza/posts/de-maelo-al-hip-hop-un-taller-para-j%C3%B3venes-con-velcro-y-awilda-sterling-pronto-e/900989883276736/.

"Diálogo entre artistas: Awilda Sterling + Zuania Minier." 2020. https://www.facebook.com/ligadearte/videos/di%C3%A1logo-entre-artistas-awilda-sterling-zuania-minier/329377314069873o/.

El Cuadrado Gris. https://www.facebook.com/elcuadradogris/videos/3569578456448333/. Last accessed July 2024.

"en-cierro." Uploaded September 12, 2016. https://vimeo.com/182447197.

"en-cierro—4ta Exploración—Un mismo tema." Área Lugar de Proyectos. July 1–29, 2017. https://www.proyectoarea.com/awilda-sterling-encierro.

Entreformas. Museo de Arte de Puerto Rico. 2021. https://mapr.org/sites/default/files/gallerynoteingles.pdf.

Estrada, Amelia. "A Way of Being: Awilda Sterling-Duprey." September 4, 2018. https://thinkingdance.net/articles/2018/09/04/A-Way-of-Being-Awilda-Sterling-Duprey-/.

Gill, Jenny. "In the Studio: Awilda Sterling." June 9, 2023. https://www.joanmitchellfoundation.org/journal/in-the-studio-awilda-sterling.

"Instituto de Cultura Puertorriqueña anunció el regreso de 'Al Son de Maelo' al MAC." *El Adoquín Periódico.* October 13, 2023. https://eladoquintimes.com/2023/10/13/instituto-de-cultura-puertorriquena-anuncio-el-regreso-de-al-son-de-maelo-al-mac/.

Joan Mitchell Foundation. "Awilda Sterling." https://www.joanmitchellfoundation.org/awilda-sterling. Last accessed June 2024.

La Calle Loíza. "De Maelo al hip-hop." Facebook post. April 21, 2015. https://www.facebook.com/lacalleloiza/posts/de-maelo-al-hip-hop-un-taller-para-j%C3%B3venes-con-velcro-y-awilda-sterling-pronto-e/900989883276736/.

"Lacks Criticality." Video uploaded November 2, 2020. https://www.youtube.com/watch?v=hfoeO28tFf4.

"Maelo en el cuerpo." Puerto Rico Art News. April 2015. https://www.puertoricoartnews.com/2015/04/danza-contemporanea-y-performance-maelo.html.

Museo de Arte Contemporáneo de Puerto Rico—MACPR. "A flor de labio." From the project "Proyecto Santurce: 30 años del MAC en el barrio." Video uploaded April 16, 2016. https://www.youtube.com/watch?v=pDk5uyueBLs.

Pagán Velez, Alexandra. "En-cierro de Awilda Sterling, una pieza que se abre a lo esencial." 80 Grados, October 27, 2016. https://www.80grados.net/en-cierro-de-awilda-sterling-una-pieza-que-se-abre-a-lo-esencial/.

Puerto Rico Art News. "20 Questions: Awilda Sterling-Duprey." November 2020. https://www.puertoricoartnews.com/2020/11/20-questions-awilda-sterling-duprey.html.

"Reggaeton Lento." Video uploaded September 5, 2009. https://www.youtube.com/watch?v=VcoOygyOx-M.

"Soy la reencarnación de un alma esclavizada." Video uploaded February 1, 2022. https://www.youtube.com/watch?v=sFhpBEI1ODg.

Temple University. Department of Dance. "Reflection/Response: Conversation and Creative Practice." Awilda Sterling-Duprey. Video uploaded September 29, 2020. https://www.youtube.com/watch?v=_FiJ8tuTvIU.

"Toques de tambor para las diosas." Video uploaded June 8, 2011. https://www.youtube.com/watch?v=ox6a6yGrHOc.

"Transparente desnudez/Transparencia, no desnudez." Video uploaded July 10, 2018. https://www.youtube.com/watch?v=7ckDYYyqqmc.

Trelles, Miguel. "Tertulia Presents Awilda Sterling-Duprey." Streamed live August 24, 2022. https://www.youtube.com/watch?v=rxfEzk_m4cY.

"Unspoken Identities." Artishock. March 9, 2023. https://artishockrevista.com/2023/03/09/unspoken-identities/.

UPR Diálogo. "Awilda Sterling presenta en-cierro en la Sala Experimental del CBA." October 26, 2016. https://dialogo.upr.edu/awilda-sterling-presenta-en-cierro-en-la-sala-experimental-del-cba/.

Velázquez Collazo, Edwin. "Ismael Rivera en cuerpo presente a través de Awilda Sterling." Puerto Rico Art News. April 2015. https://www.puertoricoartnews.com/2015/04/ismael-rivera-en-cuerpo-presente-traves.html.

"Vejigante decrépito." Video uploaded February 24, 2024. https://vimeo.com/87477480.

Whitney Museum of American Art. "Awilda Sterling-Duprey: . . . blindfolded Performance." 2022. https://whitney.org/exhibitions/2022-biennial/performances/sterling-duprey.

———. "Lacks Criticality." Posted April 22, 2023. https://www.facebook.com/whitneymuseum/videos/lacks-criticality/792620545811927/.

———. "Lacks Criticality: Awilda Sterling-Duprey. No existe un mundo poshuracán." April 10, 2023. https://whitney.org/media/55169.

———. "No existe un mundo poshuracán: Puerto Rican Art in the Wake of Hurricane María." November 23, 2022–April 23, 2023. https://whitney.org/exhibitions/no-existe.

———. "Puerto Rican Artist Awilda Sterling-Duprey Performs a 'Dance-Drawing.'" Posted June 17, 2022. https://www.facebook.com/whitneymuseum/videos/whitney-biennial-2022/3192737201046256/.

INDEX

ANASTASIA VALECCE is associate professor of Hispanic Studies in the Department of World Languages and Cultures at Spelman College.

www.ingramcontent.com/pod-product-compliance
Lightning Source LLC
LaVergne TN
LVHW091144230926
848584LV00025B/193